History, Memory
& Politics in
Postwar Japan

Published in association with the
Japan Publishing Industry Foundation for Culture

History, Memory & Politics in Postwar Japan

edited by
Iokibe Kaoru, Komiya Kazuo, Hosoya Yūichi, Miyagi Taizō,
and the Tokyo Foundation
for Policy Research's Political
and Diplomatic Review Project

LYNNE
RIENNER
PUBLISHERS

BOULDER
LONDON

Translated by
Fred Uleman, Brian Lewis, Frank Moorhead,
Stephen Suloway, and Charles Stewart

Published in the United States of America in 2020 by
Lynne Rienner Publishers, Inc.
1800 30th Street, Boulder, Colorado 80301
www.rienner.com

and in the United Kingdom by
Lynne Rienner Publishers, Inc.
Gray's Inn House, 127 Clerkenwell Road, London EC1 5DB

First published in Japanese as *Sengo Nihon no rekishi ninshiki,*
University of Tokyo Press; © 2017 by the Tokyo Foundation for Policy Research.

Library of Congress Cataloging-in-Publication Data
A Cataloging-in-Publication record for this book
is available from the Library of Congress.

ISBN 978-1-62637-877-3 (hc.)

British Cataloguing in Publication Data
A Cataloguing in Publication record for this book
is available from the British Library.

Contents

Preface

Hosoya Yūichi

With 2015 marking the seventieth anniversary of the end of World War II, many places worldwide held commemorative ceremonies and other events that year to observe the occasion and to look back not only on the war, but also on the subsequent decades. In Japan, the media and others focused particular attention on Prime Minister Abe Shinzō's August 14 statement marking the anniversary of the war's end, Korean President Park Geun-hye's August 15 Liberation Day speech celebrating the seventieth anniversary of Korea's independence from Japan, and Chinese President Xi Jinping's speech at the September 3 military parade commemorating seventy years since victory in the war against Japan.

Remembrances are important, and the way that different peoples remember their history has become a factor shaping the history of international politics in today's East Asia. Not only does history itself beget historical memory, but narratives of historical memory themselves shape history. As such, historical memory is a critical diplomatic issue that must be addressed if we are to formulate a sound foreign policy for the future of international politics in East Asia. Looking at media coverage of Japan-China relations and Japan-Korea relations, it seems there is virtually not a single aspect untouched by the rancor over historical memory, so important is the issue of historical memory to the foreign policy agenda.

Yet, even though the issue of historical memory is all over the news and is a major concern for numerous East Asian politicians and diplomats, it has yet to be adequately understood how important a research topic this is for academics as well. In the past decade alone, Japanese scholars have made major progress in unraveling and advancing our understanding of this issue. However, these results have yet to be read, much less assimilated, by the public at large.

In an attempt to rectify this situation, this book brings together an array of political and diplomatic historians to examine the issue of historical memory in postwar Japan as dispassionately and as objectively as possible. Because this is not a dry research paper but is intended for a broad readership, there is a lot of introductory material, but all of the authors have solid records as respected scholars doing quality work in their very demanding specialties. And all of us are most delighted to be afforded this opportunity to present our findings here because we share the hope that this will further the objective, dispassionate, and academically sound discussion of this very sensitive, very divisive issue in Japan.

Because much of this book is grounded in the work done by the Tokyo Foundation for Policy Research's Political and Diplomatic Review Project, it is worth providing some background on the project. The project itself was founded in 2007 by the Tokyo Foundation for Policy Research (then called the Tokyo Foundation) as part of its program of policy research, with University of Tokyo professor and Tokyo Foundation senior fellow Kitaoka Shin'ichi asked to lead its work. That was during Abe Shinzō's first stint as prime minister. On April 11, 2007, Prime Minister Abe met with visiting Chinese Premier Wen Jiabao and the two leaders issued a statement affirming their intention to build "a mutually beneficial relationship based on common strategic interests." Now, in 2020, Sino-Japanese relations are very different from what they were then, as are Japan's position in the international community and its politics and foreign policy. The project's historians have thus had a front-row-seat opportunity to review this political and diplomatic transformation.

Throughout the years since its inception, the project team met more or less monthly, with Sophia University Professor Miyagi Taizō, University of Tokyo Professor Iokibe Kaoru, and myself serving as subleaders. All three of us had previously studied under Professor Kitaoka at the Rikkyō University Faculty of Law and Politics or the University of Tokyo Graduate Schools for Law and Politics. Midway through our work we were able to welcome Komazawa University lecturer Komiya Kazuo as a fourth subleader and to begin publishing the "Diplomatic History Book Review" on the Tokyo Foundation website.

Not coincidentally, all four of us had the opportunity more than a decade earlier to take part in the discussion sessions that Professor Kitaoka convened regularly at the University of Tokyo Graduate

Schools for Law and Politics for promising researchers regardless of age or affiliation. Much of this group's collaborative research involved reviewing and discussing new publications in the field. Both the reading and the discussions were valuable learning experiences. This was suspended, however, when Kitaoka was appointed Japan's ambassador to the United Nations, and it could not be resumed after his return to Tokyo due to his extremely busy schedule. Even after he retired from his University of Tokyo post, he moved first to the National Graduate Institute for Policy Studies (GRIPS) and then to his current position as president of the Japan International Cooperation Agency (JICA).

Yet we were finally able to resurrect our study group, albeit in a different format and at a different venue, when Kitaoka was appointed senior fellow at the Tokyo Foundation and charged with launching a new research project. Among the other changes that took place, we added frontline journalists and editors as well as younger academics who were interested in learning more about Japan's political and diplomatic history, and the discussion benefited from their enthusiastic participation. All told, we like to think our study group has contributed to a better understanding of the issues involved, both for ourselves and for society at large.

Along the way, almost unnoticed, those of us in the older group, who had been graduate students or teaching assistants, moved into positions where we teach and supervise undergraduate and graduate students. Happily, some of our students have joined the study group and are more than pulling their weight. Although I may not be able to fill Kitaoka's shoes in this group, I find that, with active support from Iokibe, Komiya, and Miyagi, this has become a most invigorating and rewarding academic forum, and I am delighted that our group has grown to the point where we were able to put this book together.

Of course, the book would not have been possible without Kitaoka's leadership and support, and I would like to take this opportunity to express our profound appreciation to him. Indeed, I suspect it was largely due to his tutelage that we, each in our own way, have been able to do the very important work of passing the joy of intellectual discovery on to young graduate students and others.

I would also like to express our immense gratitude to program officer Tanaka Nobuko at the Tokyo Foundation for Policy Research, who has done so much for our research group, and to the foundation itself for supporting our work over the years. Tanaka's assistance has been a special godsend given the diversity of our group's membership and the many different subjects we pursued, and I doubt our work would have gone nearly as smoothly or we would have had this many significant opportunities to interact with the outside world were it not for her.

Most of all, I would like to express my admiration of and appreciation to the other members of the group, who, month after month, delivered stunning reports succinctly explaining the significance of the scholarly work they had read and incisively positioned it within the overall field and flow of contemporary events. Their unflagging efforts were crucial to the group's existence and growth. Most of these people have since moved on to leadership positions within their respective organizations, but they took time from already busy schedules to consistently provide invaluable intellectual insights and stimulation, for which I am most grateful.

To quote Professor Kitaoka's kind message leading off the first issue of our diplomatic history blog:

> Steady progress is being made in researching and compiling Japan's postwar diplomatic history. Drawing upon the diplomatic archives and availing ourselves of the Freedom of Information Act to pry open new information sources, we have moved from research largely reliant upon US sources to achieve a broader perspective and better overall understanding. The reality is, however, that the bulk of the research has remained the property of specialist researchers in the field and has not contributed to building the broad foundations needed for informed public debate on foreign policy's whats and whys.

Given that little has changed since he wrote this, we very much hope our book will reach the widest possible audience and will contribute "to building the broad foundations needed for informed public debate on foreign policy's whats and whys."

Introduction

Iokibe Kaoru

This book is about the historical narratives we tell ourselves. In Japan's case, the postwar narrative has been one depicting Japan as aggressor, victim, and loser. The only thing missing is that Japan has never depicted itself as having won that war. Thus we explore in the book how the three historical self-identifications have coexisted, interacted, and played out over the years.

Historical narratives are obviously not unique to the postwar period, including the narratives constructed since the war about the prewar period, and there were also prewar narratives of how Japanese saw themselves in the flow of history. Because war has always been a primary mover shaping historical memory, it is instructive to look back at the wars prior to World War II. Even a cursory listing of the wars that were pivotal events in Japanese history would have to include the late-Tokugawa and early-Meiji strife and discord leading up to and including the Boshin War, the Sino-Japanese wars, the Russo-Japanese War, and, in a more limited way, World War I. Given this, Japan's historical memories prior to World War II were of Japan winning glorious victories. This was then followed by disastrous implosion, and one of the few privileges left to Japan after the war was that of rummaging through the many historical narrative possibilities and ruminating on its historical experience, an option that has yet to be fully exploited. I would thus like to briefly, and admittedly inadequately, review Japan's historical memory as it existed in the years before defeat, and then

build upon that to look at Japan's postwar historical narratives—this
by way of grounding the subsequent discussion.

The early Meiji history was made by the forces that had won the
Boshin War. This included, quite obviously, the people who had
wanted to oust the Tokugawa shogunate and install the young
emperor not just as titular but as de facto head of state and who,
once victorious, appropriated daimyo powers and assets, even from
those daimyo who had supported their cause, in the name of national
unification. It also included the disgruntled members of the elite
class, primary among them the charismatic warriors and returning
heroes who wanted a greater share of the spoils and ultimately
ended up in opposition to the new government. And finally it
included the freedom-and-people's-rights movement members, many
drawn from the other two groups. The Boshin War—having
employed new weaponry deployed in new ways using new people
drawn from the nonwarrior classes—not only marked a decisive victory but also liberated its participants from the old class structures
and can hence be counted as one factor accounting for their radical-
ism. The fact that these people were recorded, and saw themselves,
as victorious in this great struggle then directly tied in to their later
progressive activism on the political stage.

Those opinion leaders who were wary of this progressivism
expressed their recollections of the turmoil that accompanied the
shogunate's fall and the Meiji Restoration in very measured or even
negative terms. Fukuchi Gen'ichirō (writing under the pen name
Fukuchi Ōchi)* was one of the literati who epitomized this 1870s
gradualist school in Japanese commentary, and he later penned such
works as *Bakufu Suibōron* (The Fall of the Bakufu) (published by
Minyūsha in 1883) and *Bakumatsu Seijika* (Politicians in the Late
Bakufu Era) (also Minyūsha, 1900). A former bakufu official, he was
critical of the people advocating that the shogunate be overthrown as
well as of those advocating that the barbarians be expelled.

This same conservative sensibility permeated the various political novels that inspired the freedom-and-people's-rights movement.
Kajin no Kigū (Strange Encounters with Beautiful Women) by Aizu-
born Shiba Shirō (better known as Tōkai Sanshi) (volumes 1 and 2
published by Hakubundō in 1885) depicted the shogunate's fall and

---

Note: Personal names are given in the order they appear in the original language. For Japanese, this means family name first.

the Restoration as a vicious downward spiral of conflict in which the excesses of the "revere the emperor and expel the barbarians" crowd provoked escalating responses by foreign powers and showed the Aizu forces standing heroically alone in trying, albeit unsuccessfully, to mediate between the two sides and keep things from spinning out of control. This same vicious-spiral concern and sense of warning was also a central motif in Yano Fumio's (pen name Yano Ryūkei) *Keikoku Bidan* (Young Politicians of Thebes) (published by Hōchi Shinbun-sha in 1884) and Suehiro Shigeyasu's (pen name Suehiro Tetchō) *Setchūbai* (Plum Blossoms in Snow) (Hakubundō, 1886).

Vicious spirals spread cancer-like, and it is typically very difficult to halt or reverse them. Yet there were also political novels that sought to engender a *virtuous* spiral in the hope it would have the same metastatic qualities and that the vicious and virtuous spirals would cancel each other out. Both *Keikoku Bidan* and *Setchūbai* are political novels in which youths who follow the doctrine of the mean (*zhongyong*) win over the skeptical masses with quiet fervor and persuasive speeches.

In *Kakan'ō* (Warbler Among the Flowers) (Kinkōdō, 1887), Suehiro's sequel to *Setchūbai,* he postulated trust and friendship between the public and private sectors, between radicals and moderates, at the individual level as prerequisite to this virtuous spiral. The compartmentalization of the personal and the public so that political differences do not mar personal relations was a constant theme in much of the writing at the time, and not just in the political novels. Fukuzawa Yukichi repeatedly preached the need for harmony between officialdom and the public, which he did expecting reconciliation to be possible, since he himself had longtime friends among senior court officials and opposition politicians.

This sense that the vicious spiral must not be allowed to reappear was shared by both the freedom-and-people's-rights advocates and the more conservative commentators, and they competed—in speeches, magazine articles, and more—to do those little things that would spark the start of a virtuous spiral. Indeed, such campaigns were part of the climate facilitating the promulgation of the Constitution of the Empire of Japan (the Meiji Constitution) in 1889. Even so, as the demands for democratic government grew stronger, the rift in views on how the constitution should be interpreted grew wider and it was feared that this could spark a vicious round of escalating antagonism. One of the many people to address this issue was Yoshino Sakuzō.

The *minpon-shugi* democracy that Yoshino advocated should be understood as a philosophy that would work to contain the vicious spiral by linking the opposing concepts of form and content in line with Hegelian dialectical thinking. As Yoshino famously wrote in his "Kensei no Hongi wo Toite sono Yūshū no Bi wo Nasu no Michi wo Ronzu" (An Elucidation of the Essence of Constitutional Government and a Discussion of How to Achieve Its Elegance) in the January 1916 issue of *Chūō Kōron,* the all-important spirit that it embodies, the constitution's wording aside, is the spirit of formulating national policy grounded in the will of the people at large. In this, the majority thus stands as the formal primary, yet within that form is the need for a spiritual leader. As Yoshino himself explained this in terms of Hegelian dialectical thinking (see "Hēgeru no Hōritsu Tetsugaku no Kiso" [The Foundations of Hegel's Philosophy of Law], 1905, in vol. 1, *Seiji to Kokka,* of the sixteen-volume *Yoshino Sakuzō Senshū* [Collected Works of Yoshino Sakuzō], Iwanami Shoten, 1995), the vacuous form is fulfilled by the content, yet because this content itself cannot but become form-like, it is in turn fulfilled by new content in an endless evolutionary process: Yoshino's *minpon-shugi's* wording (form) constantly fulfilled by new spirit (content) in a constant process of renewal, making it possible for the constitution, the titular majority, and the de facto ruling minority to coexist. A political historian by training, Yoshino was well aware that Europe's socialist campaigns had at times engendered vicious spirals of confrontation with the authorities and at times engendered virtuous spirals of dialogue and compromise, and it was this awareness of history that informed his *minpon-shugi.*

History is said to be written by the winners, but in Japan's case, it would better be said that, given the Meiji-Taisho milieu, the winners defined the trappings of the state while the losers, through the concept of karma, defined political manners, thereby creating a complex ground of historical awareness. The fact of a functioning constitutional government facilitated mobilization during the Sino-Japanese (1894–1895) and Russo-Japanese (1904–1905) wars. As a consequence of winning these wars, however, Japan seemed to have forgotten the spiral concept, in foreign affairs even more so than in domestic politics. Having won the wars, the imperative that developed was to consolidate the gains, yet this mentality worked against generating a virtuous spiral in Japan's relations with its vanquished opponents. The effort to consolidate the spoils set foreign policy adrift from its moorings and opened the way for the emergence of another vicious spiral. In the wake of the war with China, for example, both private and public sectors rushed to develop alliances and to support their friends on the continent. While this frenzy was intended to put the bilateral ties on a stronger, more stable basis, it also entailed risks in that different Japanese found themselves on different sides when civil strife broke out in China. In the 1911 Xinhai Revolution, for example, plans were advanced by Japanese throughout China to assist this or that faction, the end result being that Japan was accused of intervening all over the map in line with what was at best a haphazard China policy.

With the outbreak of World War I, Japan put forth its infamous "21 Demands," including recognition that it was replacing Germany on the continent, but Foreign Minister Katō Takaaki wanted Qingdao not so much to hold them long-term but more to use them to bargain with in extending the term of Japan's hold on those parts of Manchuria that it had won from Russia in the Russo-Japanese War. The foreign policy establishment that followed Katō advocated better relations with China and, albeit at different times, supported both the Kuomintang government in the south and the Duan Qirui government in the north. Yet both prongs of this policy invited denunciation, in Japan and internationally, as interventionist, and it proved impossible to achieve Japan's aims on the continent.

Turning to Russia, Japan signed agreements with Russia in 1907 and again in 1910, delineating their spheres of influence in Manchuria and pledging to respect each other's interests. A new agreement was signed in 1912 extending their spheres to Inner Mongolia. This was followed in 1916 by a fourth agreement in which they pledged to cooperate militarily in beating back any third-country challenges to their positions in China. Despite this, all of these efforts to stabilize the bilateral relationship turned to dust in the Russian revolution of 1917, and Japan dispatched troops to Siberia (1918–1922).

These events alarmed the United States and put Japan at a disadvantage in the Washington Naval Conference that President Harding convened following World War I and in the resultant Five-Power Treaty, calling for the five powers (Britain, France, Italy, Japan, and the United States) to scale back their navies, as well as the Nine-Power Treaty calling on the parties to respect Chinese territorial integrity and sovereignty on the continent. Yet this latter treaty was not entirely to Japan's disadvantage, as it also recognized Japanese interests in Manchuria-Mongolia and recognized some Japanese interests on the Shandong Peninsula, in effect consolidating some of the gains Japan had won in the Russo-Japanese War and World War I. Having signed the Nine-Power Treaty, Japan refrained from intervening in China for the next decade, and the potential for a vicious spiral was largely muted. Yet the rights that Japan had acquired by war and by treaty were the target of ferocious criticism by Chinese nationalists, and the danger of slipping into a vicious spiral of conflict was heightened when both Chinese nationalists and Chinese revolutionaries sought to have Japan surrender the rights it had earlier acquired. It is very possible this could have been averted with conciliatory policies; this then marks another critical juncture in Japanese history.

Japanese domestic politics was also very unsettled at this time. Starting in 1924, there was a run of cabinets dominated by political parties, first the Kenseikai (which later became the Rikken Minseitō) and then the Rikken Seiyūkai. Under Foreign Minister Shidehara Kijūrō's leadership, the Kenseikai pursued a foreign policy of cooperation with its neighbors. While this policy stance had broad support from the emperor, elder statesman Saionji Kinmochi, and the public at large, the constant infighting between the two parties for control of the government apparatus meant they were forever digging up dirt on each other; they spent more time on political battles than on policy issues; and the public developed politics fatigue in the face of scandal after scandal and other unsightly behavior by the politicians. Shidehara's policies were further undermined by the Seiyūkai's constant carping that he was weak-kneed and irresolute in defending Japan's interests. Things were not helped when the two leading parties failed to follow in the footsteps of Fukuchi, Fukuzawa, the political novelists, and others who had earlier moved to keep politics from being captured by the vicious spiral of power-game campaigns and failed to speak out in ways that would have held this vicious spiral at bay. With this, much of the intelligentsia became disillusioned with the Seiyūkai and the Rikken Minshutō, seeing them as more-of-the-same establishment parties, and turned their attention to the more progressive movements, be they the proletarian parties or the nationalists.

Japan-China relations became increasingly confrontational in the wake of the 1931 Mukden Incident, albeit with occasional lulls. The May 15 coup attempt, in which Seiyūkai president and prime minister Inukai Tsuyoshi was assassinated, took place the following year, 1932, marking the end of party government and ushering in a new government format amenable to military control.

The prewar historical narrative played a direct role in the formulation of Japanese government and foreign policy, and the fact that this was a historical narrative depicting Japan as a "winner" contributed to Japan's escalating confrontations and boxed in the nation's policy options. By contrast, Japan's postwar historical narrative is that of having lost the war, and this historical narrative's impact has been both more indirect and much more complex. Such indirection and complexity does not, however, imply insignificance. Looking just at the Japan–United States Mutual Security Treaty and the concurrent antiwar pacifism, both of which have been foci of contention between the conservative and the progressive forces, the structure here is clearly one of three factors working in complex interaction: the desire to rebuild following defeat, revulsion at the horrors war exacts of its victims, and remorse at the horrors Japan inflicted. All three figured importantly, but they were not, unlike the "winner" historical narrative and the policies it spawned, the direct determining factors.

Thus the inclination is to deal with the separate components of the postwar historical narrative separately, and dealing with them separately has yielded a number of outstanding analyses. Even so, looking at them cross-sectionally as integral components of a whole and how they operated era by era can also yield some interesting analyses and vivid explications of their features. That is what this book strives to do. Whether our efforts are successful or not I leave to the reader's judgment, but I would like to say a few words about the intent behind and the significance of each chapter by way of brief introduction.

Yoshida Shigeru was the leading figure in the early postwar era when Japan's foreign policy foundations were being laid, and it is only fitting that Takeda Tomoki should lead off with "The Yoshida Shigeru Years: Coming to Terms with the Issue of Historical Memory" (Chapter 1). While the old liberalists who were on record as having opposed the war constituted the immediate postwar foreign policy establishment, there were sharp differences of opinion within this group on, for example, China policy and Japanese interests in China, as well as on the Soviet Union and communism. (I suspect that these differences stemmed from their different mindsets and interests as former victors, as well as their different anxiety levels about the possibility of further defeat and ruin.) It was Yoshida who freed himself of these differences and analyzed the situation most cogently—perhaps because he was most aware and accepting of

Japan's defeat. In this, Yoshida accepted the Far Eastern Tribunal's verdict of history as well as the San Francisco Peace Treaty, and was successful in managing Japan's return to the community of nations.

Even though he achieved this at little cost to Japan, there was still a strong sense of victimhood and injustice in Japan, and the return to international society took place with no decision on how to make due amends to China and Korea, neither of which was party to the San Francisco Peace Treaty. Indeed, the issue of reparations to China and Korea had to wait until diplomatic relations were normalized with these two nations—with Korea in the 1960s and with China in the 1970s.

The 1960s and 1970s were an era of rapid growth, as laid out in Murai Ryōta's "The Satō Eisaku Years: Historical Memory in a Time of Rapid Economic Growth" (Chapter 2). Buoyed by America's Cold War strategy, Japan moved to bring legal closure to its postwar issues. This was a time of ardent introspection about the war, much of it finding outlet in such constitutional issues as state patronage of Yasukuni Shrine, the addition of Far Eastern Tribunal war criminals to the Yasukuni honor roll, and the legality of government officials' paying their respects to the mixed bag of war-dead there. The bulk of this introspection and morality debate was premised upon the idea of Japan as victim, but there was also a deep-flowing undercurrent acknowledging Japan's role in perpetrating so much horror. While this may be seen as indicative of maturity, it was not necessarily cognizant of or in agreement with how other nations saw the wartime experience. The 1978 enshrinement of the war criminals and other actions and pronouncements were seen in Japan and overseas as expressions of dissatisfaction with the legalities accompanying the war's end and were direct harbingers of today's historical memory issues.

In the 1980s, these historical memory issues developed into diplomatic flashpoints, albeit with the qualification that it was still relatively easy to finesse them politically. This is the era Satō Susumu treats in his "The Nakasone Yasuhiro Years: Historical Memory in Foreign Policy" (Chapter 3). The two points of contention that came to the fore in this era were how the war was recounted in Japanese textbooks and the propriety of paying homage at Yasukuni Shrine. On the textbook issue, Japan had the option of claiming that this was an internal matter for Japan alone to decide; on Yasukuni, Japan was able to cite earlier precedent that had gone largely unremarked. Japan did not avail itself of either option. Instead, Nakasone changed the subject and sought US, Chinese, and

Korean cooperation in constructing a great wall against the Soviet Union. Together with this, Nakasone, Miyazawa Kiichi, and others, perhaps in anticipation of China's rise, adopted conciliatory positions on history issues for public consumption that may or may not have reflected their personal opinions. As Japan then had by far the strongest East Asian economy, and both China and Korea were prepared to compromise, this approach was generally successful.

Yet Japan's historical memory issues were not restricted to its diplomatic relations with other countries. There were also major perceptual issues with Okinawa, and Taira Yoshitoshi lays out the Okinawan historical narrative and how it ties to the changes in the political structure over the years there in his "The Rift Between Okinawa and the Japanese Mainland: Historical Memory and Political Space" (Chapter 4). Okinawa under US occupation had developed its own political parties independent of those elsewhere in Japan prior to the 1971 reversion, but the mainland's conservative/progressive battle lines spread to Okinawa, albeit in a somewhat different context, about the same time that talk of reversion became real. In this, the progressive view of Okinawan history—that Tokyo had regarded Okinawa as expendable in the final stages of the war, that Okinawa was disregarded in the San Francisco Peace Treaty process, and that the Okinawan people's wishes counted for nothing in the reversion arrangements—was widespread because the conservative camp shared this historical experience and popular narrative. Indeed, it may be said that dialogue between Okinawa and Tokyo was possible only because there were central government figures who understood this Okinawan perspective and thought it deserved some accommodation.

That shared awareness was seriously weakened, however, with the end of the Cold War, the enervation of the progressive forces, and Japan's generally conservative drift outside of Okinawa even as Okinawa itself moved further to the left in opposition to the continuing presence of so many US military facilities minus their Cold War justification. This pattern persists even today, with each new base-linked grievance recharging Okinawa's shared historical narrative and feeding the sense of alienation from and frustration with the mainland. Returning us to the realm of international relations, Satō Susumu reminds us that establishing good personal relations between national leaders is not sufficient to heal today's rifts.

In seeking to address the broad sweep and implications of contemporary historical memory issues, we have opted not for issue-specific chapters but rather for a panel-discussion format with Hosoya Yūichi moderating and panelists expert in the prime areas of concern: Kawashima Shin (China), Nishino Jun'ya (Korea), and Watanabe Tsuneo (the United States). The record of the first discussion, held shortly before Prime Minister Abe Shinzō released his statement on the seventieth anniversary of the war's end, is in Chapter 5,"Is Reconciliation Possible? The Outlook for Japan-China, Japan-Korea, and Japan–United States Relations." Among the many topics discussed are why China and Korea, which had previously played down the history issue, have recently become more aggressive on it, and where the potential flashpoints are in the seemingly placid Japan-US relationship.

These same experts gathered again a little over half a year after the Abe Statement; the record of this discussion is in Chapter 6, "Historical Memory and International Relations in East Asia: The Abe Statement in Retrospect." The discussants start by outlining the process leading to the Abe Statement and then look at the Chinese, Korean, and US reactions to it. A specialist in British history, Hosoya supplements this with an extensive commentary on historical memory issues as they have played out in Europe. Drawing all of this together, they explore the outlook for Japan's relations with the different countries involved. One takeaway from this discussion is that values politics (including history), which used to be largely a distant second to jockeying over power and interests, is becoming a significant independent variable in its own right.

For readers who want to delve deeper into these issues, we offer Chapters 7 (Hosoya's "Historical Memory and International History: A Guide for Further Reading") and 8 (Komiya Kazuo's "Key Sources on the Postwar Era"), both of which briefly review the academic literature. All in all, this is an extravagantly ambitious book.

Values politics may have come to be an independent variable because victor narratives have come to define international politics in East Asia. Yet what kind of victor allows values politics to run rampant or subjects policy freedom to historical memory considerations? Most likely a victor dissatisfied with the results of the victory. A victor who has won a complete victory can afford to be magnanimous. Prewar Japan was a victor dissatisfied with the outcomes and hence felt it necessary to constantly stress its victor's status. This was particularly acute after Japan lost its position on the Liaodong Peninsula, which it had won in the Sino-Japanese war, to the Triple Intervention of 1895. Not having received reparations from Russia, Japan was unhappy with the limitations on the leaseholds it had wrested from Russia and turned increasingly assertive—which did not end well.

China, Korea, and Russia won their wars against Japan, but they do not have the same claim to winner status that the United States has. Russia, for example, won its battles in Asia Pacific but then went on to lose the Cold War. Korea feels it did not receive adequate reparations because it concluded its peace treaty with Japan in the midst of the Cold War and under a discredited regime. China's situation has the added kicker that its economic development came thirty years later than Japan's and is even now tapering off. Another factor in the Korean case, of course, is that Korea was a Japanese colony and thus could not take part in the war against Japan as an independent nation. Overlaying all of this is the fact that China and Korea were major victims in the war.

By contrast, Japan won the postwar when it achieved rapid economic growth and its democracy took root. And if one delves into the root factors accounting for these achievements, it is very possible the prewar self-identification as a winner carried over across the war's divide and figured as a factor here. Even though I wrote at the outset that Japan has never depicted itself as having won World War II, only a minority of historians today would dispute the notion that there are some aspects in which prewar Japan was successful. This may make it all the more difficult for Japan's neighbors to be magnanimous "good winners." Even though crisis management has averted the worst for now, the historical memory issue is today a complex mix of many issues leading easily to bickering and brawling. What hints does this all-too-inadequate history of the problem hold for us?

First is the need to be accurately cognizant of the immediate power relationships and interests before us. While values politics is emerging as an independent variable, relations are still largely defined by the balance of power among Japan, China, Korea, and the United States. Once that is understood, it is easy to escape the bewilderment and unease that comes of asking why "the other side" is so unreceptive to your own historical narrative. In the discussion sessions, Watanabe quite rightly stresses the absolute importance of being fully aware of the other person's circumstances, to which I would simply add that these "circumstances" are both objective and subjective.

Second, Japan should not just explain and defend its postwar historical narratives but also learn and share the lessons of its prewar historical narratives. As part of this, we should revive the idea of karma. Having itself been an unsated winner, Japan killed the virtuous spiral before it could get traction by being overly focused on the "spoils of war" idea. Japan is thus ideally positioned to provide advice, if it will, should other countries be at risk of repeating this sad history. The true victor is not the victor who nurses grievances and dissatisfaction but the victor who sets a virtuous spiral in motion.

Karma is self-propagating in that it both goes out and comes back. If a virtuous cycle can be initiated, everyone can come out a winner. Conversely, if it is a vicious cycle that is initiated, everyone is a loser. While this is not that difficult to understand in theory, people are somehow reluctant to follow through unless it ties to specific and detailed remembrances and visions.

Japan is looking ahead to commemorating the 150th anniversary of the Meiji Restoration, and this anniversary will very likely trigger an outpouring of broad-brush and succinct summations of the past century and a half of Japanese history. Indeed, this present work may be considered an effort to summarize Japan's postwar history. The important thing is not whether or not these histories are published but whether or not the right lessons are learned from them.

One more lesson that should be revived and shared from the prewar years is that of delineating and distinguishing between the public and the private selves. In the immediate context, this means not cutting corners in the rush to structure a politically virtuous cycle but spending the time necessary to lay the groundwork for this virtuous cycle by promoting greater interaction, exchanges, and cooperation in the economic, cultural, academic, and other realms.

Academia—arguably the furthest thing from politics—must strive to win politics' awed respect. It is essential that scholars continue to build a record of meticulous research into what happened when, where, and why. The 150th anniversary, the 200th anniversary, or even the 250th anniversary is no excuse for slipshod summations. Having tried to live up to this high standard, we would appreciate reader comments, criticisms, and corrections on where we have fallen short.

1

The Yoshida Shigeru Years

Coming to Terms with the Issue of Historical Memory

Takeda Tomoki

Discussions of the issue of historical memory, focusing on what guilt Japan bears for its war of aggression against its neighbors and its colonial rule and how Japan perceives and fulfills its responsibilities, have intensified since the 1980s. A series of events symbolizing the historical reconciliation between Japan and the United States occurred in 2015–2016 and there were hopes for a ripple effect on historical settlements with neighboring countries, yet this issue has yet to be resolved even today.[1]

This issue does not seem amenable to resolution with postwar historiography,[2] primarily because it is often debated without considering the results of postwar historiography. Since the end of World War II, historians in Japan and the other countries concerned have steadily advanced research on the actual conditions during the war. As a result, virtually no historians today still believe that Japan was innocent of aggression during the war. Paralleling this, some researchers have produced dispassionate analyses of how the Allies discriminated against Asian peoples and sometimes themselves committed atrocities. Reconciliation at the academic level should not be impossible if it is grounded in such mutual understanding.

If no progress is made on reconciliation at the political level regardless of the actual progress toward reconciliation in academia, there must be various dynamics at work that go beyond the realm of historical positivism. In fact, the historical perception issue came into full focus in the 1980s because that was when these dynamics began to fully exert themselves,[3] and the period discussed in this chapter, from around the time of defeat in the war up until the 1950s (hereinafter the occupation and independence period), has been treated as a blank space, or at most a prehistory to the historical memory problem.

Nevertheless, this was a period when the issue of how to understand the history of the war had an important impact and was highly political, although in a different sense than later, in the 1980s. Furthermore, among the various points of contention that were debated during this period, there were even debates that put forth the fundamental question of how to understand the war. The purpose of this chapter is to describe the different paths to the historical narrative during this occupation and independence period.

These can be summarized using the image of three streams: the path to the Tokyo Trials (the International Military Tribunal for the Far East), the path continuing to the San Francisco Peace Treaty system, and the path leading from the attitudes of the "Old Liberalists" around the end of the war to the Investigation Council for the War. The first and second paths are relatively well known. For the third path, the relevant materials have been republished in recent years and the research is only just beginning.[4] In contrast to the first and second paths, which exhibit what might be called a "heteronomous" historical narrative, the third path provided the possibility for Japan to draw its own independent conclusions about this history. While that was not ultimately achieved, this chapter looks at the possibilities and limitations of Japan's efforts to produce an independent coming-to-terms with the historical memory issue.

Who are the Old Liberalists? Like "the Reverse Course" and "the Conservative Reactionary," "Old Liberalists" is a journalistic term that was used after the war and has no rigorous academic definition. What the Old Liberalists had in common were criticism of the rise of the military before and during the war, denunciation of the path to war, and advocacy of freedom of speech. After the war, however, they defended the emperor system and were critical of Japan's movement toward socialism; and as the occupation and independence period passed, they were criticized by the postwar left as being "conservative."[5]

Nevertheless, it was none other than the Old Liberalists who advocated an independent Japanese analysis of the war's history during this period. To consider the possibility of such an independent analysis and the reasons that it failed to be undertaken is to posit that the interpretation of history is sometimes so political or dogmatic that the emotions cannot be overcome and the reality cannot be understood or accepted. Of course, there were also differences among the Old Liberalists. Considering, however, that Japan is frequently criticized for not itself having rigorously analyzed the war gone wrong, tracing the potential of the efforts by the Old Liberalists, who were uncomfortable with Japan's path to war, in order to scrutinize and verify that history, is itself significant.

Finally, while their argument was not grounded in the postwar peace-loving-nation position symbolized by Article 9 of the constitution, it developed overlapping that understanding in part.[6] This convergence is an interesting aspect of the historical memory issue in this period.

From around the time of Japan's defeat in the war, the Old Liberalists attempted to intrinsically grasp the truth of the way the war played out and consider the state of the postwar Japanese nation. What sort of historical lessons did this forensic effort lead to, and how was it related to the historical view of the Tokyo Trials and to the San Francisco Peace Treaty system?

The Historical View of the Tokyo Trials and the San Francisco Peace Treaty System

Historical Overview of the Tokyo Trials

The occupation and independence period ran from around Japan's defeat in the war through the subsequent occupation leading to the recovery of Japanese independence. The first event related to the historical memory problem during this important period is the path to the Tokyo Trials.[7]

The Tokyo Trials were war crimes trials that took place from 1946 through 1948, in which eleven of the Allied powers deliberated the responsibility of twenty-eight Japanese leaders under international law. The Allied powers had been planning to try the losing side for war crimes even before the war ended, and the Axis powers expected to be tried if they lost. What was not known was what procedure would be followed and what character those judgments would take. There was a debate among the Allied powers themselves, and initially the dominant opinion was in favor of adopting the summary-execution style used with the Nazi leaders (US treasury secretary Henry Morgenthau was a strong advocate of this approach).

Summary execution, however, was criticized as medieval and bar-baric, and the "civilized judgment" approach (championed by US war secretary Henry Lewis Stimson) of designating war criminals and having them stand trial was adopted.

At the London Conference (International Conference on Military Trials), which took place from June through August 1945, three war crimes were recognized: crimes against peace, ordinary war crimes, and crimes against humanity. In the end, it was decided to adopt the format in which defendants facing charges related to these three crimes would stand trial. The crimes against peace were charges under international law of planning, preparing, initiating, and waging aggressive war, or participating in a conspiracy to accomplish the same; and the crimes against humanity were charges under interna-tional law of inhumane acts committed against any civilian popula-tion, including those committed before the war and against citizens of one's own country, or persecutions on political, racial, or religious grounds. These were both ex post facto laws.

The Potsdam Declaration (Proclamation Calling for the Surren-der of Japan) was issued on July 26, shortly before the end of this London Conference. The Japanese government's intention to accept this declaration was conveyed on August 14, and the Instrument of Surrender was signed on September 2. The stipulation in Paragraph 10 of the Potsdam Declaration that "stern justice shall be meted out to all war criminals, including those who have visited cruelties upon our prisoners" became the legal basis for the Allied powers to try Japanese as war criminals.

These three stipulations were applied at the Nuremberg Trials (which began November 20, 1945) and came to be applied to the tri-als against Japan as well. The Tokyo Trials began on May 3, 1946, and judgment was pronounced on twenty-five of the defendants on November 12, 1948 (three having been excluded from judgment or having died before the trials were concluded).

The Tokyo Trials, which were conducted over a period of two and a half years, placed the responsibility for the war on "war criminals." The trials prescribed three war crimes and had the historical perspec-tive of judging Japan's acts starting from the 1928 Huanggutun Inci-dent as a war of aggression, meaning that the historical perspective was that the war was launched by war criminals, that they were not only conventional war criminals but also war criminals guilty of the crime of jointly conspiring and waging global invasion, and that the war was the crime of "aggressive war" for which Japan alone should be punished.

This perspective was the essence of the historical view of the Tokyo Trials, and this historical viewpoint was presented in "Tai-heiyō Sensō-shi" (History of the Pacific War), which was run serially in the leading Japanese newspapers from late 1945 through the start of 1946 (December 8–January 7) and subsequently published in book form. This account viewed the war as a continuation from the Mukden Incident and emphasized the crimes of Japanese militarists (including their abuse of power, deprivation of citizens' freedom, and inhumane treatment of prisoners and noncombatants); criticized the atrocities of the Japanese army; and was read by a considerable portion of the population.[8]

Historical Narrative as a Means of Integrating Japan Within the International Community

The confrontation between the Tokyo Trials' view of history and opposing historical perspectives did not surface during the occupation and independence period but emerged only in the 1980s.[9]

How were the Tokyo Trials perceived through the occupation and independence period? In fact, the Tokyo Trials were seen as an atonement obligation imposed on a defeated Japan, and the faithful execution of that duty was seen as one of the few means for Japan to gain reacceptance by the international community.

International law expert Taoka Ryōichi understood this and was well aware of the problems with this trial, including its character as victor's justice and its violation of the *nulla poena sine lege* principle (that one cannot be punished for something that is not prohibited by law at the time it is done). Nevertheless, he wrote just before the war trials began at Ichigaya: "From a policy perspective, these trials are a good policy in that they are emotionally satisfying for the people of the belligerent nations." Taoka explained: "This 'the people of the belligerent nations' refers not only to the citizens of the victorious nations but also to the citizens of the defeated nation who were deceived, driven into war, blindfolded, and pushed to the depths of ruin." He added that transcending the boundaries between the victorious and defeated nations by "having those proven truly responsible for leading Japan into war take personal responsibility to atone for the vast blood spilled in this war through judgment by an international court" is "consistent with popular sentiment worldwide."[10] Having the Tokyo Trials identify the war criminals and decide the severity of their punishments was seen as one of the few methods for the decent people of Japan, which was being denounced as an aggressor nation, to have common identification with the international community.

It was Yoshida Shigeru who presented the concept of recognizing the errors leading to the war as an effective means of diplomacy. In a policy speech on November 8, 1949, after the Tokyo Trials had concluded and the new constitution had been promulgated, Yoshida— who had become one of the most influential people in Japan—said that firmly establishing the peace treaty demanded that Japan "demonstrate both domestically and overseas that Japan is a nation of democracy and civilization that can hold its head up as a member of the international community." He added: "The only route to guarantee the security of Japan is, as solemnly declared in the new Constitution, to renounce war, to take the initiative in disarming as a demilitarized nation, and to promote understanding of Japan by the civilized world against the background of the worldwide public love of peace." In other words, Yoshida's understanding was that regaining the international community's trust and ensuring the nation's security as a peace-loving nation were inseparable.

This foreign policy line put forth by Yoshida was clearly based on the peace-loving-nation doctrine, but the greatest factor supporting this logic was "remorse over the past." As he put it:

> When I consider the facts of Japan's defeat in the war in depth, I believe the fact that Japan lacked sufficient knowledge of the international situation, overestimated its own military preparations, and had no hesitation in disrupting world peace sullied our history, hindered the rise of the nation, brought unprecedented misery to the Japanese people having them lose their children, husbands, and parents, and made the world their enemy. It is precisely not having armaments that guarantees the safety and happiness of the Japanese people and leads to international trust. I also firmly believe that having no armaments is sufficient reason for Japan to be proud of itself as a peace-loving nation before all the world. Consequently, I hope all citizens will work toward this end, and I have no doubt the Japanese people will see the way forward.[11]

This speech clearly fuses the three aspects of citizens' diplomacy, promotion of reconciliation, and national security around the core of "remorse over the past."

The San Francisco Peace Treaty System

The next important item is the legal framework following the conclusion of the San Francisco Peace Treaty. Hatano Sumio calls this the San Francisco Peace Treaty system. There were initial efforts toward peace under Ashida Hitoshi, but little progress was made, and reconciliation and Japanese independence were left to Yoshida's leadership. The San Francisco Peace Treaty system provided the structure for the postwar arrangements among governments from the San Francisco Peace Treaty through to the Treaty on Basic Relations between Japan and the Republic of Korea and the normalization of relations between Japan and the People's Republic of China (PRC).[12]

While an explanation and examination of this system would take us well beyond the period covered by this chapter, it was this system that provided the legal framework for settlements among governments, which means that, while they may seem to be unrelated, the treaty and the historical perception issue are closely intertwined. In fact, Article 11 of the San Francisco Peace Treaty refers to the Tokyo Trials in stipulating: "Japan accepts the judgments of the International Military Tribunal for the Far East."

Japan signed the peace treaty in September 1951, with Yoshida as its plenipotentiary, and achieved a return to the international community with its commitment to observe the treaty's provisions. In that sense, the San Francisco Peace Treaty is, from the viewpoint of the historical memory issue, an extension of the Tokyo Trials. Also in that sense, the Allied powers' intent to appropriate justice to themselves alone as the "victors" or "civilized countries," and US strategic designs in the Cold War, were at work in these two paths.[13]

Japanese diplomacy from the Tokyo Trials through the San Francisco Peace Treaty and on to 1956 was a diplomacy of faithfully cooperating with the Tribunal and striving to regain the trust of the international community while knowing that the questions of Japan's war responsibility and how it should be judged remained heavy on everyone's minds, as evidenced in the Yoshida remarks quoted earlier, because it was the only way to "guarantee the safety and happiness of the Japanese people."

The policy statement that Yoshida released in 1956 marking the fifth anniversary of the signing of the San Francisco Peace Treaty was an eloquent summation of his foreign policy. In it he noted that there were still numerous unresolved problems left over from the war, among them the resumption of diplomatic ties with the Soviet Union, the fulfillment of reparation obligations, the conclusion of commercial accords, General Agreement on Tariffs and Trade (GATT) membership, and the normalization of diplomatic relations with both China and Korea. In addition, he characterized the two issues of Japanese yet to be repatriated from captivity and the repatriation of Japanese in

Micronesia and on the Ogawasara islands as especially uppermost in his mind. So intent was he on regaining the international community's trust that he made no specific mention of historical memory issues.[14]

Before and After Japan's Defeat

The previous section looked at two important factors for considering the historical memory issue during the occupation and independence period, but here I would like to return to 1944 when the war was still taking place and review the activities of the Old Liberalists, which should be considered the third path. This I will do by tracing the establishment of one small research center in Tokyo.

Kiyosawa Kiyoshi and Establishment of the Japanese Foreign Relations History Research Center

The Nihon Gaikō-shi Kenkyūjo (Japanese Foreign Relations History Research Center)—a small research unit inside the publishing house Tōyō Keizai Shinpōsha—was launched in December 1944. Organized by Kiyosawa Kiyoshi, a journalist who had been active during the prewar period and was a well-known commentator, the center was just a small research group he hosted. It operated for only a short period of time and left no major accomplishments. Nevertheless, the center cannot be overlooked because it was an effort inside Japan while the war was still raging to examine the facts and to identify where the errors of the war lay.

Kiyosawa's diary provides an account of the developments leading to the establishment of the research center.[15] This is first mentioned on December 28, 1943, a little more than a year before the center was actually founded: "I wrote a proposal for the establishment of a Japanese Foreign Relations History Research Society. I am doing something that I have hoped for a long time; at the same time, it is something that prepares for my future livelihood." Kiyosawa submitted that proposal to Tōyō Keizai the following day, December 29.

Just after the turn of the year, on January 3, 1944, Kiyosawa visited Takagi Rikurō (vice president of the Sino-Japan Enterprise Company), a businessman who was an old friend and who was known for being very knowledgeable about China. Kiyosawa went to ask for financial support to establish the research center. Takagi suggested he consult Kobiyama Naoto of the South Manchuria Railway Company.

Kiyosawa wrote that this was "a good idea," and on January 26 he wrote that he "consulted with Kobayashi and Mitsui concerning the business of the Japanese Foreign Relations Society." "Kobayashi" was Kobayashi Ichizō, the founder of the Hankyū Railway, and "Mitsui" was Mitsui Takao of the Mitsui clan. He subsequently requested, but was refused, a consultation with the Ōkura zaibatsu (business conglomerate) (September 27, 1944, diary entry). Two months later, on November 20, Kiyosawa asked former foreign minister Shidehara Kijūrō to give the address at the opening ceremony for the center, to be held on December 5.

Kiyosawa's diary entry for the day of the ceremony states that twenty-three people took part. "It happened to be on the same day as the funeral service for Dr. Onozuka Kiheiji, which made it impossible for Hozumi Shigetō and Rōyama Masamichi to join us." The research center was probably launched with around two dozen members, and while Kiyosawa did not mention where the opening ceremony took place, Ashida Hitoshi's diary for that day puts it at Tōyō Keizai.[16]

Kiyosawa himself also gave a speech that day in which he enumerated collecting accounts of diplomats' experience, doing distinctive research on diplomatic history, compiling a diplomatic history dictionary, and translating material into English as the four main activities the center would undertake (December 5, 1944, diary entry). Kiyosawa declared that he would not accept any compensation for this work. The research center was supposed to be a way of earning his livelihood, but Kiyosawa was prepared to work at the center pro bono, even though he was the de facto director, so determined was he to do this.

Research on Wartime History and the Old Liberalists

Kiyosawa was a leader in establishing and operating the Japanese Foreign Relations History Research Center. But why was he so engaged in diplomatic history research during the war? Before the war, Kiyosawa had advocated maintaining Japan–United States relations and had been critical of the prowar and right-wing factions who led the process leading to war against the United States. In the diary that he began keeping after the war broke out, Kiyosawa never tired of criticizing people who incited expressions of anti-foreignism. He singled out Tokutomi Sohō, Kanokogi Kazunobu, and other central members of the Dai-Nihon Genron Hōkokukai (Greater Japan Patriotic Press Association), as well as those who opposed Japanese foreign policy from the 1920s on, especially former diplomat Honda Kumatarō and other hawkish right-wing journalists who loudly criticized the policy of cooperation with the United States and noninterference in China as advocated by Shidehara Kijūrō.[17]

However, Kiyosawa did not criticize the right-wingers in public, lest his criticism be considered excessive and he be subjected to a crackdown by the government. Instead, he bundled up his resentment and threw himself into historical research.

First, he wrote the two-volume *Nihon Gaikō-shi* (History of Japanese Diplomacy) (1941). The following year, these two volumes were expanded and published as a combined edition, which was the first overview of modern Japanese diplomacy written in the modern era. While there may be some details that do not stand up in light of today's research, this was a superb book with a solid view of history that still captivates many diplomatic historians. The diplomatic time-lines and other materials that formed the heart of his subsequent *Nihon Gaikō Nenpyō Narabi ni Shuyō Bunsho* (Japanese Diplomacy Chronological Tables and Important Documents) (Hara Shobō, 1953) were also based upon research done during this period. That work, an essential guide for researchers of Japan's diplomatic history, was not published before his untimely death during the war but was ultimately purchased by the Ministry of Foreign Affairs and finally saw the light of day only after the war.[18]

In addition, it can be verified that Kiyosawa agreed to serve as managing director of the Kokusai Kankei Kenkyūkai (International Relations Research Society), led by Ishibashi Tanzan for "advancing research in the history of foreign relations" (April 10, 1944, diary entry), and often listened to lectures and discussions at meetings arranged by the Ministry of Foreign Affairs and other gatherings. It seems clear that the Japanese Foreign Relations History Research Center was another expression of his interest in this subject.[19]

This research center is significant here because it appears that the prewar liberals who were blocked during the war were assembled in full force. From the diary entry when the center was founded, the membership included:

FORMER DIPLOMATS: Shidehara Kijūrō, Matsuda Michikazu, Yanagisawa Ken, Tamura Kōsaku, and Shinobu Junpei.
JOURNALISTS, WRITERS, AND SCHOLARS: Ishibashi Tanzan, Kuwaki Genyoku, Suzuki Bunshirō, Itō Masanori, Takahashi Yūsai, Obama Toshie, Baba Tsunego, Takayanagi Kenzō, and Matsumoto Jōji.

Businessmen: Mitsui Takao, Iida Seizō, Takagi Rikurō, and Miyagawa
   Saburō.
Politicians and bureaucrats (including former politicians and
   bureaucrats): Uehara Etsujirō, Ashida Hitsoshi, and Ayusawa Iwao.

The members came from many different walks of life, but they
all kept their distance from the militarists and ultranationalists during
the prewar period and the war and stayed true to their liberal position. As such, the Japanese Foreign Relations History Research Center served as an umbrella organization for the Old Liberalists who
were oppressed before and during the war.

Interview with Shidehara Kijūrō

Regardless, the research center did not last long, and it closed without achieving any substantive accomplishments. Kiyosawa's sudden
death from pneumonia complications was fatal for the center as well.
The only real clues to the center's historical perspective that remain
are Kiyosawa's diary and a record of an interview with Shidehara
Kijūrō, who attended the center's opening ceremony.[20]
   As topics for the interview, Kiyosawa selected the Washington
Naval Conference, which may be considered the highlight of Shidehara's diplomatic career, and Japan-China relations. Shidehara, who
continuously supported Japanese foreign policy after World War I as
a vice minister, ambassador to the United States, and foreign minister, spoke frankly to Kiyosawa about the difficulties in political coordination inside the United States in holding the Washington Naval
Conference, US concerns about the Anglo-Japanese alliance, and the
split between Japan and the United Kingdom regarding foreign policy toward the United States. Shidehara had gained the confidence of
US secretary of state Charles Evans Hughes when he was the Japanese ambassador to the United States, and he made no secret of the
fact that Hughes had secretly consulted him on exchanges with UK
cabinet secretary Maurice Hankey.[21]
   The Manchurian situation before and after the Mukden Incident
was another area of interest. Shidehara said: "Eugene Chen [Chen
Youren in Chinese] came to Japan, and we held discussions. [Note:
The British-born Chen was the foreign minister of the Guangzhou
government when Wang Jingwei was premier.] . . . Chen came to
Tokyo in July 1931 and came to see me right away. As soon as I sat
down, I said to him in jest 'I hear you have come to sell Manchuria.

I do not know if you have a written commission to do this or not, but even if you have made all the necessary preparations, we have one condition: We want the right to throw all the Manchurians into the Bohai Sea.' Hearing this, Chen laughed. . . . After a while, Chen turned serious and said that there was some truth to my joke." Shidehara then told Kiyosawa what Chen had told him:

> Chen wanted to create a special status for Manchuria. He said Zhang Xue-liang was using 80 percent of the revenues on the military, but this was foolish because the Japanese army would immediately put down anything that might happen even if he expanded the military. So Chen said, in essence, the governor-general system should be abandoned in Manchuria and replaced with a high commissioner structure [this high commissioner structure apparently referring to the high commissioner system used by the UK in the Commonwealth]. The high commissioner would have no military authority and would maintain public peace with police patrols. . . . Chen proposed a structure whereby China would maintain sovereignty with the high commissioner appointed by Japan with Chinese nominal approval.

Looking back at how the conflict of interests over Manchuria (and Mongolia) became a pivotal issue in Japanese diplomatic history, this proposal from some of the forces in China prior to the Mukden Incident is of great interest. Shidehara's real reason for relating this episode, however, was that the question of Manchuria was brought to Japan once again immediately after the Mukden Incident. Shidehara says that Chen made the following remarks after the Mukden Incident: "It is most unfortunate that this [the Mukden Incident] happened, but there is one good aspect. The high commissioner system I spoke of before can now be realized. If Zhang Xue-liang is pushed out, Manchuria will be cleaned up. This should afford a good opportunity to do that. I want to ask what Japan intends to do." Shidehara added: "Aside from the proposal for dealing with Manchuria, the plan Chen brought included a proposed alliance between Japan and China, and he said that unifying these two might constitute a proposal for smoothing Sino-Japanese relations."

We know, of course, that neither a high commissioner system nor a Sino-Japanese alliance to maintain some equality and linkage between Manchuria and Japan was put in place during the 1930s. What did happen were the forced establishment of Manchukuo, the consequent conflict with the League of Nations, the invasion of North China, and the outbreak of total war with China—all of which paved the way to the broader world war.

It is particularly noteworthy that Shidehara and Kiyosawa, who had this conversation near the end of the war, were very critical of the events following the Mukden Incident. Shidehara continued to be proud of Japan's China policy in the 1920s when he served as minister for foreign affairs, but his discomfort with Japanese foreign policy during the 1930s is clear here.

Commonalities and Differences Among the Old Liberalists

Unease with the 1930s

Today, the history of the war is taught assuming qualitative differences between Japanese foreign policy in the 1920s and in the 1930s. This understanding is widely shared among all Japanese, as is plainly illustrated, for example, by Prime Minister Abe's statement issued on August 14, 2015. Consistent with this understanding, the history texts stress the Great Depression or the shock of the Mukden Incident as triggering the change and contrast the international cooperation in the 1920s with the international community's subsequent breakup into blocs, Japan's isolation, and Japan's closeness to Italy and Germany in the 1930s. Given that Shidehara was at the forefront of advocating international cooperation in the 1920s, it may seem only natural that he was discomforted by Japan's 1930s foreign policy shift. In addition to founding the Japanese Foreign Relations History Research Center, Kiyosawa was intent on leaving a record of modern Japan's enduring desire for international cooperation. As proof of this, and also demonstrating his frustrations with the 1930s, Kiyosawa was planning to follow his talk with Shidehara by interviewing Makino Nobuaki, one of the plenipotentiaries at the Paris Peace Conference and part of the faction working for friendly relations with the United Kingdom and the United States during the 1930s (February 10, 1945, diary entry).

Yoshida was another person who was obviously dissatisfied with Japanese foreign policy in the 1930s and during the war. Just before Hirota Kōki appointed him minister for foreign affairs, Yoshida was blocked from taking that position by the army because his father-in-law was Makino Nobuaki and because Yoshida was favorably inclined toward the United Kingdom and the United States. Yoshida met frequently with Kiyosawa and Shidehara, and they had many congenial discussions during the war.[22]

Nevertheless, the Old Liberalists cannot be pigeonholed politically simply based upon whether they identified with the 1920s or the 1930s. Rather, it is necessary to consider what they had in common and what issues divided them.

The Distance Between the 1920s and the 1930s

Shidehara, who was known to be an advocate of international cooperation, viewed the issue of Japanese interests in Manchuria and Mongolia in absolutist terms. At the time of the Mukden Incident, Shidehara was foreign minister in the Wakatsuki Reijirō administration, which was being spun about by the Kwantung army and the Japanese Korean army. Despite that, Shidehara was second to none in his defense of Japanese interests in Manchuria and Mongolia. Kiyosawa's close friend Baba Tsunego described Shidehara after the Mukden Incident as follows:

> [A visitor] asked Shidehara if he had any advice going forward on China. Shidehara responded that China does not recognize Manchukuo's independence and is doing what it can at the League of Nations, but that is the height of foolishness. He said Manchukuo independence is the reality, and China's saying they will rescind that independence may be an interesting theoretical exercise but is already outside the realm of political practicality.[23]

Conversely, what did the people responsible for Japanese foreign policy in the 1930s and during the war think? One such person was Shigemitsu Mamoru. After the Mukden Incident, Shigemitsu served as vice minister for foreign affairs, Japanese ambassador to the Soviet Union, and ambassador to the UK. He was appointed minister for foreign affairs in April 1943 and was known for advocating an Asian Monroe Doctrine and Greater East Asia Co-Prosperity Sphere diplomacy.

Kiyosawa was fiercely critical of Shigemitsu. When Shigemitsu became foreign minister in the Tōjō Hideki cabinet, Kiyosawa wrote: "Shigemitsu is a grand opportunist. To date he has written reports from London and Moscow (on international affairs and policies) following the tone of the military. He is a leading social climber" (April 21, 1943, diary entry). Kiyosawa later wrote: "Whether Shigemitsu was in the USSR or in London, he always said whatever would please the people in power. This is not admired by the younger government officials" (December 9, 1944, diary entry). Kiyosawa all but calls Shigemitsu a warmonger.[24]

However, Shigemitsu, whom Kiyosawa criticized, and Shide-hara, whom Kiyosawa respected, maintained friendly relations as government officials and China hands from the mid-1920s up until the time of the Mukden Incident. While recognizing the limits of Shidehara's diplomacy, Shigemitsu took pride in supporting Shide-hara's foreign policies during the 1920s and worked hard to pro-mote international cooperation. Toward the end of the war, the two also exchanged views regarding the postwar framework.[25] While Shigemitsu certainly had a far more aggressive foreign policy ori-entation than Shidehara did, they were not in complete opposition through the final stages of the war.

On the other hand, Kiyosawa, who was a proponent of interna-tional cooperation, wrote in his diary on December 30, 1943:

> The so-called stubborn foreign policy is succeeding. This would be so if it stopped at a certain fixed point. It would succeed if Japan had stopped at the Manchurian Incident, Italy in Ethiopia, and Germany at the Munich Conference. In Italy's war in Ethiopia, the League of Nations admitted failure and the neutral nations [of World War I] officially discontinued their blockade [June 25, 1936]. The problem is whether or not these various nations should have stopped there.

This entry is fully in line with the statement Shigemitsu made at a meeting of intellectuals (the Sannenkai) organized by his secretary, Kase Toshikazu, toward the end of the war. There, Shigemitsu said: "It would have been perfect had the military stopped with the Muk-den Incident."[26] In other words, the Japanese foreign policy gap between the 1920s and the 1930s was surprisingly small. The Old Liberalists had a realistic perspective toward the outside world before the war and during the war and may be said to have developed a realistic policy doctrine rather than looking at history through rose-colored ideological blinders.

Anticommunism

The Old Liberalists basically shared their anticommunism. Yet there were individual differences as well as commonalities in this as well. For example, Kiyosawa had an intense hatred of the wartime anti-intellectualism that called the Americans animals ("amemals," as it were) and blamed the international situation on a Jewish-communist plot, and he attributed such thinking to a combination of feudalism and communism (December 20, 1943, diary entry). In that sense,

Kiyosawa hated both the extreme right and the extreme left, but he tended to appreciate the intellectual activities of the left in preference to the anti-intellectual rightist words and deeds.[27]

Fierce anticommunism is evident, conversely, in the Konoe Jōsōbun (Report to the Emperor, by Konoe Fumimaro) written in February 1945.[28] This report, which was colored by a conspiracy view of history, states that the post-Mukden history was a conspiracy hatched by the many secret communists in the faction controlling the army and calls for Japan to surrender to the United States before a communist revolution occurs. Yoshida, who was close to Kiyosawa, was involved in writing this report, and the report's underpinnings reflect his pro–United Kingdom and pro–United States worldview. Yoshida's fixation on communist plots also provided justification for his favoring the United Kingdom and United States after the war.[29]

Nevertheless, in the 1930s, Shidehara—who also favored the United Kingdom and the United States—was involved behind the scenes with the revision of the Soviet-Japanese fisheries agreement to ease tensions between Japan and the Soviet Union following the conclusion of the Anti-Comintern Pact and was clearly not that concerned about communism.[30] Kiyosawa was also sympathetic to the efforts to get the Soviet Union to mediate peace with the United Kingdom and United States during the war (March 31, 1944, diary entry). Yoshida, Kiyosawa, and Shidehara stayed in touch throughout this period, but it was Yoshida's anticommunism that stood out in the late stages of the war. Yoshida promoted left-wing intellectuals and worked with them to deal with the immediate postwar crisis, but he ultimately ended up leading the conservative camp in its confrontations with the reformists.[31]

What of Shigemitsu? In fact, it was just after Shigemitsu was appointed ambassador to the Soviet Union that Shidehara devised plans with the Soviet Union, and it was while Shigemitsu was minister for foreign affairs that Kiyosawa had hopes the Soviet Union would mediate a peace initiative with the United Kingdom and the United States. Shigemitsu was also responsible for the normalization of diplomatic relations with the Soviet Union after the war. Shigemitsu had a long and close foreign policy involvement with the Soviet Union, but that did not mean he was particularly sympathetic. Shigemitsu's distaste for the Soviet Union was sometimes more intense, but never less, than Yoshida's. Although Shigemitsu maintained contact with the Soviet Union for diplomatic reasons, he was intensely anti-Soviet because he understood, better than Yoshida did, the impact of the social leveling and socialism that had spread in Japan before and during the war. More than an emotional reaction against communism, Shigemitsu's distaste was based upon a dispassionate analysis of events anticipating the historical conditions leading to the welfare state. After the war, he became the president of the Kaishintō party, which emphasized policies for small and medium enterprise and social security, and led the progressive forces in confronting the conservatives and seeking a realignment of the political structure.[32]

Errors in Japan's China (Asia) Policy

While the Old Liberalists had much in common in how they understood and approached international cooperation, national interests, and ideology, they had differences at the policy-statement level as to how to achieve international cooperation, how to protect and grow national interests, how to respond to emerging communism, and how much to emphasize the need for broad social policy. There were also significant differences in their China policy prescriptions, differences that have yet to receive their due attention.

Regarding China policy, it was Shidehara, and even more so Shigemitsu, who emphasized the errors in modern Japan's Asia policy. In the 1930s, Shidehara's advocacy of a realist foreign policy led him to also be critical of Japan's China policy. When the Second Sino-Japanese War broke out in the summer of 1937, Shidehara received word of a peace plan (the German intermediation plan prior to the launch of the Trautmann mediation) that had been approved by the German ambassador, and immediately took it to the Ministry of Foreign Affairs. However, it was rejected by then–minister for foreign affairs Hirota Kōki. Shidehara reportedly told East Asia Bureau chief Ishii Itarō, with whom he was close: "It is most unfortunate that this had to be put to someone who does not understand foreign policy." When the Abe Nobuyuki cabinet was formed, Shidehara submitted his own plan for handling the Second Sino-Japanese War through his old friend Ōdaira Komatsuchi.[33]

Shidehara's strong interest in Sino-Japanese relations continued after the war. In a lecture, Shidehara explained: "Ever since I entered government service, and in fact even before that, I have strongly believed in the need for friendly cooperation and understanding between Japan and China. That is how I felt then, and that is how I feel today."[34]

Shigemitsu's comments around the time of Japan's defeat go further. He had made similar comments in March 1945, but he commented to newspaper journalists on August 28, prior to the signing of the Instrument of Surrender:

> Japan's position in the world today is very different from what it was in the Meiji era. While working just as hard as during the Meiji era, we must not make the same mistakes they made in the Meiji era. . . . Of the three major Meiji era failings [the one I want to address] is, while the word bothers me, the *"chankoro"* [chink] policy. Although the First Sino-Japanese War was unavoidable, we continued to call Chinese people *"chankoro"* even after that, illustrating how provincial the Meiji era was.[35]

While there were many people saying that Japan's prewar China (Asia) policy was a mistake, Shigemitsu's comments are significant as the earliest postwar example of remorse over modern Japan's China (Asia) policy from inside the Imperial Japanese government system. It was around the same time that the prewar commentator Murobuse Kōshin, who served as a member of the Constitution Investigation Association, wrote in the November 1945 inaugural issue of the magazine *Shinsei:*

> That we need to look hard and clear at our responsibility for the war is in part to fulfill our duty to the world. We must especially remember what we have done in the name of the state to the 400 million peaceful people of China. We took Manchuria from China, bound it with the iron chains of our military, called it a utopia, took Manchuria and Mongolia, devastated northern China, . . . murdered hundreds of thousands of people, and burned homes. The crimes we committed in this war were horrendous. On the other hand, clarifying the responsibility for this war will deliver the Japanese people from slavery, recover our human dignity and consciousness, and launch a new Japan with a new spirit and order.[36]

It is worth noting that, as opposed to remorse as a government policy, this hints at a model for what might be called "ethical remorse"—especially since the foreign policy line put forth by Yoshida was completely lacking in an understanding of Japan's prewar China (Asia) policy as mistaken.

As seen, the Old Liberals' words and deeds evidenced a diversity and depth that cannot be simply dismissed as "conservative" and "antiquated." What is important from the perspective of this chapter is that the Old Liberals were remorseful, each from his own perspective, regarding Japan's prewar colonial rule and foreign aggression. The image that Japan's remorse was forced on the Japanese by the Tokyo Trials and the San Francisco Peace Treaty system has no basis in fact, and there was a very real possibility Japan might have independently looked back on the war and examined its own errors in ways that differed from the Tokyo Trials and the San Francisco Peace Treaty. These efforts to ascertain the facts of the war were systematized under Shidehara Kijūrō, who unexpectedly became prime minister in November 1945, in the establishment within the cabinet structure of the Investigation Council for the War.

The Investigation Council for the War: Possibilities and Limitations

The Investigation Council for the War was established inside the cabinet by the Shidehara administration on November 24, 1945. Abolished by the first Yoshida administration on September 30 of the following year, it was active for less than a year. The council was initially named the Council on the Investigation of the Greater East Asia War but had to be renamed when use of the term "Greater East Asia War" was prohibited in official documents as of January 1946.[37]

The direct cause for establishing the council was a statement by the navy on October 5, 1945, at a government-wide meeting of all ministries organized by the Central Liaison Office. The navy had begun looking into the facts of the war with approval of the occupation General Headquarters (GHQ) and the Supreme Commander for the Allied Powers (SCAP) and wanted the cabinet or the Ministry of Education to take over as the responsible party inside the government (this request was probably made on the assumption that Japan's military forces would be disbanded). This work was taken over by the Cabinet Investigation Bureau on October 15, which then proposed compiling a history of World War II. Given the opposition to compiling a war history, it was decided on October 30 that the bureau should be limited to collecting materials and thoroughly investigating the causes of the war and the reasons for defeat. At the same time, "preventing a recurrence of the errors made in Japan's defeat" was added to the bureau's mandate. Then, in November, the Cabinet Investigation Bureau was reorganized as the Cabinet Councilors Office and the Investigation Council for the War was established. It is significant that the military's desire to compile a history of the war was taken over by the cabinet and that the cabinet established the Investigation Council for the War this way.[38]

Proposals by the Old Liberalists

However, that is not the whole story behind the establishment of the Investigation Council for the War, as there were also many proposals made before and after defeat to look into what really happened. Important among them were those from Shidehara, who was prime minister when the Investigation Council for the War was established. Unhappy with the course of Japanese foreign policy in the 1930s, Shidehara wrote a proposal titled "Shūsen Zengosaku" (Making the Best of Defeat) in August 1945, right after Japan's defeat, and distributed it to a wide range of people, including Yoshida. In this, Shidehara presented five policy proposals, writing of the need to "make clear to each and every Japanese the gravity of the situation brought about by defeat" and stating that this demanded that the government "investigate the causes of our defeat and publish the conclusions." While it was not yet clear that he would become prime minister, it is clear that Shidehara thought the political turmoil over Japan's unprecedented defeat should be prevented by "remorse over the past," and it was the result of Shidehara's leadership as prime minister that "remorse over the past" became one purpose of the Investigation Council for the War.[39]

Ashida Hitoshi, who had joined Kiyosawa in establishing the Japanese Foreign Relations History Research Center during the war, also viewed "remorse over the past" as an important task for the postwar government and saw it as closely connected to the rebirth of the state and the recovery of international trust. On September 4, 1945, Ashida wrote "Dai-Tōa Sensō wo Furi Naru Shūketsu ni Michibikitaru Gen'in narabi ni sono Sekinin no Shozai wo Akiraka ni Suru tame Seifu no Toru beki Sochi ni kansuru Shitsumon" (Questions Regarding the Measures to Be Taken by the Government to Clarify the Causes Leading to the Greater East Asia War's Disadvantageous Conclusion and to Assign Responsibility for the Same) and submitted it to the Higashikuni Naruhiko administration. Ashida believed that "those who neglect self-criticism and harsh introspection, whether an individual or a state, invite their own downfall," and after the defeat he wrote: "The first step toward a true regeneration of the Japanese people is for the Japanese to calmly reconsider the entire past process while facing the current difficulties and making this an opportunity for national remorse." In addition, he said: "I firmly believe that the world will acknowledge our noble spirit if we do this."[40]

Ashida's thinking clearly foreshadows the 1949 Yoshida policy speech mentioned earlier. In fact, Yoshida, who was foreign minister when the Investigation Council for the War was established, told Aoki Tokuzō, who served as the council's secretary-general: "The Allies are trying to put the Greater East Asia War criminals on trial and looking into the causes and facts of the war in detail, but Japanese have a very what's-done-is-done attitude regarding responsibility for the war. This is unacceptable, and we Japanese must ourselves clarify the causes and facts of the war and solemnly and deliberately ascertain the reasons for Japan's defeat so as to prevent a recurrence of such mistakes."[41] The eighty-ninth session of the Imperial Diet deliberated establishing the Investigation Council for the War, and Matsumura Giichi, Saitō Takao, and others, despite their differences of opinion regarding scope and methodology, were all positive regarding the work itself. While the background to the establishment of the Investigation Council for the War included an upsurge of support at the national leadership level, most of them were people known today as Old Liberalists.

Composition of the Investigation Council for the War

One has only to look at the list on page 92 of Tomita Keiichirō's "Haisen Chokugo no Sensō Chōsakai ni Tsuite" to see that the Investigation Council for the War included a large number of Old Liberalists:

President: Shidehara Kijūrō (prime minister)
Vice president: Ashida Hitoshi (member of the House of
                        Representatives)
Secretary-general: Aoki Tokuzō (president of the People's Bank)

SUBCOMMITTEE 1 (POLITICS AND FOREIGN POLICY)
Chairman: Saitō Takao (member of the House of
                      Representatives)
Vice chairmen: Ōkōchi Kikō (member of the House of Peers)
                      Katayama Tetsu (member of the House of
                      Representatives)
Main members: Takagi Yasaka, Matsumura Giichi, and Suzuki
                      Bunshirō

SUBCOMMITTEE 2 (MILITARY AFFAIRS)
Chairman: Iimura Jō (former provost marshal)
Vice chairman: Tozuka Michitarō (former chief of the Yokosuka
                      Naval District)

SUBCOMMITTEE 3 (FINANCE AND ECONOMICS)
Chairman: Yamamuro Munefumi (former chairman,
                    Mitsubishi Trust Company)
Vice chairman: Watanabe Tetsuzō (former professor, Tokyo
                    Imperial University)
Main members: Obama Toshie and Arisawa Hiromi

SUBCOMMITTEE 4 (IDEOLOGY AND CULTURE)
Chairman: Baba Tsunego (president, *Yomiuri Shimbun*)
Vice chairmen: Watsuji Tetsurō (professor, Tokyo Imperial
                    University)
                    Nakamura Kōya (former professor, Tokyo
                    Imperial University)
Main members: Watanabe Ikujirō and Abe Shinnosuke

SUBCOMMITTEE 5 (SCIENCE AND TECHNOLOGY)
Chairman: Yagi Hidetsugu (president, Osaka Imperial
                    University)
Vice chairman: Shibata Yūji (professor, Nagoya Imperial
                    University)

Interestingly enough, Shidehara initially asked the prewar liberals Makino and Wakatsuki to serve as president of the Investigation Council for the War.[42] It was only on February 26, 1946, after many twists and turns, that Shidehara accepted the council presidency, with Ashida Hitoshi as vice president and Saitō Takao, who was well known for his antimilitarist stance, as chairman of the subcommittee responsible for political and foreign policy questions. Baba Tsunego, Watanabe Tetsuzō, Takagi Yasaka, Ōuchi Hyōe (who resigned soon afterward), Obama Toshie, Watsuji Tetsurō, and others were appointed subcommittee chairmen and members. An initial proposal believed to have been prepared by Chief Cabinet Secretary Tsugita Daizaburō also listed Tsurumi Yūsuke, Abe Yoshishige, and Hasegawa Nyozekan as candidates. Like the Japanese Foreign Relations History Research Center before it, the Investigation Council for the War had a strong lineup of Old Liberalists.[43]

The Perils of Pursuing Responsibility

However, the same Old Liberalists who promoted "remorse over the past" and felt this should include "political responsibility" had their differences here just as they did during the war period. One of the main points of difference was over how far to pursue individual responsibility. For example, Shidehara and the government felt strongly that the entire nation was at fault and that all of the people bore war guilt. This may have been a holdover position from the Higashikuni Naruhiko administration, but it was underpinned by the belief that, as Shidehara explained in the Diet: "Just in general, for us to pursue specific individuals as responsible for the war would be akin to washing blood with blood among the Japanese people and is not a desirable approach."[44]

Yet the issue of individual responsibility was actively debated at the eighty-ninth session of the Imperial Diet. Saitō Takao was one of the people who argued for individual responsibility. He said: "I think the fundamental responsibility for the war today lies with two people: General Tōjō and Prince Konoe. Of course, it is not only these two who are responsible for the war. There are many others. But it was these two who held the reins of political power and were fundamentally responsible for causing this war, and there is no one in the world who thinks differently." Significantly, this statement was applauded.[45]

If this line of thinking is pursued to its logical conclusion, however, it soon runs up against the question of the Emperor's responsibility. The Investigation Council for the War settled on sixty-eight items for study and set itself the task of investigating everything from the rise of the military, the oppression of the media, and insufficient education to specific individual causes. Elucidating these accumulated errors could lead to the question of who is ultimately responsible over the long term, and to whether that was not the emperor. Saitō argued that Konoe and Tōjō were responsible, but since they were the emperor's advisers, this responsibility would also accrue to the emperor.

While all of this was going on, GHQ/SCAP presented a draft for the new constitution in mid-February 1946, and the national polity was being pushed to change.[46] As the war criminals' trials continued, the decision not to try the emperor was finally conveyed to Chief Cabinet Secretary Tsugita Daizaburō by Bonner Fellers on March 20, 1946. This decision was made in April, but Tribunal president William Webb argued for looking at the emperor's role even after the Tokyo Trials started later that month. This situation made it difficult to go into war responsibility in any depth when the main priority was on preserving the national polity (i.e., the Imperial institution).[47]

Differences Regarding Causes of the War

The Old Liberalists also disagreed on what they saw as the causes of the war. For example, Saitō, who never stopped arguing that Konoe and Tōjō were responsible, stated: "It goes without saying that the Greater East Asia War ultimately stemmed from the Second Sino-Japanese War, and that the Greater East Asia War would never have happened were it not for the Second Sino-Japanese War. Accordingly, if the responsibility for the Greater East Asia War lies with General Tōjō, then responsibility must also lie with Prince Konoe, who was responsible for the Second Sino-Japanese War." Here, Saitō is expressing what may be called the etiology of the Second Sino-Japanese War, and this is yet another manifestation of the same personality trait that led to his resigning from the Diet for his criticism of the Second Sino-Japanese War.[48]

Ashida Hitoshi developed a different argument. According to Ashida, the war "arose from policy errors around the time of the Mukden Incident." Ashida explained: "Had the Japanese Empire wanted to resolve the Mukden Incident peacefully and avoid international isolation . . . we should have made arrangements with the UK and the Chiang Kai-shek government, which were eager to compromise at that time, and with France and Italy, which were not interested in the Manchuria issue, and then begun negotiations with the US and the USSR."

Instead, the Japanese Empire became more and more isolated internationally and allied with Germany and Italy, and "associated the East Asia issue with the struggle for world domination even though geographical conditions made mutual assistance almost impossible." In other words, Ashida said the war was caused by Japan's diplomatic isolation after the Mukden Incident. Ashida, who quit the Ministry of Foreign Affairs and became a politician after the Mukden Incident, never wavered from this position.[49]

Another individual who was outspoken at the Investigation Council for the War was Baba Tsunego. Baba's basic stance was that starting the war was a mistake in the first place, and he often attributed this to Japan's basic ignorance of "the global situation"—which he then blamed on the repression of free speech in the prewar period. In addition, Baba said that Japan's defeat was ultimately attributable to Japan's prewar international isolation and that the reasons for that isolation show the way to "constructing a nation of peace." In short, Baba said that a nation of peace had to be premised upon freedom of speech, and it was Baba who made Yoshida's nation-of-peace argument from the media position.[50]

The Pacific War in History
and in International Relations

The nature of the argument put forth by the Meiji historian Watanabe Ikujirō, who was a member of Subcommittee 4 (ideology and culture), was slightly different. Watanabe felt that Japan should reflect on its past in the context of its history since the beginning of the Meiji era, and he subsequently elaborated on this in his book *Taiheiyō Sensō no Rekishiteki Kōsatsu* (Historical Observations on the Pacific War).[51]

As Watanabe said at the Investigation Council for the War, he was unhappy that the discussion focused on the idea that the war was sparked by the Japanese military's despotism and prejudice, and he "could not help but feel great doubts and regrets regarding these discussions." These doubts and regrets arose because he could not rule out the questions "Can any major war that determines the fate of a nation be caused by only some of the people and only some members of a certain class without the support of internal and external circumstances (which may have been misunderstood)?" and "Can citizens really be moved by deception and propaganda alone?"[52]

Where, then, did Watanabe place the blame? "Looking over this war within the flow of Japanese history," Watanabe "tried to discover the causes and sources of the war in the history of the Meiji Restoration or in the Japanese character," and paid "special interest and inquiry to how the same things that were credited for the nation's rise could later be blamed for the nation's fall."[53]

In other words, Watanabe noted that the push for overseas expansion supported Japan's development during the Meiji era, but the backwardness of the domestic political system subsequently promoted overseas adventurism and gave birth to Japan's errors starting with the Mukden Incident. "Within the glorious achievements of the Meiji Restoration and the construction of the new Japan . . . or within the everyday-life problems that arise from the Japanese character, the national land area, and the population, there existed special causes for the development and prosperity of the state that were also causes for the war and the major source of Japan's miserable defeat and disaster."[54]

Watanabe said that "prior success became subsequent failure, the cause of the earlier prosperity became the cause of the later crushing defeat and the present unhappiness," and noted that overseas relations "require extremely careful preparations and arrangements.

Otherwise, the consequent harm is beyond contemplation. . . .
Japan's internal and external politics since the Mukden Incident
saw entirely too much misuse and abuse in the preparations and
arrangements stage." He viewed mistakes by Japan's leaders and
the loss of "the guiding principles of government" as the causes of
the war.[55]

Watanabe was not the only one who thought that the type of
aggression starting with the Meiji-era expansion to the continent was
the foundation for national development but also was the cause of the
war and the reason for the tragedy of Japan's defeat. Baba was
another person who held this view, and he urged Watanabe to speak
about understanding the war in historical perspective at a joint meeting of Subcommittees 3 and 4. At that time, Baba also commented:

> When Saigō Takamori and others advocated a punitive expedition
> to Korea in 1873, that also meant expansion to the Asian continent.
> I think expansion to the continent and the development of the
> Japanese people arose from the human instinct to expand outward
> by any and all means. Is it right to denounce this indiscriminately
> by calling it imperialism? If this be imperialism, then all countries
> were imperialist. Do you believe that the cause of war therefore
> lies with every country, or was it inherent in some special charac-
> teristic of the Japanese people? I would like to hear [from Watan-
> abe] regarding this point.[56]

Baba is also interesting for having spoken about Japan's China
policy during the 1920s, when he said: "Japanese may have acted
badly in Manchuria and around China, but the Chinese also treated
the Japanese horribly. . . . My thinking is that if Japan had straight-
forwardly appealed to the League of Nations or elsewhere and made
clear how much the Japanese were being downtrodden before the
Mukden Incident, Japan might not have caused the Mukden Incident
and could have exercised better judgment. Or the Second Sino-
Japanese War might have been avoided."[57] While I have not been
able to confirm this, *Tomimasu Shokutaku Taiheiyō Sensō Ron*
(Tomimasu Essays on the Pacific War) (March 1946) reportedly says
that US and Chinese policies in the 1920s bear some of the responsibility for the Mukden Incident while also noting the error of letting
the military run amok and Matsuoka's foreign policy mistakes during the 1930s. That is in line with Baba's comments, as it highlights
the need to understand the facts of the war in the international context, and is akin to suggesting that all of the nations concerned
shared responsibility for the war.[58]

Conclusion

As we have seen, Japan had a wealth of intellectual diversity during the Imperial era as well, and some intellectuals began trying early on to view the war dispassionately and to identify the errors made and the areas for retrospection. In the end, however, those objectives were not realized.

First, it was around this time that Japanese public opinion turned to complete denial of the latent "fertility" of Imperial Japanese politics. That may have been due to the influence of the Tokyo Trials' version of history, or it may have resulted from the emergence of the so-called fascism historical view. In February 1946, in a speech delivered at a campaign rally in Moscow, Stalin defined the world war just ended as a "war among capitalist countries" and "an anti-fascist war," and said the war against fascism was the defining characteristic of World War II.[59] The research on fascism ("Nihon Fashizumu to sono Teikōsen" [Japanese Fascism and Its Line of Resistance]) that was published in serial format in the magazine *Chōryū* (Currents) starting in January 1948 was representative of how academicism approached this issue of fascism in history at that time. Led by the coauthors of this research article, intellectuals denied both the diversity and the potential of the Old Liberalists; and the Old Liberalists also began to distance themselves from the savagery of the "New Liberalists."[60]

Second, it has been noted that Japan was truly on the cusp of great changes and there was absolutely no leeway for the government to choose a "third way" on the historical narrative issue. In fact, the Investigation Council for the War was abolished due to opposition from the Soviet Union and the British Commonwealth (Australia) on September 30, 1946, during the first Yoshida administration. Apparently there was concern that study of the war might lead to preparations for the next war, and Yoshida had already tentatively decided to abolish the council that August. In the end, the new Japan solemnly accepted the verdict of the Tokyo Trials and chose the path laid out by the San Francisco Peace Treaty.

Third, it is important to recognize the influence of Yoshida's style and how it led the new Japan down this path. Yoshida may be said to have remembered Suzuki Kantarō's advice: "In war, you must either win well or lose well. A carp does not move a muscle once it is placed on the cutting board, even when a knife touches it. I want you to lose well in that manner."[61] Yoshida's foreign policy—which restored Japan to membership in the community of nations and led to its becoming a wealthy country that could hold its head up in the international community—was well aware of the Old Liberalist thinking and efforts, but Yoshida completely accepted the "victors' history." In that sense, it may be said that Yoshida sowed the seeds of the future historical memory problems.

Nevertheless, it was by accepting those conditions that Japan was ultimately able to return to the family of nations. Moreover, starting around 1948, the international situation suddenly turned favorable to Japan's restoration. The spread of the Cold War to Asia transformed Japan and the United States—which had reviled each other and fought to the death just a few years before—into firm allies in Asia. Finding ways to understand the diverse discord and differences that underlay the war was no longer an issue. The Yoshida Shigeru era was a time when it was acceptable for Japan to choose—and Japan did choose—to avoid any independent historical postmortems.

Yet it cannot be denied that Yoshida failed to recognize that Japan's response to Asian nationalism, which was obvious soon after Japan's defeat, was in error. When Rhee Syngman visited Japan in January 1953, Yoshida said: "The past errors happened because of Japanese militarists. I assure you such will never happen again." Behind this statement was Yoshida's understanding that "it is wrong to say Japanese rule brought nothing but suffering to the Korean people. On the contrary, Japan contributed to Korea's economic development and to improving the people's lives, and that should be given its fair due." Yoshida probably thought the same regarding China. As noted earlier, there were major differences between Yoshida on the one side and Shidehara and Shigemitsu, who were aware of the errors of Japan's prewar Asia policy, on the other.[62]

Nor was Yoshida very interested in "carving out an independent foreign policy" as advocated by Shidehara and Shigemitsu after the war. After resigning as prime minister, Shidehara became Speaker of the House of Representatives, where he worked to forge a nonpartisan foreign policy including both the Liberal Party and the Socialist Party so as to avert the kind of party acrimony that had been so disastrous in the run-up to the war. In line with this, Shigemitsu planned, once he became the president of the Kaishintō party, to build a nonpartisan foreign policy structure with Yoshida. However, Yoshida, although also a former diplomat, was indifferent toward this idea and it came to naught because the key to postwar Japanese politics was majority rule and Yoshida had the majority.

Having the majority, it was Yoshida's aversion to the Socialist Party that shut down Shidehara's nonpartisan foreign policy plans.[63]

He called the Japan–Soviet Union negotiations being advanced by Shigemitsu in the Hatoyama administration "out-in-left-field negotiations" and did not hesitate to brand negotiating with the Soviet Union a "national disgrace."[64] Yoshida's anti-Soviet, anticommunist stance became even more pronounced after the war, and his political stance was the very model of "conservatism" in the conflict between the conservatives and the progressives. Unsurprisingly, this political confrontation reflected the different readings the conservatives and the progressives had of history during the 1950s. This was another facet of the Yoshida Shigeru era.

Notes

1. Resources that can be relied upon to provide a good outline of the historical perception issue include Hatano Sumio's *Kokka to Rekishi: Sengo no Rekishi Mondai* (The State and History: Postwar Japan's History Issues) (Tokyo: Chūōkōron Shinsha, 2011); Ōnuma Yasuaki's *Rekishi Ninshiki to wa Nanika* (What Is Historical Awareness?), interview by Egawa Shōko (Tokyo: Chūōkōron Shinsha, 2015); and Tōgō Kazuhiko and Hatano Sumio, eds., *Rekishi Mondai Handobukku* (History Issue Handbook) (Tokyo: Iwanami Shoten, 2015). Unless otherwise noted, the understanding of the issue in this chapter is based on these works. For other resources, see Chapters 7 and 8.

2. History is an academic field that focuses on "how" and "why" questions, and it is thus on a somewhat different plane than the historical awareness issue of guilt and responsibility. Moreover, any questioning of guilt and responsibility must be accompanied by recognition and forgiveness, which means the historical memory issue is a foreign policy issue or an international issue specific to a given region. Regarding this point, see Antony Best's "Yōroppa kara mita Ajia no Rekishi Ninshiki Mondai" (The Seventieth Anniversary of the End of the Pacific War: A European Perspective) in *Chūō Kōron* (September 2015), drawing on postwar reconciliation in Germany.

3. The academic findings of Japanese historians have been published in various forms for scholars and the general public. See Chapter 7 for an introduction to such findings. For references in English see, for example, Loyd E. Lee, ed., *World War II in Asia and the Pacific and the War's Aftermath, with General Themes* (Westport: Greenwood, 1998).

4. Hirose Yoshihiro, ed., *Sensō Chōsakai Jimukyoku Shorui* (Investigation Council for the War Secretariat Documents), 15 vols. (Tokyo: Yumani Shobō, 2015).

5. Two recent works that mention the postwar Old Liberalists are Oguma Eiji's *"Minshu" to "Aikoku": Sengo Nihon no Nashonarizumu to Kōkyōsei* ("Democracy" and "Patriotism": Postwar Japanese Nationalism and Publicness) (Tokyo: Shinyōsha, 2002); and Ueda Miwa's *Jiyū Shugi wa Sensō wo Tomerarerunoka* (Can Liberalism Stop War?) (Tokyo: Yoshikawa Kōbunkan, 2016).

6. Some leading works on the nation-of-peace argument are John Dower's *Embracing Defeat: Japan in the Wake of World War II* (New York: Norton,

1999); Koseki Shōichi's *Heiwa Kokka Nihon no Saikentō* (Rethinking Japan As a Nation of Peace) (Tokyo: Iwanami Shoten, 2002); Wada Haruki's *"Heiwa Kokka" no Tanjō: Sengo Nihon no Genten to Henyō* (Birth of a Nation of Peace: Origin and Transformation of Postwar Japan) (Tokyo: Iwanami Shoten, 2015); and Toyoshita Narahiko's *Shōwa Tennō no Sengo Nihon* (The Emperor Shōwa's Postwar Japan) (Tokyo: Iwanami Shoten, 2015).

7. The following account was prepared referring to Awaya Kentarō's two-volume *Tokyo Saiban e no Michi* (Path to the Tokyo Trials) (Tokyo: Kōdansha, 2006); and Higurashi Yoshinobu's "Tokyo Saiban" (Tokyo Trials), in Tōgō and Hatano, *Rekishi Mondai Handobukku*.

8. Nakaya Ken'ichi, trans., *Taiheiyō Sensō-shi Rengōgun Sōshireibu Minkan Jōhō Kyōikukyoku Shiryō Teikyō Hōten Jiken yori Mujōken Kōfuku made* (The Pacific War History Materials Provided by GHQ Civil Information and Education Section from the Huanggutun Incident to the Unconditional Surrender) (Tokyo: Takayama Shoin, 1946).

9. Ōnuma, *Rekishi Ninshiki to wa Nanika*, p. 19.

10. Taoka Ryōichi, "Senpan Saiban ni Tsuite" (Regarding the War Crimes Trial), *Shinsei* no. 6 (June 1946), p. 21.

11. From Yoshida Shigeru's policy speech at the sixth extraordinary session of the Diet (House of Councilors) on November 8, 1949. Database: Sekai to Nihon, Nihon Seiji, Kokusai Kankei (The World and Japan, Japanese Politics, and International Relations) (Tokyo: University of Tokyo Institute of Advanced Studies on Asia, Tanaka Research Office).

12. For an outline of the occupation period and Yoshida foreign policy, see Kusunoki Ayako's *Yoshida Shigeru to Anzen Hoshō Seisaku no Keisei Nichibei no Kōsō to sono Sōgo Sayō 1943–1952* (Yoshida Shigeru and the Formulation of Security Policy: Japan–United States Concepts and Their Interaction, 1943–1952) (Kyoto: Minerva Shobō, 2009); and Kusunoki Ayako's *Gendai Nihon Seiji-shi 1: Senryō kara Dokuritsu e 1945–1952* (Political History of Modern Japan 1: From Occupation to Independence, 1945–1952) (Tokyo: Yoshikawa Kōbunkan, 2013). On the San Francisco Peace Treaty system, see part 1 of Hatano, *Kokka to Rekishi,* which presents a clean summary of the main points. For a more detailed presentation of the fundamental points of the occupation and independence period, see Hatano Sumio, ed., *Nihon no Gaikō: Sengohen* (Japanese Foreign Policy: Postwar), vol. 2 (Tokyo: Iwanami Shoten, 2015).

13. There was also harsh debate within the prosecution team regarding the political nature of the Tokyo Tribunal. See Higurashi Yoshinobu, *Tokyo Saiban* (The Tokyo Trials) (Tokyo: Kōdansha, 2008). Regarding Japanese foreign policy during the Cold War, see Kusunoki, *Yoshida Shigeru;* and Hatano, *Kokka to Rekishi.*

14. Yoshida Shigeru, "Heiwa Jōyaku Goshūnen wo Mukaete" (On the Fifth Anniversary of the Peace Treaty) (September 8, 1956), later published in Yoshida Shigeru, *Kaisō Jūnen* (Recollections of Ten Years), vol. 4 (Tokyo: Shinchōsha, 1958), p. 188. The quotation is from *Kaisō Jūnen.*

15. Kiyosawa Kiyoshi, *Ankoku Nikki* (Tokyo: Hyōronsha, 1980). Hereafter, quotations from the diary are presented in the main text with only the diary entry date. This diary has been published in translation as *A Diary of Darkness: The Wartime Diary of Kiyosawa Kiyoshi,* translated by Eugene Soviak and Kamiyama Tamie (Princeton: Princeton University Press, 1999).

Although the Soviak-Kamiyama work does not include all diary entries, this work defers to their translation when that is available.

16. Fukunaga Fumio and Shimokōbe Motoharu, eds., *Ashida Hitoshi Nikki* (Ashida Hitoshi Diary), 5 vols. (Tokyo: Kashiwa Shobō, 2012). Quotations from the diary are presented in the main text with just the diary entry date.

17. See Kitaoka Shin'ichi, *Zōhoban Kiyosawa Kiyoshi Gaikō Hyōron no Unmei* (Fate of Kiyosawa Kiyoshi's Diplomatic Criticism), expanded ed. (Tokyo: Chūkō Shinsho, 2004).

18. See Kitaoka Shin'ichi, "Gaikōkan Shusshin Sōri no Rekishi Ishiki" (Historical Awareness of a Diplomat Who Became Prime Minister), in Yoshida Shigeru Memorial Foundation, ed., *Ningen Yoshida Shigeru* (Yoshida Shigeru the Person) (Tokyo: Chūō Kōronsha, 1991). Also see Kitaoka's *Zōhoban Kiyosawa Kiyoshi Gaikō Hyōron no Unmei.*

19. Kiyosawa was very interested in Japan–United States relations. He listened to a speech by former Japanese ambassador to the United States Nomura Kichisaburō and confirmed the possibility of a compromise in the Japan–United States negotiations; heard from Sakamoto Naomichi (Sakamoto Ryōma's nephew, who was engaged in educational activities at the France branch of the South Manchuria Railway) that it was Matsuoka Yōsuke who ruined the Japan–United States negotiations; and wrote about this in his diary (August 9, 1944).

20. This record is in the biographical documents compiled by Kishi Kuramatsu, who was Shidehara's secretary after the war. "Shidehara Kijūrō Danshaku Kō Washinton Kaigi no Rimenkan Sonota" (Baron Shidehara Kijūrō Manuscript: Inside View of the Washington Naval Conference) (Tokyo: Ministry of Foreign Affairs Research Bureau, Section 1, date unknown), and "Nisshi Mondai no Omoide Shidehara Kijūrō Danshaku Kōjutsu Kiyosawa Kiyoshi Hikki" (Baron Shidehara Kijūrō's Statements on Memories of the Sino-Japanese Issue As Recorded by Kiyosawa Kiyoshi) (date unknown), both in Shidehara Heiwa Bunko, National Diet Library, Tokyo, Modern Japanese Political History Materials Room, Collection R-18. The record does not have dates in the main body, but Kiyosawa's diary indicates the interview took place on December 19 and 24, 1944, and January 8, 1945.

21. One very recent work regarding this period is Nakatani Tadashi's *Tsuyoi Amerika to Yowai Amerika no Hazama De* (Sailing Between Strong America and Weak America) (Tokyo: Chikura Shobō, 2016).

22. See Kitaoka Shin'ichi, "Yoshida Shigeru no Senzen to Sengo" (Yoshida Shigeru Prewar and Postwar) in *Nenpō Kindai Nihon Kenkyū* (Modern Japanese Research Annual), vol. 16 (Tokyo: Yamakawa Shuppansha, 1994); and Kitaoka, "Gaikōkan Shusshin Sōri no Rekishi Ishiki."

23. *Shidehara Kijūrō* (Shidehara Kijūrō) (Tokyo: Shidehara Peace Foundation, 1955), pp. 563–564.

24. During the war, there were direct and indirect exchanges between Shigemitsu and Kiyosawa as part of the scheme to form positive public opinion toward the United Kingdom and United States, which was called "Japonicus" in the *Nippon Times* (today's *Japan Times*). Nevertheless, impressions remained unchanged. Takeda Tomoki, "Gaimushō to Chishikijin 1944–1945: 'Japonikasu' Kōsaku to Sannenkai" (The Ministry of Foreign Affairs and Intellectuals, 1944–1945: The "Japonicus" Scheme and the Sannenkai), pts. 1–2 in *Tōyō Kenkyū* nos. 181, 187 (2011, 2013).

25. *Shidehara Danshaku to Daitōa Sensō Waheikan Kiyosawa Kiyoshi Shuki* (Baron Shidehara's Views on Peace in the Greater East Asia War: Kiyosawa Kiyoshi's Memoir) (Shidehara Heiwa Bunko, R-12).

26. Tomizuka Kiyoshi, *80nen no Shōgai no Kiroku* (Record of My Eighty Years) (private publication, 1975), entry from March 11, 1945.

27. See Yamamoto Yoshihiko's *Kiyosawa Kiyoshi no Seiji Keizai Shisō: Kindai Nihon no Jiyū Shugi to Kokusai Heiwa* (Kiyoshi Kiyoswa's Political and Economic Thinking: Modern Japanese Liberalism and International Peace) (Tokyo: Ochanomizu Shobō, 1996); and Yamamoto Yoshihiko, *Kiyosawa Kiyoshi sono Tagen Shugi to Heiwa Shisō no Keisei* (Kiyosawa Kiyoshi: Formation of His Pluralism and Peace Ideology) (Tokyo: Gakujutsu Shuppankai, 2006).

28. "Shōwa 20nen 2gatsu 14nichi Konoe Kōshaku Tenki Hōshi no Sai Jikyoku ni kanshi Sōjō no Yōshi" (Summary of Prince Konoe's Report to the Emperor Regarding Current Affairs on February 14, 1945), in Kido Diary Research Group, *Kido Kōichi Kankei Bunsho* (Writings Concerning Kōichi Kido) (Tokyo: University of Tokyo Press, 1966), pp. 495–497.

29. Shōji Jun'ichirō, "Konoe Jōsōbun no Saikentō: Kokusai Jōsei Bunseki no Kanten Kara" (Reconsideration of Konoe's Report to the Emperor: From an International Affairs Analysis Perspective), in *Kokusai Seiji* (Japan Association of International Relations) 109, issue on "Shūsen Gaikō to Sengo Kōsō" (The Foreign Policy of Defeat and Postwar Structures) (1995).

30. *Shidehara Kijūrō,* pp. 499–503.

31. On relations between Yoshida and left-wing intellectuals, see Takahashi Hikohiro's *Nihon Koku Kempō Taisei no Keisei* (Formation of Japanese Constitutional System) (Tokyo: Aoki Shoten, 1997).

32. See Takeda Tomoki, *Shigemitsu Mamoru to Sengo Seiji* (Shigemitsu Mamoru and Postwar Politics) (Tokyo: Yoshikawa Kōbunkan, 2002). During his time as ambassador to the Soviet Union (1936–1938), Shigemitsu had embassy personnel conduct an analysis of the Soviet Union and reported this to Japan. See Takeda Tomoki's "Kaisetsu" (Commentary) in Shigemitsu Mamoru Kinenkan, ed., *Shigemitsu Mamoru Gaikō Ikenshoshū* (Collection of Shigemitsu Mamoru's Diplomatic Opinion Papers) (Tokyo: Gendaishiryō Shuppan, 2010).

33. *Shidehara Kijūrō,* pp. 505, 511.

34. Shidehara Kijūrō, "Watakushi no Shinakan" (My Views on China), March 25, 1946 (Shidehara Heiwa Bunko, R-18).

35. Etō Jun, ed., *Shūsen Shiroku* (Historical Record of the End of the War), vol. 1 (Tokyo: Kōdansha, 1989), pp. 217–218. Shigemitsu made a similar statement at a meeting of the Sannenkai on March 15, 1945. Tomizuka, *80nen no Shōgai no Kiroku,* entry for March 15, 1945.

36. Murobuse Kōshin, "Arataneru Hi no Tame ni" (For a New Day), *Shinsei* inaugural issue (November 1945).

37. Unless otherwise noted, this account of the Investigation Council for the War is based on Tomita Keiichirō's "Haisen Chokugo no Sensō Chōsakai ni Tsuite: Seisaku wo Kenshō suru Kokoromi to sono Zasetsu" (The Investigation Council for the War Immediately After the War: Policy Verification Efforts and Their Frustrations) (National Diet Library, Tokyo, Research and Legislative Reference Bureau *Refarensu,* January 2013).

38. If a history of the war is to be more than a military history, it should naturally be compiled postwar. Partial results were compiled by the Ministry

of Demobilization. The reports through number 36 are reprinted in Tanaka Hiromi (editor-in-chief), Commentary, Second Bureau of Demobilization Liquidating Department, ed., *Taiheiyō Sensō Kaisen Zenshi* (History Prior to the Outbreak of the Pacific War) (Tokyo: Ryokuin Shobō, 2001). The commentary there and "Koramu no. 3: Shūsengo ni Okeru Sensō Chōsa oyobi Shijitsu Chōsa" (Column 3: Postwar Investigations into the War and the Historical Facts), JACAR Glossary, https://www.jacar.go.jp/glossary/fukuin -hikiage/column/column3.html, suggest that the army and navy investigations began earlier than indicated in Tomita, "Haisen Chokugo no Sensō Chōsakai ni Tsuite," and were complex. I would like to leave this for another time.

39. Shidehara Kijūrō, "Shūsen Zengosaku" (Making the Best of Defeat), in *Shidehara Kijūrō.*

40. Ashida Hitoshi, "Dai-Tōa Sensō wo Furi Naru Shūketsu ni Michibik-itaru Gen'in narabi ni sono Sekinin no Shozai wo Akiraka ni Suru tame Seifu no Toru beki Sochi ni kansuru Shitsumon" (Questions Regarding the Measures to Be Taken by the Government to Clarify the Causes Leading to the Greater East Asia War's Disadvantageous Conclusion and to Assign Responsibility for the Same), in *Ashida Hitoshi Kankei Bunsho* (Writings Concerning Ashida Hitoshi), documents section, p. 160. There are two versions of this document with different wording but the same purport.

41. Aoki Tokuzō, *Sensō Chōsakai no Hossoku kara Haishi made: Moto Sensō Chōsakai Jimukyokuchōkan Aoki Tokuzōshi Dan* (Conversations with former Investigation Council for the War Secretary-General Aoki Tokuzō from the Launch Through the Abolition of the Investigation Council for the War) (Shidehara Heiwa Bunko, R-12).

42. Tomita, "Haisen Chokugo no Sensō Chōsakai ni Tsuite," p. 90. On Kiyosawa's intent to interview Makino at the Japanese Foreign Relations History Research Center, see the "Before and After Japan's Defeat" section of this chapter.

43. Ōta Ken'ichi et al., eds., *Tsugita Daisaburō Nikki* (Tsugita Daisaburō Diary) (Okayama: Sanyo Shinbunsha, 1991), p. 162.

44. Shidehara Kijūrō, "Dai 89kai Shūgiin Honkaigi Gijiroku" (Proceedings of the 89th Plenary Session of the House of Representatives), November 28, 1945, in Teikoku Gikai Kaigiroku Database, National Diet Library, http://teikokugikai-i.ndl.gov.jp.

45. Saitō Takao, "Dai 89kai Shūgiin Honkaigi Gijiroku" (Proceedings of the 89th Plenary Session of the House of Representatives), November 28, 1945, in Teikoku Gikai Kaigiroku Database, National Diet Library, http://teikokugikai-i.ndl.gov.jp.

46. Regarding revising the constitution, see Koseki Shōichi, *Shinkenpō no Tanjō* (The Birth of Japan's Postwar Constitution) (Tokyo: Chūō Kōronsha, 1997). Later listed by Chūkō Bunko, currently available as *Nihonkoku Kenpō no Tanjō* (Translation) (Tokyo: Iwanami Gendai Bunko, 2009).

47. *Tokyo Saiban e no Michi,* p. 171.

48. Ibid.

49. Ashida Hitoshi, "Kansō" (Impressions), in *Ashida Hitoshi Kankei Bunsho,* documents section, p. 161. These are believed to be impressions compiled in his later years. The relevant portion is: "My humble opinion going back to the Mukden Incident which I have expressed [in this questionnaire] . . . was not

first released to the world today, after the defeat in the war. . . . It is my cherished opinion. In retrospect, since 1932, when I retired from the government in reaction to the Mukden Incident, I have earnestly, firmly held this assertion, with a deep desire to save our motherland from the prospect of mad upheaval."

50. See Baba's statement in "Sensō Chōsakai Dai 4 Bukai 1 kai Gijiroku Sokkiroku" (Draft Minutes of the Proceedings of the 1st Meeting of Subcommittee 4 of the Investigation Council for the War), April 23, 1946, in *Sensō Chōsakai Jimukyoku Shorui,* vol. 6.

51. Watanabe Ikujirō, *Taiheiyō Sensō no Rekishiteki Kōsatsu* (Historical Observations on the Pacific War) (Tokyo: Tōyō Keizai Shimpōsha, 1947).

52. Ibid., pp. 1–2.

53. Ibid., p. 4.

54. Ibid., p. 34.

55. Ibid., pp. 132–133.

56. *Sensō Chōsakai Dai 4 Bukai 1 kai Gijiroku Sokkiroku,* p. 255.

57. Ibid., p. 270.

58. Yui Masaomi, "Senryōki ni okeru Taiheiyō Sensō kan no Keisei" (Formation of Views on the Pacific War During the Occupation), *Shikan* 130 (1994), p. 7.

59. This speech was translated in *Sekai Shūhō* in April 1947. It is introduced in Hirano Yoshitaro's "Stārin Gichō no Dainiji Sekai Taisen ni taisuru Shisō" (Chairman Stalin's Thoughts on the Second World War), in *Sensō to Heiwa no Shiteki Bunseki* (Historical Analysis of War and Peace) (Tokyo: Yakumo Shoten, 1949).

60. This serial included, for example, Tsuji Kiyoaki's "Kakkyo ni Nayamu Tōchi Kikō" (Government Organs Worried About Defending Their Authority) and Maruyama Masao's "Gunkoku Shihaisha no Seishin Keitai" (Psychological Makeup of Military Rulers), *Chōryū* (May 1949). The effort to locate the origins of a unique Japanese fascism in the Konoe administration, even while recognizing that administration's diversity as atypical of a totalitarian state and recognizing that it lacked the strength of leadership Nazi Germany had, seems to exhibit both a strong ethical basis and the influence of a specific historical understanding of the Tokyo Trials and Stalin.

61. Yoshida Shigeru, *Kaisō Jūnen* (Recollections of Ten Years), vol. 1 (Tokyo: Shinchōsha,1957), pp. 116–117.

62. Nakanishi Hiroshi, "Yoshida Shigeru no Ajiakan: Kindai Nihon Gaikō no Aporia no Kōzō" (Yoshida Shigeru's Views on Asia: Structure of Japanese Diplomacy's Aporia), in *Kokusai Seiji Yoshida Rosen no Saikenshō* no. 151 (2008), p. 25.

63. Regarding the efforts Shidehara and Shigemitsu made for nonpartisan diplomacy, see Takeda Tomoki, "Sengo Nihon no Gaikō Seisaku Kettei to Seitō no Seisaku Chōsei Kinō: Kenkyūshi Riron Hōhōron" (Determination of Postwar Japan's Foreign Policy and the Policy Coordination Function of Political Parties: Research History, Theory, and Methodology), in Oku Kentaro and Kōno Yasuko, eds., *Jimintō Seiji no Genryū: Jizen Shinsasei no Shiteki Kenshō* (Headwaters of LDP Politics: Historical Examination of the Preliminary Review System) (Tokyo: Yoshida Shoten, 2015); and *Shigemitsu Mamoru to Sengo Seiji,* pt. 2.

64. *Kaisō Jūnen,* vol. 4, pp. 188–189.

2

The Satō Eisaku Years
Historical Memory in a Time of Rapid Economic Growth

Murai Ryōta

History-textbook depictions, prime ministers praying at Yasukuni Shrine, the comfort women: all of these have long been recognized as historical memory issues of international concern. But looking at Japan's postwar history a little more closely, their framing and handling differs importantly from period to period, just as the question of how history is to be understood at any given time varies depending upon Japan's international situation at the time. Looking at what is loosely termed the Satō Eisaku years, which followed Yoshida Shigeru's time, this chapter attempts to clarify the era from the early 1960s to the late 1970s.

During the 1950s, Japan was making a new start after having lost the war and was under pressure to adopt a specific understanding of history—a reading that was consistent with its experiences leading up to and during the war and was thus easy to accept as Japan concentrated on repairing its foreign relations and working out reparations agreements. Later on, though, in the 1980s the Yasukuni Shrine question became an international issue and the question of historical memory emerged as the central foreign policy issue it is today. Between these two decades, Japan accomplished a remarkable economic recovery and won the reversion of Okinawa. Japan was looking anew at how to live in the international community and considering what path it should take after accomplishing this rapid growth.

There are four dimensions to Japan's understanding of history. The first is an internal understanding of history: the way postwar Japan saw Imperial Japan stripped of its overseas colonies and a "collapsed empire."[1] The question of memorials for the war-dead is one obvious expression of this inward-looking view, and there was later the question of public attitudes to the war as seen in the textbook controversy.

Second, there was the way the empire was understood in hindsight. Japan's defeat not only led to remorse over a war of aggression but also involved disowning the time spent as a colonial power and maintaining very altered relationships with areas formerly subject to Japanese Imperial rule. These included the people and governments of Taiwan, the Korean Peninsula, the Kwantung leased territory, and Micronesia.

Third was the question of reconciliation with the aggrieved nations of Asia. This was particularly crucial with countries such as China that had borne the brunt of the Japanese aggression and countries that had been battlefields or occupied, many of them in Southeast Asia but also including India, the Philippines, and Australia. Many of these had been colonies before the war but were independent nations after the war.

Fourth was the question of reconciling with those wartime adversaries in the West that were themselves colonial powers. Because the post–San Francisco Peace Treaty international order was led by the United States, which was itself anticolonial, this was also a question of compatibility with the international order. All of these dimensions have to be considered together lest we miss the complete picture or overlook some underlying issues.

Shortly after the war ended, Yoshida was prone to getting up early and walking up to an escarpment where he had an unobstructed view as far as the horizon. The vast expanses of red soil with even the weeds burned off from the bombing were a sobering sight, and he was often heard to mutter: "When will we ever get this cleaned up and the houses built up again? Even twenty years might be a stretch."[2] Later, in a speech accepting the San Francisco Peace Treaty, Yoshida said that a new Japan would be born from the rubble of the old Japan. Looking at it twenty years later, what did this new Japan look like and where was it going?[3] This chapter represents a hunt for clues to answering this question within the context of the times.

Post-Anpo Soul-Searching: The Postwar, the Cold War, and Rapid Economic Growth, 1960–1964

A Practical Response to Dealing with Postwar Problems

Looking back from the present, there are two myths associated with the 1960s. One is the myth of Japan as a great economic power, and the other is the myth that this was a golden age for the Liberal Democratic Party (LDP). Both are based on hindsight, and both diverge from how people saw the situation at the time. It is true that the foundations for Japan's rapid economic growth were laid starting in 1958, and it is also true that the LDP was founded in 1955 and stayed in power without a break until 1993, but Japan was rocked by major political instability in 1960 due to the riots protesting the security treaty. The anti-treaty Japan Socialist Party (JSP) was supported by the working class, and this made them a formidable opposition party. In the lead-up to 1970 and the debate over the security treaty's rollover extension, fresh protests further fueled the conservative versus progressive confrontation. There was fierce rivalry between the LDP and the JSP within what is called the 1955 structure. As Ikeda Hayato, Satō Eisaku, and others who succeeded Yoshida as prime minister worked their way along an economic path based on cooperation with the United States, they were subject to constant carping and criticism from both right and left.

Following the 1960 Anpo demonstrations protesting the Japan–United States Security Treaty, the first development in response to the demands of the Cold War was to strengthen ties with the United States and the countries of Western Europe. The Berlin Wall, that symbol of East-West confrontation, was built in August 1961, and the Cuban Missile Crisis occurred in October 1962. Inaugurated in January 1961, the administration of President John F. Kennedy worked to restore the ties between the United States and Japan and, wary of the security treaty disturbances as making Japan the weak link in the Western camp, worked with Japan to strengthen the economy and promote the building of good relations between Japan and Western Europe.[4] For Japan, this meant substantial progress through economic reconciliation.

The Ikeda (Hayato) administration worked on the problem of the Thai special yen, the problem of the government appropriation for relief in occupied areas, the Burma compensation review negotiations, negotiations regarding Korea's right to make claims against Japan, and other pending issues.[5] To an extent, the Cold War worked in Japan's favor in the peace treaty negotiations. Since it was thought that the excessive reparations demanded of Germany following World War I had been a cause of World War II, reparations were limited to such as allowed Japan a viable economy.[6] Japan worked out agreements with Burma, the Philippines, Indonesia, and South Vietnam and paid reparations from 1955 to 1976. In the same period, it worked to settle other problems by carrying out what could be called quasi-reparations with economic cooperation and payments in lieu of reparations as part of the postwar settlements with Laos, Cambodia, Thailand, and more.

The Singapore and Malaysia blood-debt problem starting in 1962 is particularly noteworthy.[7] When a mass grave of hundreds of victims of the Japanese occupation was discovered in Singapore in February, the Japanese government did not dispute the charge that the occupation had murdered large numbers of Chinese, and Prime Minister Ikeda expressed his heartfelt regret when Lee Kuan Yew of Singapore came to Japan.[8] At the same time, given that Singapore had been a Crown colony and the UK had given up the right to seek compensation, Japan argued that there was no legal basis for any Singaporean claims. However, given Singapore's separation from the merger agreement and Malaysia, Japan entered into negotiations. After prolonged talks, an agreement was reached in 1967 to settle the issue "completely and finally" with a combination of grants and loans.[9] In addition to insisting on putting this within a legal framework, the Japanese position was also shaped by a desire to achieve an appropriate balance with other regions and the political situation in the recipient country.

At home, the governing party and the opposition were in sharp disagreement over the compensation question, with the opposition JSP criticizing the government as insufficiently contrite and not interested in atoning for the wrongs done. In the case of the question of the Thai special yen, for example, the JSP opposed the government's effort to promote the payment as having the characteristics of compensation and maintained that it was just another vehicle for the direct export of Japanese capital aimed at securing imperialistic hegemony in Southeast Asia.[10] In this, the JSP advocated that Japan be unarmed and peaceful but that the need to stabilize people's lives argued against any further burden of compensation, thus seeking an end to compensation.[11] This attitude emphasized Japan's rebirth but could be seen as at odds with the thinking of the international community.[12]

The Development of Introspection
and Damaged Communities

As time passed and with rapid economic growth enabling more and more people to escape abject poverty, a change also took place in their introspection. Following the war, Marxist historical interpretations questioning social and economic structures were mainstream in Japanese historical academia, but political science was orientated toward modernization and was critical of Japan's special characteristics and holdover feudal elements, with Maruyama Masao a leading figure in this scholarship.[13] In 1961, Edwin Reischauer, also a historian, arrived as the US ambassador. Reischauer thought highly of Japan's modernization and initiated a discussion about considering it a model for newly emerging countries.[14]

Of course, history is not a straight-line story, and work continued on empirical research into the war's causes and course. Published by the Japan Association of International Relations in 1962–1963, *Taiheiyō Sensō e no Michi* (Japan's Road to the Pacific War), in seven volumes plus a separate volume of appendixes, is a scholarly elucidation of the mechanisms of aggression, researching the process from right before the Mukden Incident to Pearl Harbor. Under the terms of the San Francisco Peace Treaty, Japan accepted the verdict of war crimes handed down by the Allies at the Tokyo Trials. However, research by independent historians sometimes supported and sometimes contradicted the official history narrative on the planning and timing of this aggression. A great variety of theories have been evoked to explain "the war." Hayashi Fusao published *Dai-Tōa Sensō Kōteiron* (A Positive View of the Greater East Asia War), while Ienaga Saburō brought lawsuits in 1965 over how future generations should be taught Japan's history and contesting the screening of his school textbooks.

The question of memorials for the war-dead also came to the fore. Before and during the war, the central establishment for memorializing the fallen dead was the Imperial Shrine of Special Status, called Yasukuni Shrine, but Yasukuni's link with the state was cut during the US occupation reforms, though it was allowed to survive as a religious judicial person.[15] The first priority for the bereaved families was surviving, but once survival was assured, they sought government support for the enshrinement of lost family members at Yasukuni Shrine. All Class B defendants (accused of war crimes) and Class C defendants (accused of crimes against humanity) were included.[16] Symbolic overseas missions were mounted to bring back soldiers' remains, and the Chidorigafuchi National Cemetery was established in 1959.[17] In July 1963, the Ikeda administration decided to confer decorations on war survivors, and the conferring of honors on those fallen in war, which had been stopped by GHQ in April 1947, was revived the following January. Similarly, following the restoration of independence, a government-sponsored national memorial service for the war-dead was held in Shinjuku Gyoen park in 1952. This was moved to the Hibiya Kōkaidō (Tokyo Metropolitan Hibiya Public Hall) in 1963. Also in 1963, Tokunaga Masatoshi, a member of the House of Councilors who had been a navy lieutenant at war's end and who served as general secretary of the Japan War-Bereaved Families Association, sought to have a memorial service held every year for all of the nation's fallen, saying: "Japan has its peace constitution and has declared that we will make war no more, and this will be one more action in support of that." As for where he thought this ceremony should be, he suggested the open spaces in front of the Diet building or in front of the emperor's residence as possibilities.[18] Following this, a memorial service was held every year. In 1964, the service was held within the grounds of Yasukuni Shrine, but when this became an issue in the Diet the following year, the ceremony was moved to the Nippon Budōkan.[19]

Writing in 1964, Prime Minister Satō said of his own wartime experience: "My recollections of those days are all memories of a terrible defeat. . . . Even if I do not speak of this miserable situation, all of us shared the same horrendous experiences and have the same memories."[20] Experiences differed with place, age, and situation, but Prime Minister Satō saw the experience of defeat as common to all Japanese.

Normalization of Relations with Korea, the Vietnam War, and the 1970 Security Treaty, 1965–1969

Normalization of Relations with Korea

The 1964 Tokyo Olympics proclaimed to all the world that Japan had recovered from the hellfire of war and, with the symbolism of the emperor as honorary president, Japan achieved a return to the international stage. However, 1964 was not all gold. China carried out a nuclear test on October 16, and the Gulf of Tonkin incident in Vietnam in early August led the United States to start bombing North Vietnam the following February.

Such was still the situation when the Treaty on Basic Relations between Japan and the Republic of Korea was signed in June 1965 and the Satō administration achieved diplomatic normalization. Fourteen years had passed in preparatory negotiations, with the highest hurdle being the issue of the right to demand reparations, but the United States was very concerned about the Cold War and strongly urged the treaty be signed. Ōhira Masayoshi, foreign minister in the Ikeda administration, and Kim Jong-pil, director of the Korea Central Intelligence Agency, agreed that there would be a $300 million grant, a $200 million interest-bearing loan, and a $100 million commercial loan in quasi-compensation, which was later supplemented to top $300 million US in commercial loans.[21] Efforts were made to meet Korea's quantitative expectations, and the settlement was affirmed to be "complete and final." In February 1965, Foreign Minister Shiina Etsusaburō, speaking at Kimpo International Airport, said: "There have been unfortunate times in our two countries' long history. This is truly regrettable, and we are deeply remorseful."[22]

There was strong opposition to the treaty in both countries. In Korea, criticism of President Park's "low profile" foreign policy on Japan led to the imposition of martial law. In Japan, looking ahead to 1970, when the security treaty with the United States would come up for renewal, normalization was criticized as hardening the division between North and South Korea and having a militaristic character. The LDP and the JSP were in full standoff mode in the Diet, with the JSP seeking to have personal property claims "settled based on the evidence" and issuing a declaration disowning the treaty.[23] Prime Minister Satō, speaking on national policy at a cabinet town hall in Kanazawa on September 26, spoke of Japan's dedication to preserving freedom and devotion to peace. On the normalization of relations with Korea he said he thought lingering doubts and anxiety that Japan might not have entirely forsaken its old ways had complicated the negotiations.[24] Almost immediately after this, on September 30, there was a coup in Indonesia totally upending the situation in the region.[25]

"Peace-Loving" Japan Searching for a National Memorial in the Shadow of the Vietnam War

In August 1965, Prime Minister Satō visited Okinawa and said that the postwar period will not have ended for Japan until Okinawa is returned. In August 1967, at a cabinet town hall in Wakayama, he spoke of his impression of the memorial services for the war-dead, saying: "The scars of war are no longer visible in Japan. Yet it must be admitted that there are fallen spirits throughout the land, and it is when you stand before those spirits of the fallen that you feel the scars of wars past." In this, he was stressing the importance of maintaining Japan's identity as a "peace-loving nation" that would develop a flourishing economy founded on democratic politics.[26] All this while the Vietnam War fanned Japanese antiwar feelings, the university disturbances spread, and the left-right confrontation grew more intense.

Yoshida Shigeru's state funeral in 1967 became an opportunity to look back at developments since the war, just as the 1968 celebrations marking the Meiji Restoration's centennial were an opportunity to reflect on how Western civilization had been digested and absorbed, on the great sacrifices that had been made, and on the outlook for the future.[27] There was strong criticism that it was the Meiji Restoration's centennial and not the twentieth anniversary of the new constitution that was being celebrated, and the occasion sparked the publication of voluminous historical materials and fueled much honest discussion transcending political, national, and other differences. There was also a broadening of resource availability, one example being the August 1968 *Kurashi-no-Techō* (Notes on Daily Life, vol. 96), a special issue gathering readers' reminiscences of life during the war.

While all of this was happening, the question of establishing a memorial for the war-dead became mixed up with the question of having the state manage Yasukuni Shrine. The Japan War-Bereaved Families Association, for example, gathered 23.4 million signatures on a petition seeking state support for Yasukuni Shrine and in April 1966 held a national convention for war-bereaved families for realizing state support for Yasukuni Shrine.

As symbolized by the *akagami* (red postcard) draft notices, young men had been torn from their everyday lives and sent to the battlefield. In 1968, the work of bringing back these soldiers' remains from overseas began again. However, plans to honor the dead ran up against a constitutional problem in the interpretation of the separation of state and faith. While there were quite a number of people who unthinkingly assumed out of habit that Yasukuni Shrine would be the center for commemoration, labor unions and citizen activists strongly supported the constitutional separation, and there were many who feared a rebirth of militarism and nationalism. In addition, religious groups who valued their newfound religious freedom and many others strongly opposed Yasukuni Shrine quite apart from this left-right rivalry. Central to these opposing parties' activities were legal battles in the courts. Among the many lawsuits filed were the Tsu *jichinsai* lawsuit contesting a public authority's use of public money for a ground-breaking ceremony, the Minoo suit contesting city plans to provide public land for a memorial to the loyal dead, and the Iwate Yasukuni suit over government officials attending Yasukuni Shrine ceremonies. Also in relation to the constitution, the final report of the Constitution Research Council, set up in 1957, was delivered in July 1964. Prime Minister Satō said that he would like to spend time thinking about the constitution with the people, effectively shelving the question of amending the constitution.

When Yasukuni Shrine approached the centennial of its founding in 1969, the LDP submitted a bill to the House of Representatives finessing the question of reconciling state support with the constitution by saying that the name "Yasukuni Shrine" notwithstanding, it was not a religious judicial person and decisions about the war-dead would be made by the prime minister in line with standards set down by government ordinance and based on proposals from Yasukuni Shrine. As such, the shrine would be subject to oversight by the prime minister and would thus be under democratic control.[28]

Normalization of Diplomatic Relations with China and the Constitutional Debate After the 1970 Anpo Protests, 1970–1975

Normalization of Diplomatic Relations with China

The same Satō administration that later engineered the agreement for Okinawa's 1972 reversion rode out the widespread protests and effected the automatic extension of the security treaty with the United States in June of 1970. That same year (1970), the Osaka World Expo was held celebrating "Progress and Harmony for Mankind" and the song "Sensō wo Shiranai Kodomo-tachi" (Children Who Have Never Known War) became popular. A new generation had arisen, and the change was striking. In November 1970, the first postwar national election was held in Okinawa, preceding reversion. In this election, the LDP vied for support by invoking the war-dead: "This is the last year you will be memorialized under American rule. We have come to pledge to the brave spirits buried here that we will build a peaceful world free of war. Starting next year, we will be 100 million compatriots together striving hand in hand to build world peace."[29] This was a campaign speech, but it was basically in line with what the prime minister was saying elsewhere. With Japan experiencing rapid economic growth and having developed into an economic power, concern was being voiced both within Japan and overseas that the world might see a revival of militarism. Satō chose a path leading to Japan's being an economic power but not a military power. Citing Japan–United States cooperation, he spoke out for being a nonnuclear, solely defensive power.[30] As Satō explained it: "Japan's very raison d'être as a nation is to enrich mankind and to be ourselves treated equitably by the international community, and that is the kind of country we aspire to build."[31]

In the autumn of 1971, the emperor visited Europe again, fifty years after his earlier visit as crown prince. The English monarch unusually took the opportunity to restore the Order of the Garter and all other orders rescinded during the war.[32] However, one person threw a coat at his carriage in London and another threw a thermos at his car in the Netherlands, highlighting the deep-seated resentment and other personal issues that were not amenable to bilateral settlements by government lawyers.

The Tanaka Kakuei administration was formed soon afterward, and diplomatic relations with China were normalized in September 1972 in the wake of the dramatic Sino-American rapprochement. In this, Japan recognized the People's Republic of China as the sole legal government of China, and China renounced any demand for war reparations. The Japan-China Joint Communiqué declared: "The Japanese side is keenly conscious of the responsibility for the serious damage that Japan caused in the past to the Chinese people through war, and deeply reproaches itself."[33]

The Japanese opposition parties and public opinion welcomed the normalization of diplomatic relations with China, but there was some discontent within the LDP about how Taiwan had been treated. Despite the rapid economic growth Japan was enjoying, China's renouncing any claim to reparations had been a precondition for the normalization, given the vast scale of injury inflicted on China during the war. At the same time, the Chinese government was taking the danger of war with the Soviet Union seriously and knew it had to improve relations with both Japan and the United States. Faced with a population that was not anxious to reconcile with Japan, the Chinese government explained: "The Japanese militarists invaded China and inflicted great damage on the Chinese people, but at the same time they inflicted great damage on the Japanese people as well." In this explanation, it clearly distinguished between the broad swaths of Japanese people and the small coterie of militaristic elements.[34]

During the occupation, the term "Greater East Asia War" was banned and the term "Pacific War" was put into vogue. Gradually, however, the sense of responsibility for the damage done in East Asia increased, and the general public, who had been seen as victims, began to be seen also as responsible for this carnage. In 1972, Honda Katsuichi produced a book called *Chūgoku no Tabi* (Travels in China) in which he accused the Japanese forces at the Chinese front of war crimes.

In January 1974, Prime Minister Tanaka visited Southeast Asia, only to be met with widespread anti-Japanese demonstrations blaming the whole of Japan for the war's horrors. This sense that all citizens shared in the guilt for imposing terrible damage contributed to understanding the reality and to sustaining restraint during the process of growing into a great power. That said, had the problem been mishandled, it could have resulted in diluting the leadership's responsibility. Then in 1974, former prime minister Satō was awarded the Nobel Peace Prize. Also in the same year, US president Gerald Ford visited Japan, followed by Queen Elizabeth II the next year.

Constitutional Questions About Memorializing the Dead at Yasukuni Shrine

The Yasukuni Shrine bill was brought forward every year between 1969 and 1974, but it always failed to pass. During the 1974 debate, the Legislation Bureau of the House of Representatives issued a position paper on the constitutionality of the Yasukuni Shrine bill, saying the bill would not run afoul of the constitution if the shrine abandoned such generally religious features as the "*nihai, nihakushu, ippai*" (bow twice, clap twice, and bow once) ritual specific to Shinto worship. With this "would not run afoul if" opinion, the LDP passed the bill on its own in the House of Representatives but failed to get the necessary support in the House of Councilors.[35] The House of Councilors election immediately following this produced a near equal balance of government and opposition parties in the Diet. At this, the War-Bereaved Families Association and the Association of Shinto Shrines, while not abandoning the effort to transfer Yasukuni to national management, shifted their emphasis to gaining formal visits such as by the emperor and foreign delegations. Emperor Shōwa and successive prime ministers had visited the shrine after the war, but it was Prime Minister Miki Takeo in 1975 who first visited on the August 15 anniversary of the war's end, and this timing cemented the shrine's association with World War II—an association that had been assumed but ambiguous despite the overwhelming number of World War II dead enrolled at this ancient shrine whose establishment dated back to the Meiji era.

To avoid charges that he was in breach of the constitution, Miki emphasized that he was attending in his private capacity, saying "as an individual" to distinguish this from his official visit to the Chidorigafuchi National Cemetery. This started a new debate as to whether visits were private or official, and the debate within Japan became increasingly complicated.

In the autumn of 1975, the emperor visited the United States, where he referred to "that unfortunate war for which I am deeply sorry."[36] After returning home on November 21, he then visited Yasukuni Shrine, explaining that he was visiting as a private individual. Amid the nonstop tumult among the Japanese people, this became the emperor's last visit, and there have been no further visits by the emperor.

Social Upheaval and the Enshrinement of Class A War Criminals, 1975–1980

Great Power Status Underpinned by Contrition

Even though the Vietnam War ended in April 1975, the flames of war in East Asia did not die down. Vietnam invaded Cambodia in December 1978 and China invaded Vietnam the following February. The Soviet Union then invaded Afghanistan in December, and the Cold War grew frostier. With the international order being called into question like this, Prime Minister Miki attended a conference of the heads of state of the leading Western powers (the Rambouillet Summit) in November 1975 and went on record saying that Japan would continue to defend freedom and democracy no matter what challenges it faced.[37] This was seconded in August 1977 when the Fukuda Takeo administration laid out its Southeast Asia policy (in what was called the Fukuda Doctrine), stating that Japan sought not to become a great military power but to emphasize heart-to-heart relations. The Japan-China Treaty of Peace and Friendship was concluded the next year (1978), and Deng Xiaoping visited Japan in October to exchange documents of ratification.

At a banquet welcoming him, Prime Minister Fukuda spoke about the war to say it had been a truly deplorable event, and Deng accepted this. While in Japan, Deng inspected the most modern factory facilities, and Nippon Steel's Inayama Yoshihiro and other business leaders encouraged the proactive transfer of technology to China in strong support for China's economic development.[38] Following this, the Ōhira administration encouraged Australia to take the lead in birthing the Pacific basic cooperation concept (this to avoid any suspicion that it signaled a rebirth of the Greater East Asia Co-Prosperity Sphere), promoted yen loans to China, and supported China's reform and opening-up policy.

Yasukuni Shrine's Independent Policy as a Religious Judicial Person

While the government and the general public were working to allay suspicions and improve relations with Japan's Asian neighbors, an April 19, 1979, newspaper reports revealed that Tōjō Hideki and other Class A war criminals (convicted of crimes against peace) had been entered in the Yasukuni Shrine lists the previous year. The former military personnel in the War Victims' Relief Bureau at the Ministry of Health and Welfare had taken the initiative in 1966 and forwarded shrine name cards for all un-enshrined military personnel to Yasukuni Shrine. After largely completing the enshrinement of the Class B and Class C war criminals in 1970, a meeting of the Yasukuni Shrine parishioners' representatives decided to go ahead with Class A enshrinement. However, this was postponed by Yasukuni's main priest, Tsukuba Fujimaro. When Tsukuba died suddenly in 1978, however, his successor, Matsudaira Nagayoshi, hurriedly pushed the enshrinement through. Matsudaira said later: "I have long believed that the spirit of Japan cannot be revived so long as we accept the Tokyo Trial verdict that only Japanese are at fault."[39] In the process of carrying out this enshrinement, Yasukuni Shrine adopted unprecedented secrecy and staked out an independent path of its own as a religious judicial person.

Prime Minister Ōhira attended the shrine's annual spring festival immediately after this news broke, but this did not change the dynamics of the issue either in Japan or overseas. Then, in 2006, a memo by Tomita Tomohiko, former grand steward of the Imperial Household Agency, came to light revealing that the emperor had opposed the enshrinement and had intentionally not taken part in subsequent shrine ceremonies.[40]

Conclusion

Although this era saw not only the resolution of questions regarding reparations but also the normalization of diplomatic relations with both Korea and China, laying the legal grounds for reconciliation with all but North Korea, the domestic debate over constitutional issues grew more heated and the way was paved for a rash of disputes to emerge as international flashpoints in the years ahead. I noted four such dimensions at the start of this chapter, but it was not just these four that became issues. Lurking behind reconciliation between nations are always regional circumstances, personal experiences, and the future. Politics is not everything, but I want to draw attention to the buildup of public and private efforts for reconciliation that took place in this decade.

Japanese often remark that seventy years have passed since the end of the war. The fact that Japan has gone seven decades without being responsible for another war, let alone a war of aggression or revenge, has been a good thing not only for Japan but also for the region and the world as a whole. There is, however, the danger that this pat phrase "since the end of the war" may seem to describe an uneventful period and may invite the illusion that events inevitably unfolded as they did. In fact, there were remarkable changes in Japan's situation and concerns in each of the subperiods, and the international community's perceptions and responses also changed over the years. In Japan, there are different and complex "postwars" depending on the region and the standpoint, and the flow of postwar time has been very different from one country to another within the East Asia region.

It would be a mistake to either trivialize the historical memory issues or to rush to make them top-priority political and diplomatic issues. Rather than such knee-jerk responses, we need carefully thought-out efforts for reconciliation and mutual assistance based upon the building up of mutual trust both domestically and internationally. Party politics has a major role to play in this by enabling the people to be fully cognizant of the historical facts and context, enabling Japan to find an equilibrium between the popular sentiment and the national interest, and promoting the formation of popular consensus at home and harmonious cooperation within the international community.

Notes

In the course of my research, I received assistance from the Kakenhi Grants-in-Aid for Scientific Research, JP15H03325.

1. Asano Toyomi, *Teikoku Nihon no Shokuminchi Hōsei: Hōiki Tōgō to Teikoku Chitsujo* (Law Enforcement in the Japanese Colonies: The Integration of Jurisdiction and Imperial Order) (Nagoya: University of Nagoya Press, 2008).

2. Aso Kazuko, "Musume no Tachiba kara" (A Daughter's Perspective), in *Yoshida Shigeru 10nen Kaisō* (A Decade's Recollections of Yoshida Shigeru), vol. 4 (Tokyo: Chūōkōron-sha, 1998), p. 337.

3. University of Tokyo Institute for Advanced Studies on Asia (Tanaka Akihiko's office and Matsuda Yasuhiro's office) and University of Tokyo Graduate School Interfaculty Initiative in Information Studies (Harada Shiro's office), Database: Sekai to Nihon (The World and Japan), http://www.ioc.u-tokyo.ac.jp/~worldjpn.

4. Yoshitsugu Kōsuke, *Ikeda Seikenki no Nihon Gaikō to Reisen: Sengo Nihon Gaikō no Zahyōjiku 1960–64* (Japanese Foreign Policy Under Prime Minister Ikeda and the Cold War: The Parameters of Postwar Diplomacy, 1960–64) (Tokyo: Iwanami Shoten, 2009).

5. Ōhira Masayoshi, *Ōhira Masayoshi Zen Chosaku-shū* (The Complete Works of Ōhira Masayoshi), vol. 2., edited by Fukunaga Fumio (Tokyo: Kōdansha, 2010), pp. 62–72.

6. Database: Sekai to Nihon; Kitaoka Shin'ichi, *Monko Kaihō Seisaku to Nihon* (The Open-Door Policy and Japan) (Tokyo: University of Tokyo Press, 2015).

7. Satō Susumu, "Tai-Shingapōru/Marēshia Kessai Mondai to Sono Kaiketsu" (Resolving the Blood-Debt Issue with Singapore and Malaysia), *Journal of East Asian Studies* (Nishōgakusha University) 38 (March 2008); Ikeda Naotaka, "Shingapōru Kessai Mondai to Nihon no Taiō" (The Singapore Blood Debt Problem and the Japanese Response), *Kokugakuin University Institute for Japanese Culture and Classics Annual* 94 (September 2004).

8. Satō, "Tai-Shingapōru/Marēshia Kessai Mondai to Sono Kaiketsu," p. 47.

9. Speaking in the Diet following a visit to Singapore in 1966, Satō's foreign minister, Shiina Etsusaburō, summarized the issue: "There is still a lot of resentment against Japan over the well-known blood debt problem—the killing of a large number of Chinese. Actually, they are saying that some kind of compensation must be paid to put this matter to rest. . . . That's what they are saying." Then he reported: "There are a lot of financial details involved for us, but this is such an important issue, so we looked at this again here and, when I was there, managed to contain the problem amicably and without incident." ("Minutes of the Committee on Foreign Affairs," House of Councilors, following the closing of the 52nd Diet session, November 18, 1966). Here and following, Diet minutes were accessed through the Full-Text Database System for the Minutes of the Diet (http://kokkai.ndl.go.jp).

10. Gekkan Shakaitō Editorial Board, *Nihon Shakaitō no 30nen* (JSP 30-Year History), vol. 3 (Tokyo: Shakai Shimpō, 1975), p. 9.

11. Japan Socialist Party Policy Council, ed., *Nihon Shakaitō Seisaku Shiryō Shūsei* (Collected JSP Policy Documents) (Tokyo, 1990), pp. 42–43.

12. See also Kitaoka, *Monko Kaihō Seisaku to Nihon.*

13. Fukunaga Fumio and Kōno Yasuko, *Sengo towa Nanika: Seijigaku to Rekishigaku no Taiwa* (What Does Postwar Mean? Dialogue Between Political Science and History), vols. 1–2 (Tokyo: Maruzen, 2014).

14. Edwin Reischauer, *Nihon Kindai no Atarashii Mikata* (A New View of Modern Japan) (Tokyo: Kōdansha, 1965).

15. For a recounting of questions swirling about politics and memorials for the dead in postwar Japan, including prior research, see Murai Ryōta, "Sengo Nihon no Seiji to Irei" (Politics and Memorial in Postwar Japan), in *Kokkyō wo Koeru Rekishi Ninshiki: Nitchū Taiwa no Kokoromi* (History Across Borders: Attempting a Japan-China Dialogue), edited by Liu Jie, Mitani Hiroshi, and Yang Daqing (Tokyo: University of Tokyo Press, 2006). A host of other valuable research has also come out, including Akazawa Shirō, *Yasukuni Jinja: Semegiau Senbotsusha Tsuitō no Yukue* (Yasukuni Shrine: The Future of Conflicted War Memorials) (Tokyo: Iwanami Shoten, 2005); Hata Ikuhiko, *Yasukuni Jinja no Saijin-tachi* (The Enshrined at Yasukuni Shrine) (Tokyo: Shinchōsha, 2010); Itō Tomonaga, *Ki wo Terawazu: Rikugun Shō Kōkyū Fukkan Miyama Yōzō no Shōwa* (Shōwa War Department Adjutant General Yozo Miyama: An Ordinary Man) (Tokyo: Kōdansha, 2009); and Mainichi Shimbun Yasukuni Reporting Group, ed., *Yasukuni Sengo Hishi: A-Kyū Senpan wo Gōshishita Otoko* (Yasukuni's Secret Postwar History: The Man Who Enshrined the Class A War Criminals) (Tokyo: Kadokawa, 2015). For resource material, see National Diet Library Research and Legislative Reference Bureau, *Yasukuni Jinja Mondai Shiryō Shū* (Yasukuni Shrine Problem Archives) and *Shinhen Yasukuni Jinja Mondai Shiryō Shū* (Yasukuni Shrine Problem Archives), new ed. (Tokyo: 1976 and 2007).

16. In 1952, the Act on Relief of War Victims and Survivors was enacted, survivor pensions and condolence moneys were paid, and the Public Officers Pension Act was amended to allow reinstatement of the public service assistance fee in 1953. Many members of the military were recognized as war victims and economic relief was extended even to convicted war criminals. The Japanese government treated war criminals as not liable to punishment within Japan and included them in financial support associated with the legal dead. That said, there was a clear distinction between ordinary war-dead and war criminals, as well as between Class A war criminals and Class B and Class C war criminals with regard to enshrinement in Yasukuni Shrine. Murai, "Sengo Nihon no Seiji to Irei"; and Itō, *Ki wo Terawazu.*

17. The symbolic facility at the Chidorigafuchi National Cemetery and the grave of the unknown soldier were expected to memorialize the war-dead, but as a result of proposals put forth by Yasukuni Shrine and the Japan War-Bereaved Families Association, a process was put in place resulting in Chidorigafuchi being limited to serving as a resting place for the ashes of the unknown soldier. Murai, "Sengo Nihon no Seiji to Irei"; and Itō, *Ki wo Terawazu.*

18. "Minutes of the Committee on Social and Labor Affairs," 43rd Diet session, House of Councilors, March 5, 1963.

19. When the Chidorigafuchi National Cemetery was completed in 1959, a memorial service was held for the fallen veterans in the presence of the emperor, and memorial services were also held when soldiers' remains were brought back to Japan. (Explanation by Yamamoto Asatarō, Government Committee, "Minutes of the Committee on Social and Labor Affairs," 43rd Diet session, House of Councilors, March 5, 1963. Refer to the National Diet Library Research and Legislative Reference Bureau, 1976.) Minister of Health and Welfare Nishimura Eiichi, answering a question in the House of Representatives, Committee on Social and Labor Affairs, in July 1963, said: "Whether they will continue to be at the Tokyo Metropolitan Hibiya Public Hall or whether they will be held somewhere else is still a question for the future. But whatever happens, it is essential the ceremonies be held somewhere with no whiff of religion about it. It would be inappropriate for the ceremony to have a religious taint." ("Minutes of the Committee on Social and Labor Affairs," 43rd Diet session, House of Councilors, July 5, 1963.)

20. Satō Eisaku, *Kyō wa Asu no Zenjitsu* (Today Is the Day Before Tomorrow) (Tokyo: Face, 1964), pp. 172–175.

21. Lee Jong Wong, Kimiya Tadashi, and Asano Toyomi, eds., *Rekishi toshiteno Nikkan Kokkō Seijōka* (History of Japan-Korea Normalization of Diplomatic Relations), vols. 1–2 (Tokyo: Hōsei University Press, 2011); and Kimiya Tadashi and Lee Won-deog, eds., *Nikkan Kankei-shi 1965–2015* (History of Japan-Korea Relations, 1965–2015), vol. 1, *Seiji* (Politics) (Tokyo: University of Tokyo Press, 2015).

22. Shiina Etsusaburō Tsuitō-roku Kankō-kai (Shiina Etsusaburō Memorial Record Publication Society), ed., *Kiroku Shiina Etsusaburō* (The Shiina Etsusaburō Record), vol. 2 (Tokyo, 1982), p. 49. The Japan-Korea Joint Communiqué of February 20, 1965, states: "Foreign Minister Lee explained that the feelings Korean people have toward Japan arose because of the unfortunate relationship existing between the two countries at a particular time in the past. Japanese Foreign Minister Shiina Etsusaburō noted Foreign Minister Lee's statement and said that he felt regret and deep remorse about past relations. Shiina Etsusaburō gave his opinion and expressed his strong conviction that the prosperity of the two free peoples based on justice, equality, and mutual respect can be ensured by sincerely promoting talks between the two countries and establishing a new friendly relationship." Database: Sekai to Nihon.

23. Japan Socialist Party Policy Council, *Nihon Shakaitō Seisaku Shiryō Shūsei,* pp. 504–506.

24. Prime Minister's Office, *Satō Naikaku Sōri Daijin Enzetsu Shū* (Collected Speeches of Prime Minister Satō Eisaku) (Tokyo, 1970), p. 66.

25. Miyagi Taizō, *Kaiyō Kokka Nihon no Sengo-shi* (Japan's Quest for Stability in Southeast Asia) (Tokyo: Chikuma Shobō, 2008).

26. Prime Minister's Office, *Satō Naikaku Sōri Daijin Enzetsu Shū,* p. 150. Prime Minister Satō's inscription on a memorial stone was unveiled in April 1966 at Hifū-no-Oka at Haebaru-cho, Okinawa. Yoshida Shien, *Chiisana Tatakai no Hibi: Okinawa Fukki no Urabanashi* (Small Battles Daily: The Inside Story on Okinawa's Reversion) (Tokyo: Bunkyō Shōji, 1976), p. 201.

27. Prime Minister's Office, *Satō Naikaku Sōri Daijin Enzetsu Shū,* pp. 214–215.

28. National Diet Library Research and Legislative Reference Bureau, *Yasukuni Jinja Mondai Shiryō Shū,* pp. 146, 150.

29. "Election Materials, 1970" (documents of the Council for Okinawa's Reversion to Japan, Okinawa Prefectural Archives).

30. Murai Ryōta, "1970nen no Nihon no Kōsō: Aratana Nihon e no Toikake ni Kotaete" (Japanese Thought in the 1970s: Answering Questions for a New Japan), in *Daini no Sengo no Keisei Katei* (Japan's Second Postwar Restart), edited by Fukunaga Fumio (Tokyo: Yuhikaku, 2015); and "Minutes of the Budget Committee," 64th Diet session, House of Councilors, December 15, 1970.

31. Prime Minister's Office, *Satō Naikaku Sōri Daijin Enzetsu Shū,* p. 321.

32. Kimizuka Naotaka, *Joō Heika no Burūribon: Eikoku Kunshō Gaikō-shi* (Her Majesty's Blue Ribbon UK Decoration Diplomacy) (Tokyo: Chūōkōron-Shinsha, 2014).

33. Database: Sekai to Nihon. Speaking at a dinner reception, Prime Minister Tanaka said: "Over the past several decades Japanese-Chinese relations have regrettably passed through unhappy times. During these times, Japan has caused the people of China a great deal of trouble and I wish to express again my feelings of deep remorse." But the term "trouble" became an issue. Hattori Ryūji, *Gaikō Dokyumento: Rekishi Ninshiki* (Diplomacy Documents: Historical Awareness) (Tokyo: Iwanami Shoten, 2015), p. 135.

34. Murai, "Sengo Nihon no Seiji to Irei" (p. 303); and Etō Naoko, *Chūgoku Nashonarizumu no Naka no Nihon: Aikokushugi no Henyō to Rekishi Ninshiki Mondai* (Japan in Chinese Nationalism: Changes in Patriotism and the Problem of Historical Memory) (Tokyo: Keisō Shobo, 2014).

35. National Diet Library Research and Legislative Reference Bureau, *Yasukuni Jinja Mondai Shiryō Shū,* pp. 171–176; and Murai, "Sengo Nihon no Seiji to Irei." Had the Yasukuni Shrine bill been passed and shrine management been taken over by the state, this would likely have been criticized as a display of nationalism and conservatism, but at the same time the government would have become directly involved in the enshrinement decision, probably resulting in the Class A war criminals not being enshrined. History seems full of unintended consequences.

36. Takahashi Hiroshi, *Ningen Shōwa Tennō* (Emperor Shōwa: Human Being) (Tokyo: Kōdansha, 2011), p. 359.

37. Database: Sekai to Nihon.

38. Ezra Vogel, *Deng Xiaoping and the Transformation of China* (Cambridge: Belknap of Harvard University Press, 2011), pp. 294–310.

39. Murai, "Sengo Nihon no Seiji to Irei" (p. 302); and Itō, *Ki wo Terawazu;* and Mainichi Shimbun Yasukuni Reporting Group, *Yasukuni Sengo Hishi.*

40. Mikuriya Takashi, *Kingendai Nihon wo Shiryō de Yomu: Ōkubo Toshimichi Nikki kara Tomita Memo made* (Readings in Modern Japanese History: From Ōkubo Toshimichi's Diary to the Tomita Memo) (Tokyo: Chūōkōron-Shinsha, 2011); and Hata, *Yasukuni Jinja no Saijin-tachi.*

3

The Nakasone Yasuhiro Years
Historical Memory in Foreign Policy

Satō Susumu

Nakasone Yasuhiro's views on the Greater East Asia War were dichotomous. On the one hand, he understood it as a war of aggression in Asia. On the other, he believed it was a war of defense against the United States and the United Kingdom for Japan's very survival. In particular, he was critical of the invasion of China as an extension of the "21 Demands" Japan had sent the Republic of China (RoC) in 1915 and believed that the Mukden Incident and other expansionist actions by the local military authorities in contravention of Tokyo's nonexpansion policies were evidence of aggression. He also understood that Japan's actions in Southeast Asia were not motivated by any desire to liberate Asia from colonialism but were undeniably aggression aimed at securing resources. The fact that Nakasone held such views almost certainly helped him in negotiations with Asian countries to resolve the historical perception problems that arose in connection with Yasukuni Shrine and history textbooks during his tenure as prime minister.

Later, Hosokawa Morihiro said much the same thing when he held a press conference shortly after taking office as prime minister in a non-LDP coalition government in 1993. There, he clearly stated that he considered the war to have been a war of aggression and a mistake. He believed that the countries that had suffered at Japan's hands undoubtedly saw its behavior as aggression, and that many Japanese shared this perception. Hosokawa personally considered the war to

65

have been primarily one waged against China, as well as an attack on the Korean Peninsula and Southeast Asian countries. Since Japan's invasions of these countries in pursuit of its own interests resulted in countless victims, it was undeniably a war of aggression. On the other hand, the fact that the war was also a war between Japan and the United States appears to have not impressed Hosokawa very much.

As such, Hosokawa's views were significantly at odds with those held by Ishihara Shintarō. During the war, Ishihara fled when he came under machine-gun fire from a US fighter, but on raising his head after the attack apparently ended, saw a Japanese fighter chasing the US plane away. This experience, he said, inspired his own nationalistic awakening. More specifically, it moved him to believe that a nation can protect its citizens only if it is strong. From Ishihara's perspective, the war was a war between Japan and the United States. Likewise, for the Japanese on the home front—most of the Japanese who were not in active service but still suffered in the US air raids—the war was primarily a war between Japan and the United States, which naturally encouraged the perception that they, too, were war victims.

Hosokawa did not pay an official visit to Yasukuni Shrine on the August 15 anniversary of the end of World War II, an event that took place soon after he took office as prime minister. Not only did he suspect that such visits violated the constitution's separation of state and religion, but he also thought that paying reverence at Yasukuni with the Class A war criminals enshrined there would be open to misunderstanding and would fuel distrust of Japan's expressions of remorse about the war. Hosokawa did not believe that other countries would understand how the prime minister of a country that had accepted the judgments of the International Military Tribunal for the Far East (the Tokyo Trials) and the San Francisco Peace Treaty could visit Yasukuni Shrine and pay respects to the Class A war criminals among other deities. Keeping the situation from becoming worse is obviously not the same as resolving it, but it is safe to say that a prime minister who prioritizes international perspectives this way would generally not do anything to make the historical memory dispute worse.

What Would a Resolution of the History Issue Look Like?

Miyazawa Kiichi, who preceded Hosokawa as prime minister, drew attention to his considerable concern over China's evolution into a military and economic superpower when he handed over the office to Hosokawa. While he was prime minister, Miyazawa also mentioned (to Singapore's Lee Kuan Yew and others) his misgivings about how China's phenomenal economic development would impact Japanese and East Asian security. It was during the Miyazawa administration that the emperor visited China in 1992 in a bid to promote friendship between Japan and China. Miyazawa recalls that the atmosphere during the visit was very good, as the people in Shanghai, for example, spontaneously approached the visitors in a friendly spirit. People from all walks of life had smiles on their faces, welcoming the visitors wholeheartedly. Miyazawa appears to have accepted at face value reports that the emperor and empress's heartfelt feelings touched each and every individual and that wonderful scenes of naturally friendly exchanges ensued. This imperial visit to China was widely seen as an attempt by Miyazawa and like-minded people to resolve the historical memory issue and other issues affecting relations with China as it evolved into a superpower. That said, Miyazawa's comments to Hosokawa suggest a residual anxiety about China. Nakasone, the subject of this chapter, on the other hand, appears to have taken a shorter-term view, dealing with the historical perception problem as a matter of protecting the Japanophiles in China.

Even if we assume that Nakasone's own historical memories were in fact reflected in Japanese foreign policy on the historical memory problem, individual cases suggest that he trimmed Japan's foreign policy sails as the situation demanded, regardless of his own personal preferences. This chapter looks at how the government's for-the-record stance on historical issues helped defuse such diplomatic problems as arose from time to time.

Of course, the problem of historical memory only surfaces for Japan as a diplomatic issue when others take issue with the way Japan recalls and presents its history. This chapter examines how the methods used to deal with history issues affected their subsequent prolongation and escalation. As such, it looks at how the Japanese government has responded to these issues starting with the first history-textbook controversy, which surfaced during Suzuki Zenkō's time as prime minister and is considered to be the precursor of today's protracted and intense jockeying over history issues.

While there were many government responses, such sporadic diplomatic solutions were little more than stopgaps and did nothing to resolve the basic problem. This much was clear from the acerbic comments of Lee Kuan Yew, the other party in the blood-debt problem between Singapore and Japan in the mid-1960s. To the end of his life, he maintained that while Japan might be peaceful and nonmilitary, it would never truly apologize or express genuine remorse. Addressing the question of whether or not to treat diplomacy as a failure when it is unable to achieve a complete resolution of a problem as complicated and deep-rooted as differing historical narratives, this chapter contends that even if diplomacy is seen as having achieved only a partial improvement in interstate relations over a period of years or even decades, we can still consider it more of a success than would have resulted were no summit meetings held for many years because they did not offer any prospects for a complete solution. This is because the history issue is largely determined by the international climate the countries involved find themselves in at the time and is just one of many diplomatic issues that need to be addressed in a constantly changing international environment.

Origins of the Historical Memory Problem: The First History-Textbook Controversy

China and the Controversy

The fact that Japanese historical narratives were not a diplomatic issue during the 1970s raises the question: Were friendly relations maintained because the history problem did not arise, or did the history problem not arise because relations were friendly? While we need to be cautious about asserting a causal relationship between good relations and the absence of history problems, I currently tend toward the latter view because history issues were somehow not a problem when Korea needed Japan during Park Chung-hee's time or when China needed Japan during the 1970s.

It was only in the 1980s that the issue of historical narratives came to the fore, yet Japan was able to maintain friendly relations with China and Korea even then. This raises the question: Was the historical narrative issue not serious enough to impair relations with these two countries at the time, or did the Korean and Chinese leaders have reason to believe that maintaining friendly relations with Japan was important enough to offset the serious historical narrative issue? Given the existence of pressing factors that made Japan and China, and Japan and Korea, need each other, this chapter takes the position that the latter is the case. It is worth exploring these factors individually.

On June 26, 1982, the morning editions of Japan's leading news-papers published the results of the Ministry of Education's screening of Japanese history textbooks for high schools. They reported that the ministry's screening had led to the term "aggression against" China being dropped and its being called an "advance into" China. While it is acknowledged today that these reports were erroneous, they led to the organizing within China of a campaign critical of Japan and to the Chinese government submitting a furious protest to the Japanese government, shaking the Japan-China relationship to its core. The Japanese were shocked by the Chinese response, not least because it occurred immediately after Premier Zhao Ziyang had visited Japan in May–June and the two sides had agreed on the "Three Principles of Sino-Japanese Relations:" peace and friendship, equality and mutual benefit, and long-term stability.

In fact, China was then in the process of switching to its inde-pendent foreign policy. Until then, Deng Xiaoping had prioritized resistance to the Soviet threat and had sought better relations with the United States even if it meant ignoring some more minor problems. However, he was considering abandoning this policy because he was troubled by the Reagan administration's policy toward Taiwan, espe-cially its decision on arms sales. Although China was opposed to the US policy, it was forced to make considerable concessions during negotiations concerning the US-PRC joint communiqué on Taiwan announced on August 17, 1982. Deng Xiaoping decided to dissolution of partnership with the United States in July 1982 when these negoti-ations were still ongoing. Since he thought it necessary to use some-thing other than the negotiations to signal this switch to a harder line toward the United States, he chose to adopt a tougher line toward Japan, which was US-dependent, emphasizing this stronger approach to defending China's national interests at home and overseas. Masuo Chisako says Deng Xiaoping gave instructions at a July 29, 1982, meeting on Japan's historical memory controversy to hammer on the textbook issue because he suspected Japan intended to build upon this textbook issue to assert that its past actions were not aggression. How-ever, Etō Naoko says the instructions were to focus on preempting and rebutting any Japanese effort to claim the textbook issue as an inter-nal matter for Japan and to reject any criticism of "Chinese interfer-ence." With China criticizing US arms sales to Taiwan as interference in Chinese internal affairs, it is conceivable that Deng adopted a tougher stance because he feared Japan might likewise seek to label Chinese protests over the textbooks as interference in Japanese internal affairs. All these factors were behind the campaign criticizing Japan, which erupted suddenly on July 24 and ended in September.

The Japanese government was unprepared for this situation and tried to reach an early resolution at the initiative of Prime Minister Suzuki, who was due to visit China in September 1982. Overriding opposition from the Ministry of Education, which was critical of any reediting of the textbooks, Chief Cabinet Secretary Miyazawa Kiichi released a statement on August 26 saying, in part: "From the perspective of building friendship and goodwill with neighboring countries, Japan will pay due attention to these criticisms and the Government will be responsible for making the necessary revisions."[1]

While no revisions were made immediately, the statement signified that the screening criteria would be reviewed and the textbook screening schedule would be accelerated at an early stage. The Chinese side toned down its criticisms as a result of Miyazawa's statement. A "neighboring countries clause" was subsequently added to the screening criteria, stipulating that all due consideration be given to furthering international understanding and international harmony when dealing with events in modern and contemporary history that affect Japan and neighboring Asian countries.

While it is believed no textbooks have failed the screening as a result of the clause, authors and publishers have likely made sure that their narratives keep it in mind. Factions within the Japanese government therefore stressed that the screening system led by the Ministry of Education should be steadfastly maintained and that interference from foreign countries should not be grounds for revising textbook content. That said, the Miyazawa statement resulted from the fact that Prime Minister Suzuki, Chief Cabinet Secretary Miyazawa, and others followed the Ministry of Foreign Affairs in supporting the argument that the revisions should take relations with neighboring countries into consideration. As a result of the priority the Ministry of Foreign Affairs put on consideration for other countries, things calmed down temporarily.

Meanwhile, based on its experience in the Sino-Vietnamese War, China adopted what it called its independent foreign policy at the September 1982 Chinese Communist Party (CCP) congress. As Etō says, it is possible that the historical textbook controversy enabled Deng Xiaoping to discover a means of consolidating domestic patriotism and enhancing the legitimacy of Communist Party domination, as well as a convenient tool for use against Japan. Externally at least, there is little doubt that it succeeded in creating a framework that could be used to hold Japan in check at any time. Subsequently, it established a structure that allowed China to continuously admonish Japan by evoking the historical memory problem whenever Japan showed signs of leaning toward militarism. However, China also invoked it to maintain Sino-Japanese relations, making it more than just a tool for hounding Japan. It can also be argued that neither the Japanese nor the Chinese doubted the other side's intentions toward friendship and goodwill, and both accepted this as a necessary and inevitable process of readjusting Sino-Japanese relations.

Korea and the Controversy

With the Kwangju Incident of 1980 as pretext, the Korean government sentenced democratic activist Kim Dae-jung to death. The Suzuki administration opposed the death penalty for Kim and warned that it would review its relationship with Korea, including freezing economic aid, if Kim were executed. At this, Korean president Chun Doo-hwan criticized Japan for interfering in Korea's internal affairs. Kimura Kan writes that right from the start of his administration, President Chun sought $6 billion in loans as secondary damages for Japan's de facto colonial rule.[2] While the official line was that Korea sought this aid to counter the threat posed by the Democratic People's Republic of Korea (DPRK) at the time, Japan was keen to uncouple the security question from economic aid. Foreign Minister Sonoda Sunao triggered an emotional response from the Korean side that made things worse when he said he thought it strange for a borrower to throw its weight around like this.

It was at this time that the first history-textbook problem arose. Initially, Korea made virtually no response, but once it became known that China had initiated fierce protests in late July 1982, similar protests erupted in Korea. The textbook controversy attracted a great deal of attention because of fears that Japan was developing into a superpower and showing signs of resurgent militarism. As it turned out, the Miyazawa statement helped to quell these protests as well.

As soon as Nakasone Yasuhiro became prime minister in November 1982, he dispatched Sejima Ryūzō, a former Imperial Japanese Army staff officer who later became an executive adviser to Itochu Corporation, to Korea as a special envoy. Early the following year, after Sejima had worked out the details, Nakasone became the first Japanese prime minister to visit Korea and reached an agreement with President Chun over the scale of economic cooperation. Nakasone also used personal diplomacy to alleviate anti-Japanese sentiment by, for example, giving part of his speech at a banquet hosted by President Chun in Korean. Later, when President Chun visited Japan in September 1984, it is believed that Nakasone instructed the grand steward of the Imperial Household Agency to insert the word "regrettable" into the Emperor Hirohito's speech to Chun.

Nakasone thought it was necessary to hold the DPRK and the Soviet Union in check and keep Japan safe by helping to strengthen the Korean and Chinese economies. The intention was to build an Asian arc of containment against communism in Northeast Asia. Although it is not possible to clarify to what extent Japanese assistance contributed to the two countries' development, there is no doubt that Nakasone's good intentions helped minimize the historical memory problem at the time.

The Historical Memory Problem During the Nakasone Administration

Prime Minister Nakasone's Official Visit to Yasukuni Shrine

Prime Minister Nakasone caused a major diplomatic row with other countries in Asia when he followed in the footsteps of his predecessor, Prime Minister Suzuki, and made an official visit to Yasukuni Shrine on the occasion of the 1985 anniversary of the end of the war. Prime Ministers Ōhira Masayoshi and Suzuki Zenkō had both visited the shrine after it became known in April 1979 that Class A war criminals had been surreptitiously enshrined there in October 1978. Prime Minister Miki Takeo also visited Yasukuni Shrine, on August 15, 1975, while Prime Minister Suzuki Zenkō paid anniversary visits in two successive years. Logically speaking, therefore, Nakasone's visit became a problem because it was billed as official.

Yasukuni Shrine was established in 1869 to honor the spirits of war heroes who dedicated their lives to their nation. It was used by the national authorities as a device to encourage soldiers to go to the battlefront believing that they would be enshrined as venerable divinities after they were killed. Nakasone was determined to go ahead with an official visit because he reasoned that even though the war was over, the nation would be in breach of contract with its departed war heroes if he did not go. However, the fact that Class A war criminals were also enshrined there vastly complicated the situation.

Etō has found that China's initial response was to not attach too much importance to Nakasone's official visit to Yasukuni Shrine on the anniversary of the end of the war. The Japanese government explained to China and other Asian countries in advance that the official visit was not intended to promote militarism, and Nakae Yōsuke, Japan's ambassador to China at the time, recalled that nobody thought an official visit would cause such major discord between the two countries. However, the student protests in Tiananmen Square on September 18, 1985, created a major problem, and fears that this spontaneous anti-Japanese demonstration might evolve into a domestic power struggle or inflame historical controversies forced the Chinese government to take a tough line against the Japanese government. In fact, during talks with Ambassador Nakae on December 8, Hu Yaobang complained that another official visit to Yasukuni would put China's leaders in an extremely difficult position and claimed that it would be impossible to mollify the Chinese people so long as war criminals remained enshrined there.

Meanwhile, Prime Minister Nakasone feared that the potential downfall of an enlightened, pro-Japanese leader like Hu Yaobang would have a serious impact on global and Japanese interests. Before the official visit, people close to Nakasone appealed to Yasukuni Shrine to move the Class A war criminals elsewhere, but these efforts were in vain. As a result, Prime Minister Nakasone did not attend the regular autumn Reitai-sai festival at the shrine and refrained from any other official visits from 1986 onward during his term in office, including August 15 of that year.

The second history-textbook controversy, which arose at this time, also had an impact. On June 7, 1986, the Chinese government requested that the Japanese government revise statements included in a textbook that had been authored by the Nippon wo Mamoru Kokumin Kaigi (precursor to today's Japan Conference) and had passed the screening process. This time, the Ministry of Foreign Affairs played a key role in devising proposals for amendments that would satisfy both China and Korea, and the textbook in question passed the screening after revision. While China subsequently made no further demands for revisions, this by no means dispelled dissatisfaction with Japan.

Hu Yaobang, who was forced to resign as CCP general secretary in January 1987, later voiced suspicions that a third party—the Soviet Union—had engineered the dispute between Japan and China over the Yasukuni issue as part of a stratagem to cause a rift between the two countries. Hu clearly thought that winning Japan over to China's side against the Soviet threat was a vitally important diplomatic objective. Many people continue to believe that Hu's excessively pro-Japanese stance was one reason for his ouster as general secretary. According to Zhao Ziyang, however, Hu Yaobang's forced resignation was more the culmination of his deteriorating relationship with Deng Xiaoping. Despite the fact that Deng had frequently suggested an anti-liberalization movement to crack down on ideological liberalism that he thought had gone too far since the adoption of the reform and open-door policy, Hu Yaobang continued to adopt a hands-off attitude. As a result, the two drifted apart and the party elders unanimously opposed Hu Yaobang's proposals from the summer of 1986, creating a situation in which it was impossible to get anything done properly. Consequently, Nakasone was mistaken in thinking he should avoid making official visits to Yasukuni lest they strengthen anti-Japanese sentiment amid criticism that Hu Yaobang was too pro-Japanese. No matter how Nakasone acted, Hu Yaobang's fate was already sealed. Ironically, Nakasone ended up doing the right thing for the wrong reason.

Although Nakasone and Hu Yaobang both misread the situation, they were agreed that Sino-Japanese cooperation was essential for confronting the Soviet threat. The friendship between Nakasone and Hu Yaobang symbolized Sino-Japanese friendship against the background of Sino-Soviet rivalry. The Nakasone cabinet decided on a second yen loan package to China before this, but as in the earlier case, the aim was to support China's reform and open-door policies and to promote moderation and closer relations between China and the West, as well as to atone for Japan's responsibility for the war. When Nakasone visited China in March 1984, Hu Yaobang expressed gratitude to Japan for its economic cooperation with China. In response, Nakasone said: "This expression (of gratitude) is actually very humbling, as our cooperation towards China is an expression of our regret over causing great hardships during the War. Given this, cooperation towards China is a matter of course."[3] Nakasone was well aware of the need to clear up the negative legacy between Japan and China with a view to developing good long-term ties between the two countries.

The Second History-Textbook Controversy, 1986

Such was the situation when the second history-textbook controversy arose in May 1986 over Ministry of Education approval of a high school textbook produced by the Nippon wo Mamoru group. Korea's mass media and public objected vehemently, and the Chinese government voiced its own objections immediately afterward. The Ministry of Education had already demanded a great many revisions before the textbook passed the screening, but Nakasone requested further amendments after being hit by criticism from China and Korea. For its part, the Ministry of Foreign Affairs asked the publisher to abandon publication of the textbook altogether. In the end, the author yielded to instructions issued by the Ministry of Education to revise the textbook after the examination deadline, and the ministry gave notice that it had again passed the screening on July 7. Prime Minister Nakasone's instructions to the Ministry of Education to reexamine the textbook, and the demands from the Ministry of Foreign Affairs to make a large number of revisions, reflected the administration's determination to curb nationalistic public sentiment in China and Korea and maintain good relations with them.

Things quieted down for a while after these unusual measures were taken, but in July of the same year, Minister of Education Fujio Masayuki triggered a new controversy with statements criticizing the judgments of the International Military Tribunal for the Far East (the Tokyo Trials). Writing in the September 1986 *Bungei Shunjū* (one of the best-selling monthly magazines), Fujio criticized the Tokyo Trials and claimed that the Korean side was co-responsible for Korea's annexation. Both Korea and China protested, but Nakasone defused the situation by immediately firing Fujio.

While the Japanese side made every effort to stem the deterioration in Sino-Japanese relations, Etō notes that Deng Xiaoping decided around November 1986 to switch from China's "friendly" policy toward Japan to a more "measured" policy. This was before Hu Yaobang was dismissed a few months later in January 1987. According to Etō, this was because China had become distrustful as a result of dissatisfaction over economic cooperation and repeated historical narrative problems, and concern that Japan's newfound super-economy status might fuel a resurgence of militarism—a concern that pre-mirrors Japan's current concern that China's super-economy status might engender a more assertive Chinese military presence. At home, the Nakasone administration looked at how the history issues had seemingly been brought under control and managed to convince itself that Sino-Japanese relations were still in good shape, Hu Yaobang's downfall notwithstanding.

Conclusion

In dealing with history issues, it was no longer enough to express personal feelings, and it became necessary to consider the diplomatic implications of every statement and every action. In the Suzuki and Nakasone administrations (essentially from July 1980 through October 1987) short- then medium- to long-term considerations led the Japanese government to exercise restraint in dealing with historical narrative issues so as to preempt disputes with China, given China's position as a potential future threat. Politicians and diplomats were conscious of this during the Nakasone years, knew that policies to achieve this were possible, and felt that diplomatic results could be expected to some extent. Yet despite the efforts of the government and the Ministry of Foreign Affairs, the fact remains that these results cannot be considered satisfactory in hindsight. Why is this?

I suspect a hint can be found in an anecdote about memories and reconciliation concerning the Pacific War. The fighting that followed the landing of US forces on Iwo Jima on February 19, 1945, resulted in approximately 18,000 deaths on the Japanese side and approximately 7,000 deaths on the US side. Survivors of this literally life-or-death struggle held their first reunion on Iwo Jima in 1970. Subsequent reunions have since been held, and President Reagan sent a message in 1985 marking the fortieth anniversary of the battle. Why is it that the veterans of this fierce engagement can gather together at this site with no signs of animosity or bitterness? How is it possible for former enemies, who saw their close brothers-in-arms killed and who themselves lived with death as a constant companion, to forgive so easily? The fact that the two countries became allies after the war was almost certainly a factor. If this is the case, it may be possible to resolve this chicken-or-egg question by saying that the two countries' determination to create a friendly relationship is more likely to alleviate animosity triggered by past history than efforts to alleviate such historical animosity are likely to create a friendly relationship.

Seen this way, it may be argued that even though historical memory was a serious problem during the Nakasone years, it could be ameliorated through diplomatic means because China and Korea still needed friendly relations with Japan. Subsequently, Korea gradually achieved economic growth as the Soviet Union collapsed and the Cold War came to an end, and China's astonishing economic growth started at almost the same time as its primary enemy, the Soviet Union, collapsed. As a result, the two countries' need for friendly relations with Japan declined sharply. During this time, too, efforts continued to be made from the Japan side to alleviate the historical concerns of the countries of Asia, including Prime Minister Miyazawa's response to the emperor's visit to China and Prime Minister Hosokawa's expression of remorse and apologies. If anything, awareness of the need for such approaches increased as China became more powerful. By the 1990s, however, such makeshift responses no longer had the impact they used to have. Anti-Japanese public opinion is growing more important in both China and Korea, and government leaders are no longer able to keep it in check through simple affirmations of friendship.

The international environment that somehow showed the way to resolving diplomatic problems arising from differences in historical memory during the 1980s no longer exists in the twenty-first century. Greater tensions in the DPRK situation or major changes in Sino-US or Sino-Russian relations could easily create times when both China and Korea seek better ties with Japan, but such tensions in East Asia would not be good for Japan in terms of regional security. It is essential that we work to steadily improve bilateral relations without relying on external chance events, but this is becoming increasingly difficult. As mentioned at the beginning of this chapter, Asian countries used raising the problem of historical memory in the 1980s as a tool to keep Japan's rightward tilt toward militarism in check, while Japanese leaders accepted this as a necessary adjustment process. Today, however, Japanese authorities no longer see things this way, and they are more likely to assume that history issues are tools that other countries use for domestic political purposes and to solidify their anti-Japanese credentials. Even so, there is nothing to be gained from discouraging diplomacy between leaders on the grounds that total solutions are out of reach. It has to be assumed to be possible to create friendly relations over the medium term step-by-step, and it is essential all national leaders learn from the Nakasone years to engage in diplomatic self-restraint while curbing the excesses of public opinion.

Notes

1. http://www.mext.go.jp/b_menu/hakusho/html/others/detail/1318346.htm.
2. Kimura Kan, *Nikkan Rekishi Ninshiki Mondai towa Nanika: Rekishi Kyōkasho, Ianfu, Popyurizumu* (What Are the Historical Memory Issues Between Japan and Korea: History Textbooks, Comfort Women, and Populism) (Minerva Shobō, 2014), p. 20.
3. Katori Taishi Hatsu Gaimushō ate Denshin "Sori hōchū: Ko Yōhō to no Kaidan" (Telegram from Ambassador Katori to Foreign Ministry: Prime Minister's Trip to China and Meeting with Hu Yaobang), Diplomatic Archives of the Ministry of Foreign Affairs of Japan.

4

The Rift Between Okinawa and the Japanese Mainland

Historical Memory and Political Space

Taira Yoshitoshi

Toward the end of intensive negotiations over the construction of a new military facility at Henoko in Okinawa's Nago
City, on September 7, 2015, Okinawa governor Onaga Takeshi told
Chief Cabinet Secretary Suga Yoshihide that he thought they must
have lived through different postwars. In addition to signifying the
breakdown of discussions between the pro-construction central
government and the anti-construction Okinawa prefectural government, Onaga's comment arguably symbolized the relationship
between the two governments and, in a broader sense, between
Okinawa and the Japanese mainland.

In fact, the Okinawan and mainland situations during and after
the war were totally different. During the war, Okinawa was the
only place in Japan where residents were caught up in extremely
fierce ground combat. After the war, it spent an additional two
decades under US military rule after the occupation ended for the
mainland. Even after it technically reverted to Japan under the 1972
Okinawa Reversion Agreement, US military bases continued to
occupy enormous expanses of land on the islands. Nonetheless, it is
striking that the rift had become so deep that the prefectural governor felt obliged to say this. On the one hand, the Okinawan side is
dismayed that the government, and indeed the whole of the mainland, not only failed to understand Okinawa's postwar experience
but also was completely indifferent to it. Going the other direction,

the mainland populace, including the government, finds it extremely difficult to fathom Okinawa's behavior.

Other chapters in this book have looked at historical narrative issues between Japan and Korea and between Japan and China, including the comfort women and Yasukuni issues. In the case of Okinawa, however, the history per se has not become a major political issue, nor is it an international issue akin to those with Korea and China. Rather, the US military bases are the main Okinawa problem and the focus of contention with the central government. The politics of the military base issue remind the Okinawans of altogether too many past events, including the Battle of Okinawa, the postwar land requisitions, the numerous incidents involving the US military, and the history of the Ryūkyū Kingdom and subsequent *Ryūkyū Shobun* (annexation of the Ryūkyūs); these memories are both the roots of Okinawa's complaints to the central government and the foundations on which Okinawa has based its actions.

While Japan's problems with Korea and China are essentially different from the problems between the central government and Okinawa, there are nevertheless commonalities that highlight the question of how to unravel and reconstitute these twisted relationships. This chapter looks at why, in the larger context of history, the rift between Okinawa and the Japanese mainland has grown so deep and so wide in the seven decades since the end of the war. It also examines Okinawa's historical perceptions within this context. In particular, it focuses on the process whereby the political framework of conservatives and progressives emerged, developed, and transformed; looks at changes in the political space in Okinawa; and examines the underlying structure of the relationship with the mainland.[1]

Okinawa Politics and Relations with the Mainland During the Cold War

Politics Under US Military Rule

Okinawa developed a distinctive political culture as a result of its separation from Japan for the twenty-seven years from 1945 through 1972. The three main political parties in Okinawa in the 1950s were the Ryūkyū Democratic Party (RDP), the Okinawa Socialist Masses Party (OSMP), and the Okinawa People's Party (OPP). While they differed somewhat in the extent to which they distanced themselves from the US military, their positions were not that far apart, and there were times when they cooperated, typically uniting in opposition to US military base policies and sometimes forming coalitions with other groups for the "island-wide struggle."

A macroscopic view of the relationship between these parties and mainland politics at the time suggests they achieved a degree of national unity. When an Okinawan delegation went to Tokyo to demand better backup at the time of an island-wide struggle, for example, Foreign Minister Shigemitsu Mamoru responded that the problem was essentially a Japanese problem involving all of its citizens and its identity. The Okinawan demands, he said, have to be resolved not as an Okinawan issue but as an issue for all of Japan, and he approached the issue in that spirit.

Okinawa was separated from the mainland, but the island-wide struggles led to deeper relations between the two and both injected Okinawa into the mainland's conservative-progressive political framing and injected that framing into Okinawan politics. In 1959, the Okinawa Liberal Democratic Party (OLDP) was formed as the successor to the RDP and established an alliance with the mainland Liberal Democratic Party (LDP). The same year, the Okinawa Management Association was inaugurated with support from the Japan Federation of Employers Association, creating a structure whereby Okinawa's business community supported the OLDP. Meanwhile, the previously middle-of-the-road Okinawa Socialist Masses Party gradually tilted left, while the OPP strengthened its ties with the Japanese Communist Party (JCP). In 1958, the Okinawa Socialist Party (OSP) was established as an ally of the Japan Socialist Party (JSP), and three parties (the OSMP, OPP, and OSP) styled themselves as progressive parties. At about the same time, several major labor unions were formed in Okinawa with the help of mainland unions, creating a structure in which these unions supported the three progressive parties.

It is important to note, however, that even as Okinawa was influenced by the political structure on the mainland, the conservative-progressive rivalry in Okinawa was essentially different from that on the mainland. Since Okinawa had been ruled directly by the capitalist United States outside of the provisions of the Japan–United States Security Treaty, questions of capitalism versus socialism or whether to support or oppose the security treaty simply did not become points of contention. The main issue between the conservative and progressive sides was the clash over how to effect Okinawa's reversion to Japan. While the OLDP favored a gradual reversion based on tripartite discussions among Japan, the United States, and Okinawa, the progressives took a more confrontational approach, engaging in mass actions to pressure the two national governments.

This confrontation was rooted in the differences between the OLDP and the Okinawan progressive forces. The OLDP trusted the government and the LDP and focused on cooperating with them. Making no secret of their distrust of the government and the LDP, the progressive forces emphasized cooperation with mainland progressive forces. This distrust of the government and the LDP, it should be noted, actually surfaced in Okinawa only after the mainland conservative-progressive rivalry structure made its way to Okinawa.

Yet although the structural clash between conservatives and progressives was real, the primary issue in Okinawa was how to shake off US military rule, and this was underpinned by a shared nationalism favoring reversion to the motherland, Japan. In other words, Okinawa at this time was arguably in a political matrix where ideological divisions were focused on how to bring about an integrative nationalism. Similarly, while mainland conservatives and progressives were at loggerheads over the form Okinawa's reversion should take, the two sides shared a nationalism calling for Okinawa's reversion.

The Post-Reversion Political Space

Alignments with mainland political parties took full stride in Okinawa around the time the key issue of reversion became a reality in 1972. The OLDP transitioned to be the mainland LDP's prefectural federation, while on the progressive side the OSP quickly became the Socialist Party's Okinawa prefectural headquarters and the OPP became the Communist Party's Okinawa Prefectural Committee. (The OSMP remained an unaligned local political party.) Likewise, labor unions and other private sector associations proceeded to align with like-minded organizations on the mainland.

Amid these changes, the mainland ideological clash between conservatives and progressives over the security treaty and US military bases also made itself felt in Okinawa. While the progressive camp called for abrogating the security treaty and eliminating the US bases, the conservative camp indicated that it felt the security treaty protected Japan's peace and security, and it was willing to accept US bases for that purpose, albeit within limits.

The two camps' historical narratives also took root within the context of this conservative-progressive division. Specifically, the perception took hold on the progressive side that not only had the mainland sacrificed Okinawa during the Battle of Okinawa, but it had also abandoned Okinawa again when it signed the San Francisco Peace Treaty in 1951 (seen as the second *Ryūkyū Shobun*). Subsequently, the Okinawa reversion of 1972 (seen as the third *Ryūkyū Shobun*) again ignored the Okinawan views. While the conservative side showed no signs of adopting a systematic historical framing in response, it stressed that Okinawa had to "get over it" and give up its distinctive postwar feeling of victimization. Today, over four decades since reversion, the progressive camp's historical narrative is still a strong presence and, if anything, has spread into ever-deepening confrontation with the government.

That said, it should be remembered that the same conservative and progressive forces that have clashed over problems such as the security treaty at the national level have sometimes devised cross-party responses and adopted very similar courses of action at the local level—as shown in their responses to the recurrent incidents and accidents accompanying the US military presence. When US military personnel commit heinous crimes such as murder, rape, and armed robbery, or when US aircraft crash in Okinawa, the parties in the prefectural and municipal assemblies tend to form supra-party alliances and adopt unanimous censure motions.

Conservatives and progressives alike have tended to adopt similar approaches toward the two issues of scaling down the US military presence and enabling Okinawa to achieve autonomous economic development. Although the progressives want US forces to withdraw completely and the conservatives are more tolerant of the bases, both aspire to shrink the US military footprint and to extricate Okinawa from its current base-dependent economic structure.

Nevertheless, during the Cold War, when the confrontation between the United States and Soviet Union was in full swing, the progressive camp focused more on the base issue and the conservative camp more on the economy. Yet with little progress made in returning the land occupied by US bases to its Okinawan landowners, and little prospect of creating an economy not dependent on the military bases, the conservative emphasis on prioritizing the economy arguably made more sense given Okinawa's political situation at the time. In fact, post-reversion politics were in the hands of the progressive prefectural administrations of Yara Chōbyō and Taira Kōichi from 1972 through 1978, followed by the conservative governor Nishime Junji from 1978 through 1990. Irrespective of the governor's political leanings, the political matrix was such that Okinawa's problems had to be dealt with by trying to rectify the inequalities between Okinawa and the mainland and to bolster the economy.

Nishime Junji served three terms (twelve years) as governor, having formerly been an LDP-affiliated member of the mainland House of Representatives from 1970 through 1978. In the LDP, he was a member of the Tanaka faction (later the Takeshita faction), which had inherited the policies set by Satō Eisaku, one of the architects of the Okinawan reversion, and was the largest faction within the LDP. Since the faction maintained its interest in Okinawa, Nishime was truly the right man in the right place, and he drew upon his experience and contacts to take a proactive approach to Okinawa's many problems.

Okinawan Politics and Relations with the Mainland After the End of the Cold War

Rapprochement Between Conservatives and Progressives

The situation started changing in the 1990s following the end of the Cold War. The first change came in the form of growing citizen demands for scaling back the military bases. Okinawan citizens seriously questioned why the huge US bases were needed even though the Cold War had ended. Antipathy toward the bases flared up especially after three US servicemen raped a young girl in 1995. The second change was the emerging possibility that US bases might be returned on a large scale, as symbolized by the 1996 Special Action Committee on Okinawa (SACO) report on the return of 5,000 hectares of land used by the US military. With this report, the idea that the bases were inevitable faded and the return of base land began to look like a realistic proposition. The third change was a major decline in the relative importance of the bases to the economy. While base-related revenues accounted for some 15 percent of gross prefectural income at the time of reversion, this had fallen to 5 percent by the time the Cold War ended.

As a consequence of these changes, the distance that had once existed between the conservatives and the progressives shrank and they drew closer to each other. Having focused on economics until this point, the conservatives began to see the return of base land as a more realistic proposition, while the progressives, having attached more importance to the base issue, started taking more proactive positions on economic issues. Okinawa's political space thus evolved into one in which scaling back the bases and stimulating the economy simultaneously became issues of more pressing importance. This situation continued for about twenty years, from 1990 through 2010, through the progressive administration of Governor Ōta Masahide (1990–1998) and the conservative administrations of Inamine Keiichi and Nakaima Hirokazu.

With this convergence, the single question of whether to condone or condemn the relocation of the Futenma base to Henoko in Nago City stands out as the primary dispute between the conservatives and the progressives following the end of the Cold War. It is important to note that even though the conservatives were prepared to accept the relocation, their acceptance was by no means unconditional but stipulated a time limit for the use of the base. Basically, the conservatives were concerned that relations with the central government would deteriorate if they rejected relocation within the prefecture and that this would adversely impact the Okinawa development budget. Nonetheless, even they were not prepared to allow the base to become permanent, demanding a time limit on its use as a nonnegotiable condition. Yet given Okinawa's experience with US military–related incidents and accidents, the forced expropriation of land, and many other injustices associated with the US military bases, it was very difficult to win Okinawan understanding on this, even with a time limit on the base's use.

From the mid-1990s, the Okinawa problem was handled on the mainland by Prime Minister Hashimoto Ryūtarō and Chief Cabinet Secretary Kajiyama Seiroku, members of the Keiseikai (Takeshita faction), which followed the Tanaka faction's line. They were succeeded by Prime Minister Obuchi Keizō and Chief Cabinet Secretary Nonaka Hiromu. At the same time as they put forward measures to stimulate the economy in northern Okinawa, they carefully tackled Futenma's relocation to Henoko while winning the begrudging acquiescence of the Okinawan side. The Inamine prefectural administration was thus able to remain in step with the central government, even though it walked a very narrow line in the process.

However, the mainland's stance toward Okinawa changed dramatically when the prime ministership passed to Mori Yoshirō and then to his successor, Koizumi Jun'ichirō, both of whom had formerly been in the Seiwakai (formerly the Kishi faction). After concluding that the

Inamine administration had delayed Futenma's relocation, the Koizumi administration broke off discussions with Inamine and instituted a major policy switch in its approach to relocating the facility to the Henoko coast. The rift between Okinawa and the mainland immediately began to widen.

Conservative-Progressive Cooperation

This situation changed even more dramatically in the 2010s, starting when the Democratic Party of Japan (DPJ) replaced the LDP as the ruling party in 2009 and started exploring the possibility of relocating the Futenma facility outside of Okinawa. Until then, Okinawa's conservatives had reluctantly accepted relocation within the prefecture as the best of the bad options, but when they saw the outside-of-Okinawa possibility developing, they rushed to take the lead in advocating relocation outside Okinawa. Yet after vacillating for over eight months, Prime Minister Hatoyama Yukio reneged on his campaign promise not to allow the relocation of Futenma to Henoko and accepted the Henoko plan. After resigning in June 2010, he admitted in February 2011 he had cited the US Marines' deterrent effect as an excuse to justify his volte-face. In December 2012, Minister of Defense Morimoto Satoshi, an acknowledged expert on security issues, openly conceded that militarily, there was no need for Futenma's replacement to be in Okinawa, thus destroying the logic behind one of the arguments that had sustained Okinawa's conservatives. Okinawa's conservatives had taken the position that they would accept US military bases within limits so long as they were needed to ensure the nation's peace and safety. Ultimately, however, doubts and mistrust emerged as to the exact nature of the US Marines' deterrent effect that had been used to justify relocation within Okinawa, and people also began to question why Okinawa alone should bear so much of the burden of the bases when it was possible to construct alternative facilities elsewhere in Japan.

From an economic perspective too, not just conservatives but a broad range of Okinawa citizens became increasingly aware that the vast expanses of US bases were inhibiting Okinawa's economic development. The direct economic benefit from Naha's new city center, which was built on the site of a former US base, for example, is estimated to be thirty-two times greater than the base had yielded, while it is estimated the center employs ninety-three times as many people as the base did. The same trends hold for other former base sites, and everyone, conservative or progressive, has begun to recognize that the long-sought autonomous economic development independent of the US military bases is both feasible and doable.

Another key point is that this economic development has actually been achieved at a time of cutbacks in the Okinawa development budget. Ironically, the budget peaked at 470 billion yen in 1998, during the progressive administration of Ōta Masahide, who was at loggerheads with the government. By contrast, the budget was cut to something over 200 billion yen under Governors Inamine and Nakaima, who strove to cooperate with the government. This shook Okinawa's conservatives to their very foundations, since they had argued that getting the money required cooperating with the government and had sought to use this financial incentive to win the support of the Okinawan people and thus maintain their grip on power.

Having so far been prepared to tolerate relocation within Okinawa subject to certain conditions, even the conservatives now took a very different tack and joined a cross-party movement to oppose relocation within the island. This movement could be described as a second "island-wide struggle" that emerged after the ideological rift and subsequent rapprochement between conservatives and progressives.

Toward a New Political Space

Foundations of the All-Okinawa Movement

On the conservative side, these cross-party activities were led by Onaga Takeshi, who was mayor of Naha at the time and is governor as of this writing. Speaking about the supra-party movement, Onaga said that the results were the same whether it was an LDP administration or a DPJ administration in Tokyo—nothing was done about the bases in Okinawa. Since it is an all-Japan approach that works to keep the bases as they are, he said, it is going to take an all-Okinawa approach to change things.

The basis for the all-Okinawa movement was not so much ideological as it was what Onaga calls the *Uchinanchu* (Okinawan people) identity. Actually, it was Nishime Junji, called the boss of Okinawan conservative politics, who appealed to the Okinawan people to reassert their identity, shake off their inferiority complex, and show their mettle in building Okinawa. At the time of the 1970 national election, Nishime argued that Okinawa must not let itself become the poorest prefecture in Japan after reversion. Whatever happens, he insisted, Okinawa could become the leading prefecture only when all residents unite in demonstrating they have the backbone to resist the *Yamatonchu* (Okinawan for "mainland people"). Nishime also put a great deal of effort into ensuring Okinawa's culture could be sustained and developed, rebuilding Shuri Castle and establishing the Okinawa Prefectural University of Arts to promote the survival and development of traditional culture.

Seen in this light, Onaga's words and deeds—stressing his pride as an Okinawan and working to ensure that *Shimakutōba* (the Okinawan language) survived—were in no way a deviation from Okinawan conservative thinking. Onaga was very much heir to the Nishime conservative tradition. In Nishime's case, however, the competitive urge to catch up with and overtake the mainland took priority over any feelings of distrust he may have had toward the mainland. Onaga differed in that, having come through the process of catching up and overtaking the mainland, he openly displayed his mistrust of, and dissatisfaction with, the mainland.

As the popular consensus calling for the US bases to be relocated outside of Okinawa continued to be ignored, the right to self-determination advocated by the progressive camp—Okinawa's right to decide things for itself—meshed with Onaga's identity politics and began to gain traction in Okinawa. The movement for independence and autonomy also gained momentum in Okinawa, drawing upon the expanded autonomy Okinawa had enjoyed under US military rule, the history of the Ryūkyū Kingdom, and more. While different people have different goals for Okinawan autonomy, ranging from calls for Okinawa to be a special autonomous region all the way to calls for full Okinawan independence, underlying them all is disgust at the Japanese government's fundamental inability to resolve the base issue as well as frustration and anger with the overall indifference and lack of understanding shown by Japan as a whole toward the issues involved. Tellingly, the term "structural discrimination" started to be widely accepted among prefectural residents to explain the concentration of US military bases in Okinawa.

The Okinawan political space thus evolved into one in which preventing the Henoko relocation and gaining Okinawan independence and autonomy were central, dovetailing with the progressive camp's assertions. That said, it was not actually the progressives who took the initiative in redefining this political orientation; rather it was Onaga and some other conservatives, plus some members of the business community, who decided to adapt to the changing facts. Cooperating with Onaga and other like-minded people breathed new life into the progressive movement, which had been weakened under the conservative Inamine and Nakaima prefectural administrations.

The Federation of Okinawa Prefecture Liberal Democratic Party Branches, which had broken away from the all-Okinawa movement and fully embraced the Tokyo government and LDP policies, was subsequently crushed in the national elections when Henoko relocation was the main issue, thus demonstrating that Okinawa would no longer tolerate relocation within the prefecture.

The Foundations for Dialogue Break Down

One reason it became so difficult for the mainland to understand what the Okinawan side was saying and doing was that the end of the Cold War also spelled the end of the ideological rift between conservatives and progressives. As the progressives went into decline, mainland politics became more conservative—a trend standing in striking contrast to developments in post–Cold War Okinawa, where conservatives and progressives gradually moved closer together and prefectural politics became more progressive. As the mainland tilted toward the right and Okinawa tilted left, each began to view the other as different, incomprehensible, and impossible to reason with. With the shared assumptions that had once made dialogue between the two sides possible diverging, the grounds for dialogue itself started to crumble.

It was within this evolving context that the 2007 confrontation over the screening of high school history textbooks took place. The Okinawan side objected strenuously when the Ministry of Education, Culture, Sports, Science and Technology (MEXT) screening process instructed publishers to water down or delete descriptions of how the Japanese military authorities had ordered, coerced, or otherwise induced civilians to commit mass suicide during the Battle of Okinawa. This confrontation over how to depict the Battle of Okinawa coincided with Abe Shinzō's first term as prime minister, which paraded its conservative colors by passing the revised Basic Act on Education, elevating the Defense Agency to ministerial status, and enacting a national referendum act in preparation to amending the constitution. It was also a time when fierce controversies arose over depictions in textbooks of the Nanjing Incident and the comfort women.

All forty-one of Okinawa's municipal assemblies passed motions demanding the textbook revisions be retracted, while the Okinawa

Prefectural Assembly twice passed similar motions unanimously. Additionally, about 110,000 Okinawans (organizers' estimate) took part in a supra-party rally to protest the ministry's instructions. Interestingly, Nakazato Toshinobu, then a member of the LDP and Speaker of the Okinawa Prefectural Assembly, served as chair of the supra-party rally organizing committee, and Prefectural Governor Nakaima took part.

Having accepted the role of committee chair, Nakazato later recalled that this was during the first Abe administration, when the conservative platform tended to cast doubt on whether the Nanjing Massacre actually occurred and to be evasive on the comfort women issue. There was an air of crisis, he said, and a feeling that history was being distorted. Okinawa having been the only place in Japan where civilians had been caught up in fierce ground fighting, and it having been widely reported that the Japanese military murdered numerous civilians and drove others out of safe hiding, Okinawans of whatever political stripe were strongly opposed to any attempt to whitewash these experiences and trivialize their wartime memories. This was also the reasoning behind the Okinawans' refusal to buy into tales about how people had died heroically for their country or to rehabilitate the Japanese military's reputation.[2]

In considering the relationship between Okinawa and the mainland, it is also important to remember that the national solidarity—or nationalism—that developed and united the two from the 1950s through the 1960s has likely atrophied steadily over the forty years since reversion. In this context, it is easy to understand why talk about Okinawan independence arose, and why hate speech directed toward Okinawa has emerged in some quarters on the mainland.[3] The dual declines of ideology and of the nationalism that once tied the two sides together have in turn led to a structural polarization between all-Okinawa and all-Japan.

How to Overcome the Rift
Between Okinawa and the Mainland

Matters That Postwar Japan Could Not Resolve

What has caused such a deep rift to develop between Okinawa and the mainland in the seven decades since the war? The primary element here is the fact that Okinawa, accounting for only 0.6 percent of Japan's total land area, is home to 70.6 percent (18,600 hectares) of the exclusive-use US military base land in Japan. Postwar Japan has been unable to resolve the excessive burden placed on Okinawa of these bases.

To varying degrees, all the parties concerned have had a negative image of US military bases right from the start. This was true of conservative politicians such as Kishi Nobusuke and Satō Eisaku, diplomats, and progressive parties such as the socialists and communists during the 1950s and 1960s, when there were still many US bases on the mainland. US military bases covered 135,200 hectares of the mainland when the San Francisco Peace Treaty went into effect, but this fell sharply to only 8,500 hectares in the 1980s and to 7,750 hectares today. On the mainland, the negative implications of the Japan–United States relationship gradually faded as the military presence grew less visible, giving way to the more positive image embodied in the expression "Japan–United States alliance."

However, it must be remembered that the essence of the security treaty underpinning the Japan–United States alliance lies in cooperation involving goods and people. Japan provides bases (goods) while the United States provides troops (people). In other words, the essence of the security treaty is that the United States pledges to defend Japan in exchange for being provided with forward bases. Most of the key elements of this arrangement—the bases—have become less visible because they have been localized to Okinawa, thus blurring the issue for mainlanders and enabling the Japan–United States alliance to deepen and develop. When the mainland bases were scaled back in the late 1950s, large tracts of land in Henoko and other northern areas of Okinawa were requisitioned for US Marines transferred from the mainland. These Marine bases account for 72 percent (13,400 hectares) of US military bases in Okinawa, making this an especially important issue for Okinawa.

Postwar Japan as Seen from Okinawa

Tokyo has traditionally said the bases and the development subsidies are essential to Okinawa's economy, and this blunt framing has been a primary talking point for conservative willingness to condone the US military presence, within limits, on the understanding that the bases are there for Japan's defense and benefit Okinawa. Yet given the history of the Security Treaty and US military bases, Onaga Takeshi has broken with the conservatives to ask who is really getting the better of this grand bargain—who is doing whom the favors: Okinawa or the mainland? As such, Onaga has spotlighted an aspect of Japan's postwar security system that the mainland has been unable or unwilling to address head-on.

For today's Okinawan conservatives, who have so far accepted the burden of the US bases, either proactively or passively, it is wildly unrealistic for mainlanders to talk about the Japan–United States alliance or security unless they are willing to come squarely to terms with the fact that Okinawa remains saddled with most of the burden of providing bases—the bulk of the burden of keeping the nation safe.

At the same time, Onaga is also fiercely critical of people who support Japan's current constitution and claim it is Article 9 (the no-war article) that keeps Japan secure. To claim that Japan is shielded by Article 9 and will not wage war even as Okinawa has been saddled with the heavy burden of these military bases even after reversion means, he says, that the people have been led into complacency by fantasy and fabrication. In other words, Onaga is furious about the popular complacency and refusal to make any genuine attempt to deal with the excessive burden Okinawa bears.

Conclusion

Seven decades after the end of the war, the relationship between Okinawa and the mainland has moved beyond confrontation over the Henoko relocation to one where the two sides now exist in completely different political spheres. I contend that postwar Japan's inability to resolve Okinawa's excessive base burden is the main reason their political orbits do not intersect. Intellectually and practically, the key issues going forward are how to deal with postwar Japan's security arrangements, which have failed to alleviate the excessive base burden, and how to reconfigure the Okinawan and mainland political discourse.[4]

Onaga Takeshi asks rhetorically why it is necessary to revisit historical questions, and his answer is that the US base presence is an anomaly born of historical circumstances. If we are to resolve this, it is imperative we recall how things were at the time of the *Ryūkyū Shobun,* as well as during the war, and work from there. Will it ever be possible, he asks, to create a future in which Okinawans can live without constantly having their noses rubbed in the past? It all depends on whether or not their dignity is respected and these problems resolved accordingly.

Notes

1. Although I have adopted the "conservative" and "progressive" political framework in this chapter to clarify where the problems lie, a deeper analysis of the situation should reveal more about the characteristics of Okinawan politics. Additionally, much of the analysis here is based on mainland and Okinawan perspectives, which are largely the Japanese government and Okinawa Prefecture perspectives, but fuller understanding requires comparative analyses with other prefectures that accommodate (or formerly accommodated) bases.

2. The process by which the Okinawan understanding of the Battle of Okinawa took shape is an issue that needs further study taking into consideration what this chapter refers to as the changes in the political space, generational changes, and other changes.

3. What exactly was the nature of the nationalism that developed from the 1950s through the 1960s? When, and on what sort of foundations, did it take shape? And why does it seem to have atrophied? Asking these questions inevitably raises issues such as the problem of defining prewar nationalism and how it persisted, changed, and died out after the war. At the same time, these are fundamental questions that need to be included in seeking to define postwar nationalism. This is a key issue for me going forward.

4. In a separate paper (in the September 2015 *Journalism*), I discuss what form a new security framework should take in order to resolve Okinawa's excessive burden. Amemiya Shōichi also points out that the mainland's failure to accept bases has engendered a new Okinawans versus mainlanders dichotomy. At the same time, he says that dismantling and reconstituting the all-Okinawa and all-mainland mindsets to overcome this is primarily an intellectual issue. See Amemiya, "Sengo no Koekata to Kyōdōshugi" (Beyond the Way of Post-war and Kyoudousyugi), *Dokkyo Law Review* 100 (August 2016).

5

Is Reconciliation Possible?
The Outlook for Japan-China, Japan-Korea, and Japan–United States Relations

*Hosoya Yūichi, Kawashima Shin,
Nishino Jun'ya, and Watanabe Tsuneo*

The year 2015 was a milestone year in many respects: the seventieth anniversary of the end of World War II, the centennial of Japan's issuing its "21 Demands" of China, the 120th anniversary of the end of the Sino-Japanese War, the fiftieth anniversary of the normalization of diplomatic relations between Japan and the Republic of Korea, and the year of the August 14 Abe Statement, on Japan's road to war and the path it has taken since the war's end. Given all of this and anticipating the Abe Statement, it seemed appropriate to gather some experts on China, Korea, the United States, and Europe to discuss this history and its implications. This gathering took place on July 6, 2015. The record that follows is an edited transcript of the discussion.

From "Never Forgive, Never Forget" to "Forgiving Without Forgetting"

HOSOYA: Our main subject here is to ask one question: Is reconciliation possible? As far as I am concerned, this is not a difficult question, and the simple answer is: no. That is not, however, intended to end the discussion before it starts, so I would like to ask what kinds of historical reconciliation you envision, what the points of contention are, and why reconciliation appears so difficult. And then, once the issues have been identified and clarified, what kinds of new ideas and insights might enable us to overcome these issues and make reconciliation possible?

95

In this I would like to start by asking each of you how you see the issue. Could we start with Professor Kawashima, who is the expert on Sino-Japanese relations? Professor Kawashima is also a member of the Advisory Panel on the History of the 20th Century and on Japan's Role and the World Order in the 21st Century formed to advise Prime Minister Abe in advance of his statement marking the seventieth anniversary of the war's end, as well as being an outside resource author for the Foreign Ministry's *Japan-China Joint History Research Report* and heavily involved in dialogue with Japanese and Chinese historians for the Sasakawa Japan-China Friendship Fund and other organizations.

KAWASHIMA: Historians probably have no business getting involved in issues of historical reconciliation or historical awareness, but I admit to having been involved in a number of initiatives, having been perplexed by a number of issues, and having learned a number of things along the way.

Historians have, as you know, made considerable progress on discussing these issues. Much of this was in the Japan-China Joint History Research Committee, and those discussions have been very productive in furthering understanding of our different historical narratives. However, that has been among historians, and there is considerable question about what significance the program has had for the general public.

For example, the Joint History Research Committee issued a report based upon the historians' discussions and this was transmitted to the appropriate government officials on both sides, but we then got some scathing comments from the two governments, particularly the Chinese government, which objected that the report included material that it did not want made public (even though the Chinese government had been involved in promoting the joint research). So, at the government's request, the parts that they said should not be made public were redacted, to the point the report was gutted and was not nearly as useful as it should have been. And once this redacted report was released to the public and the media got hold of it, a whole host of other issues arose. The media poured over the bowdlerized reports and discovered a number of places where the Japanese and Chinese were at odds, and these then became the focus of the media reports. We were not looking to create a common narrative but had accepted the idea that different countries would have different narratives and were just trying to clarify the differences and to understand them better. But the media ignored this dialogue process and zeroed in on the differences. And that is just one example. This whole dialogue process made me acutely aware of how, when it comes to perceptions of history, we run into the problem that the discourses and the issues appear very different at the different levels: historians, governments, the media, and the public.

Other difficulties have come up recently. For example, historical records pertaining to the Nanjing Massacre and the comfort women have been submitted to the UNESCO Memory of the World Programme and are scheduled to be reviewed this September. [On October 10, 2015, the United Nations Educational, Scientific and Cultural Organization announced that the Chinese records on the Nanjing Massacre would be included in the Memory of the World Register. Action on the comfort women records was deferred.] In Japan and elsewhere, policies about history have become the focus of propaganda aimed at both internal and external audiences. And we historians can only look on and wonder what is to be done.

People who specialize in reconciliation studies hold that the first step to reconciliation is "forgiving without forgetting" what the other party did. That level has not been reached for either Japan and China or for Japan and South Korea. In China, on the political level and the public level, the situation is "never forget, never forgive," and I am afraid it will be very difficult to reach the stage of "forgiving without forgetting."

HOSOYA: What about Japan-Korea relations? This year marks the fiftieth anniversary of the normalization of diplomatic relations, and there have been a number of conferences in conjunction with this anniversary in Tokyo, Seoul, Jeju, and elsewhere. Professor Nishino has probably been to more of these than anyone else, so I would like to ask him to speak next.

NISHINO: I am not so much a historian as I am a specialist on international politics in East Asia, especially on the Korean Peninsula, together with studying modern history based on historical records.

When you think about the problems of historical reconciliation for each of Japan-China, Japan-Korea, and Japan-US, the Japan-Korea relationship has some unique properties. In the strictest legal sense Japan and Korea were not wartime adversaries. One issue in thinking of the seventieth anniversary of the end of the war is that from Japan's point of view it is a question of how to assess World War II. But from Korea's point of view, in order to give meaning to World War II, the issue is still how to assess Japanese colonial rule—the roughly thirty-five years from the 1910 annexation treaty to 1945 and the end of World War II.

The Treaty on Basic Relations between Japan and South Korea was signed on June 22, 1965, and diplomatic relations between the two countries were normalized in December of the same year. At that time, the issue of colonial rule was equivocally settled. That is, it was agreed in Article 2 that all agreements and conventions concluded between Korea and Japan on or before August 22, 1910 (the day of the annexation treaty) are null and void. Japan takes the position that the 1910 treaty was legal, and colonial rule was carried out legally, but was voided in 1965. Korea, on the other hand, claims that the treaty itself was invalid and that colonial rule was unlawful. In effect, this difference of perceptions lay hidden within the negotiations between Japan and Korea between 1951 and 1965, and a settlement was achieved using the expression "already null and void" so each of the governments could explain this to its own national assembly. On the Korean side, though, it later became a problem that the Basic Relations Treaty made no mention of "remorse" and "apology."

However, in 1998 a Japan–Republic of Korea Joint Declaration was signed by Prime Minister Obuchi Keizō and President Kim Dae-jung. I think it would be right to see this as accomplishing formal historical reconciliation between Japan and Korea. This is what you previously pointed out, when you said that historical reconciliation was "forgive but not forget." Prime Minister Obuchi used the expression "deep remorse and heartfelt apology," and President Kim Dae-jung said he valued these expressions and the important thing was to overcome the unfortunate history and build a future-oriented relationship based on reconciliation and good-neighborly and friendly cooperation. In effect, there was an attitude of tolerance on the Korean side. Why, despite this, has the problem continued to simmer? There are reasons for this on both sides, but today I want to focus on the reasons on the Korean side.

HOSOYA: It would probably be good to look at Japan-US relations next, and there is nobody better qualified to talk on this than Watanabe Tsuneo, who spent about a decade with a Washington, D.C., think tank starting in 1995 and is one of the few Japanese researchers conversant with how US policy is actually made.

WATANABE: I research and analyze Japan-US relations and national security. I am neither a historian nor an expert in diplomatic history, so I want to speak about how Americans view the historical issues as well as how the Japan-US alliance functions in the international order and how it is linked to the historical awareness issue.

If one asks which of the four countries—China, Japan, South Korea, and the US—is the most different from the others, it is the US. The US is the nation that has been the hegemon and has maintained the global order from World War II to the present day.

Japan must be careful, in considering this issue of historical recollection, that attempts to deny the Tokyo Trials and other incriminating events do not end up rejecting the Japan-US alliance or American hegemony. If they do, forces which think friction between Japan and the US is preferable can easily come to the fore. Japan must understand that it is the US that maintains the present global order and must not forget that Japan and the US have shared interests for the whole of the seventy years since the end of the war. If Japan forgets these things, the discussion could easily develop in a most unwelcome direction. Japan has to be careful not to reject its existing international relations and dig its own grave.

The leading Western media have recently focused on whether or not Japanese historical revisionists are attempting to justify Japan's aggression against China during the 1930s. It is true that there are such people in Japan. Every country has people who want to rationalize the past. Japan being a democracy which guarantees freedom of expression, it is impossible to regulate such statements.

If there were signs that Japan were actually engaged in military expansion and expansionist behavior threatening to neighboring countries and were actually raising a military challenge to the existing international order, it would be understandable that countries would be sensitive to "historical revisionism," but that is not the case.

There have been some articles labeling Prime Minister Abe a "historical revisionist." While Abe does have a conservative bent, he is also a politician who strongly supports the alliance with the US, which has built up the postwar international order. Far from challenging the existing international order, Abe supports its preservation and maintenance.

"Historical revisionism" becomes problematic because of fears that justifying past acts of aggression could lead to justifying new challenges to the international order in the future. However, it is necessary to note the paradoxical conditions whereby current concerns regarding changing the existing international order in the Asian region by force are not about Japan, but rather about China, which harshly criticizes Japan's stance on history.

Historical reconciliation is an endless process, and we must be ready for the historical memory issue to pop up again from time to time into the future. And when it does, we have to look carefully at the extent to which it threatens Japan's existence and international relations and have to address the issue dispassionately.

In February this year [2015], Greece demanded that Germany repay a loan the Nazis extracted from Greece during World War II. Greece claimed it has the right to demand 162 billion euros, equivalent to half the country's current public debt, as damages for the wartime occupation. Most people who heard this probably thought Greece was out of line with its demands. Meanwhile, Germany calmly and dispassionately dealt with this issue as "legally and politically resolved." Had the Germans jumped to some facile self-justification such as claiming "we never did any such thing," this might have taken a different course, and I think there is something we can learn from Germany's level-headed response.

As Professor Hosoya said at the beginning, historical reconciliation will not be easy. But that does not mean the effort should be abandoned. I think the question for the future will be how to minimize the disadvantages in working out a solution.

Different Historical Narratives of World War II

Hosoya: Thank you. That is very interesting background. I would like to move on to three questions Prime Minister Abe touched upon in his address to the nation in January 2015, since all three are important issues that must be addressed if we are to make 2015 a year of progress on historical memory reconciliation. To recap, the first is how Japan should demonstrate its profound remorse over World War II. This is also an issue of intense interest for our neighbors. The second is what course Japan has trod in the seventy years since the war's end. Specifically, what has been done to try to resolve this historical memory issue and promote reconciliation? Third and building upon the answers to the first two questions is what policies Japan should pursue from here on. And if I may be allowed to add a fourth, it would be to ask what hopes and expectations you have for the statement that Abe will issue in August on historical memory.

Let's start with the first one: How should we understand World War II in terms of Japan-China, Japan-Korea, and Japan-US relations?

KAWASHIMA: Professor Nishino was talking earlier about reconciliation at the political level. There is a similar situation in Japan-China relations. There were no immediate responses from China following the Murayama Statement in 1995 or again after the Koizumi Statement in 2005, but a clear reply came when Premier Wen Jiabao addressed the Japanese Diet in 2007 and expressed strong appreciation for the two statements. In terms of the wording used by the government leaders, it seemed that a certain degree of reconciliation had been reached in Japan-China relations.

There is also the series of four basic declarations by Japan and China—the 1972 Joint Communiqué, the 1978 Treaty of Peace and Friendship, the 1998 Joint Declaration on Building Partnership, and the 2008 Joint Statement on Mutually Beneficial Relations Based on Common Strategic Interests. They sustain the note of remorse that was set by the 1972 document, and the 1998 declaration states that Japan observes the Murayama Statement. It is useful to keep in mind that there have been two styles of articulating Japan-China relations, the tone of apology and reflection in the two prime ministers' statements and the tone of "reflection" in the four joint declarations. The 1998 declaration mixed the two.

Now to Professor Hosoya's hard question. Looking back through history, the modern relationship between Japan and China began with the Sino-Japanese Friendship and Trade Treaty of 1871, which put the two countries on an equal footing. Despite this, we had the First Sino-Japanese War, leading to Japanese sovereignty over Taiwan and the Penghu Islands from 1895. There was an unequal relationship under an unequal treaty, but that does not mean relations between Japan and China were worse in every respect. Japan and China faced the common challenge of becoming modern states, and Japan, which was ahead in the process of nation-building, provided a model of modernization for China. In particular, frameworks for the modern state, including the legal system and national institutions and constitutional monarchy, were absorbed as many Chinese came to Japan to study.

The turning point in the modern Japan-China relationship was Japan's presentation of the "21 Demands" in 1915. That gave rise to the anti-Japanese movement in China and other developments that led to a worsening of relations. It was in that context that the May Fourth Movement arose.

In Japan it is generally believed that policy toward China from the 1920s on was conciliatory as part of the Shidehara foreign policy in compliance with the Nine-Power Treaty from the Washington

Naval Conference. But Chinese historians disagree entirely. The Chinese view is that from the Meiji period onward, Japan consistently pursued its continental policy, steadily invading China and moving headlong toward war. In that view, the 1920s are seen as a time of economic invasion.

The divergence of historical perceptions grows more striking for the 1930s. Chinese historians view the period from the Mukden Incident in 1931 to the end of the Second World War in 1945 as an uninterrupted fifteen-year war. Their outlook assumes an underlying constant aggression. Yet many Japanese researchers take the view that the invasion triggered by the Mukden Incident ended with the Tanggu Truce in 1933 and there was a relatively peaceful interlude between 1933 and 1937, meaning that there were not fifteen years of nonstop aggression.

With regard to the ensuing world war, the divergence between Japan and China becomes huge. It has so far proved impossible to bridge the gap between the Chinese side, which thinks it scored a great victory over Japan, and the Japanese public, who mostly think Japan was defeated by the US.

Views about the United Nations are also quite divergent. The Chinese term for the UN translates literally as "allied nations." China sees the UN as the successor to the Allies of the Second World War. Having taken its seat on the UN Security Council as one of the triumphant nations, China has never had any sympathy for Japan's bid for a permanent seat on the Security Council. As for Japan's having contributed to the global community since the war, while I believe there are ample grounds in support of that claim, China flat-out rejects this idea.

At any rate, it is still not clear to what degree such historical perceptions influence actual foreign policy. In seeking to understand the historical processes prior to the Second World War, it should be possible to sort things out so long as the researchers share the historical materials and fully discuss their views. Where we go from there, however, is very different territory in terms of how the questions are framed and how the process is utilized in diplomacy. Questions of historical perception go through different phases at different times. In Chinese eyes, the question of historical perception is not a single, fixed topic but can carry different implications depending upon domestic politics, economic conditions, relations with Japan, relations with East Asia, and global foreign policy. For them, historical perception goes through phase changes over the years and decades. We need to remember that.

NISHINO: With regard to World War II, Korea still feels regret and vexation that it could not take part. If you go to anything resembling a history museum in Korea, there is always an exhibit about the provisional government of the Republic of Korea formed at the time of the March First Independence Movement in 1919. This provisional government did set up a military organization called the Korean Liberation Army in hopes of joining in the war, but Japan surrendered before it could actually see action. History might have been different had the Korean Liberation Army fought with the Allies against Japan, and this thought remains deeply rooted in Korean society. In fact, there is some debate as to where to position the provisional government of the Republic of Korea. Internationally it is seen as having been some kind of political organization but is not recognized as a government, and this greatly complicates Korean thinking about it.

As I mentioned earlier, the question of how to view colonial rule is a serious problem between Japan and Korea. The 1965 Japan-Korea Basic Relations Treaty was equivocal, but this was not a major problem between the governments until the 1990s. Since then, Korean society has increasingly rejected the way this 1965 settlement was reached.

Looking back to 1965, the Park Chung-hee administration was a government with a strong authoritarian streak which used martial law to suppress opposition movements, and it was this administration that normalized diplomatic relations. In addition, Japan provided neither the heartfelt apology that the general public sought nor the amount of economic cooperation that was expected. Of course, many Korean people concede that Japan provided seed money that led to economic development, but there is also a strong feeling that more should have been done. That is the start of the problem of how the two countries understand their shared history.

Another important issue in the Japan-Korea relationship is that, in 1965, there was some question as to which of the regimes, north or south, Japan would recognize as the legitimate government of the whole Korean Peninsula and whether room should be left for Japan to open diplomatic relations with North Korea. This relates to Article 3 of the Basic Relations Treaty. In 1965, when diplomatic relations were being normalized, this issue lay buried within Japan-Korea relations, but now the debate is breaking out. This ties into our theme today about how long this situation will continue and whether historical reconciliation is possible. I fear the reality is that full historical reconciliation will be extremely difficult.

In discussing the Korean Peninsula, however, the nature of Korean nationalism may well change if and when the division is healed—that is, if and when we have a united Korean Peninsula. This milestone of the seventieth anniversary of the end of World War II and the fiftieth anniversary of the normalization of diplomatic relations should prompt us to think carefully about what kind of relationship Japan should have with the united Korea at that time, and how we should come to grips with the issue of historical reconciliation from that point of view.

World War II Forensics
Consistent with Historical Reality

WATANABE: The issue of historical awareness between Japan and China and between Japan and South Korea is very complicated. Japan-US relations are relatively simple by comparison. Yet the Japanese psychology is rather complex. What is important is how to reach an understanding within oneself.

For example, regarding the Tokyo Trials, most people probably feel that it was to some extent unavoidable Japan should be tried, since we lost the war. Yet there are also some who assert it is wrong that the US atrocities, such as the atomic bombing of Hiroshima and Nagasaki and the fire-bombing of Tokyo, were not also tried as violations of international law.

There is nationalism on both the right and the left in Japan. The right-wing nationalism is conservative and supports the Japan-US alliance. However, this nationalism tends to want to whitewash Japan's own past, so it is anti-Chinese and anti-Korean, and in extreme cases also confronts the US. There is also presently anti-US nationalism from the left, as seen in the many people who oppose the bills related to Japan's national security. Right and left both have elements leading to anti-Americanism. As I mentioned earlier, there are a number of factors that require caution when expressing perceptions regarding historical issues. If the Japanese and US perceptions diverge, forces that would exploit this will emerge. That would not be good for Japan or the world.

Japan has a history of not understanding, or just ignoring, the global trend toward international cooperation and becoming isolated as a result. Yet this is not the path Japan followed after the war. For example, the Treaty on the Non-Proliferation of Nuclear Weapons, which entered into force in 1970 and has been signed by 190 nations, prohibits the proliferation of nuclear weapons to nations other than the nuclear weapons states (the US, Russia, England, France, and China) and requires the treaty parties to pursue nuclear disarmament negotiations. Japan has the technology to develop nuclear weapons if it so desires, but it intentionally chooses not to. That is significant.

Any revisitation of the seven decades of Japan-US relations since the end of the war includes aspects that require autopsy reports from Japan. But it could well open a Pandora's box of problems if these studies are performed with the conclusions in mind from the start and are not reality-based. If the historical forensics are not done well and carefully, there may be areas that are incompatible with the international order that Japan depends on and the US hegemony which underpins it. It is imperative we recognize that the world we live in and humanity as a whole are less than ideal and come to terms with this reality.

The point in which Japan-China and Japan-Korea relations differ from Japan-US relations is that South Korea and China did not have democratic systems when the postwar reconciliations took place. Even though there were intergovernmental agreements, there was not sufficient discussion or understanding at the citizen level. The US was a democratic state before, during, and after the war, and Japan became a democracy after the war, which guaranteed an environment for free discussion among citizens and made comparatively open discussions regarding the different historical narratives possible. In that sense as well, historical reconciliation between Japan and South Korea and between Japan and China is more difficult than that between Japan and the US.

Government-to-Government Reconciliation vs. People-to-People Reconciliation

HOSOYA: What about my second question: How are we to understand Japanese policy in the seven decades since the war's end? What has Japan done? What have we not done? And in answering this, I would like to hear first about Japan-China relations.

KAWASHIMA: It has been announced that a military parade will be part of the Victory Day celebrations in Beijing on September 3, 2015, known in China as the "anniversary of victory in the war against fascism and Japan." Why is Victory Day on September 3? Because Japan signed the Instrument of Surrender aboard the USS *Missouri* on

September 2 and the Kuomintang government held its victory parade in Chongqing the next day. After the Kuomintang were driven off the mainland, the Communist Party first set August 15 as the commemoration day, but it later aligned with the Soviet Union in designating September 3 as Victory Day. Now, under a measure adopted last year by the National People's Congress, September 3 is Victory Day and December 13 is a National Memorial Day for Nanjing Massacre Victims.

Let me briefly run through the history of bilateral relations from the end of World War II up to the present. At war's end in 1945, there were over a million Japanese soldiers in mainland China. The first task for the Chinese was to disarm them and return them to Japan without fuss, which included efforts by both the Kuomintang and the Communist Party to repatriate Japanese forces quickly and smoothly.

The People's Republic of China was formally established on October 1, 1949, and the Kuomintang subsequently set up its government-in-exile in Taipei. Japan had to pick one side or the other for negotiating peace and establishing formal ties. Taipei very much wanted Japan to recognize it as the sole legitimate government of China. Beijing wanted to somehow maintain ties with Japan, even if Japan joined the Western camp in recognizing Taipei. With those motivations, neither side was in a position to harshly condemn Japan. However the PRC had to maintain its wartime propaganda stories about how it had won the war, and so the postwar education curriculum remained highly critical of Japan.

Right from the end of the war in 1945, Chiang Kai-shek espoused "military-civilian dualism," which laid the responsibility for the war on military leaders rather than the people at large, and portrayed most civilians and ordinary soldiers as victims. Mao Tse-tung also embraced this idea. Yet Chiang was preparing to demand reparations from Japan, having worked out the amount as no less than 51.5 billion dollars. Then with the shift in US occupation priorities, the Allied powers basically agreed to waive rights for reparations from Japan, which was done by most of the nations that signed the San Francisco Treaty. Chiang followed suit, opting to waive reparations under the Treaty of Peace between Japan and the Republic of China of April 28, 1952.

Just when East Asia was being pulled into the Cold War, Japan recognized the Republic of China as the official government of China. Ever since, great weight has been given in Republic of China–Japan affairs to Chiang Kai-shek's policy of *yi de bao yuan* (repaying evil with good). That approach led many in Japan to express gratitude for Chiang's benevolence. Until he died in 1975, Japanese politicians would mention the phrase whenever they met with him. Chiang Kai-shek did not talk about the war. The "repay evil with good" slogan worked as a sort of incantation, and it definitely had an effect, at least on relations between Japanese politicians and the Kuomintang.

Eventually the Communist Party in Beijing, while detesting Japan's alliance with the US and recognition of Taipei, began to embrace military-civilian dualism. Taking citizens off the hook might have been meant to appeal to the Japanese public and spark a movement for diplomatic recognition of Beijing, or as Mr. Watanabe has suggested, it might have been part of an attempt to counter US influence by forging links with the anti-American movement and reformist political groups.

Beijing did support the anti-American movement in Japan through connections with the various China-Japan friendship associations and progressive forces. At the time, neutralizing Japan was a key strategic goal for Beijing. Historical narrative issues did not necessarily come to the fore in the Japan-China friendship movement, yielding to more strategically vital concerns about Japan-China relations or US-Japan-China relations. In that context, for Japan, the term "Japan-China friendship" carried implications of reflection upon past history and genuine openness to cooperation with China. This was another term that cast a useful spell.

Yet even while they claimed to differentiate military and civilian responsibility, the Communist Party and the Kuomintang alike conducted educational programs with a strong anti-Japanese slant. Conversely, even as they taught at home that their having won the war against Japan was grounds for their own legitimacy, Taipei and Beijing each sent Tokyo the message that Japan should side with it. And so it went through the 1950s and 1960s. During that period there was the "repay evil with good" link between Chiang Kai-shek and Japan while Japan-PRC relations included "Japan-China friendship" as a concept and a movement. These were symbolic incantations that served to suppress disagreements over history issues, and both sides (i.e., Japan and China and Japan and Taiwan) invoked them to ward off discord. There is no comparable phrase in Japan-China relations today.

Unfortunately, during the 1950s and 1960s, when many Japanese intellectuals were feeling remorseful about the war and subscribed to the idea of war responsibility, there were not enough personal exchanges between them and the PRC, with which Japan did not have diplomatic relations, or the Republic of China in Taipei. Thus international exchanges failed to consolidate reconciliation in East Asia.

It should be noted that neither the RoC nor the PRC had a democratic government when it normalized relations with Japan; not the RoC when the Treaty of Peace was signed in 1952 nor the PRC when relations were normalized in 1972. Which is to say that their people were not involved in the process of setting national policies for reconciliation with Japan. The fact that key neighbors were not democratic is a point of difference from the German situation. As the lands around Japan democratize, the issue of postwar reckoning, both internally and internationally, will inevitably arise anew from the grassroots.

Actions taken by an authoritarian government are not based on public opinion and will ultimately be ineffective. Japan has to face that. No matter how much Japan may insist that there has been legal and diplomatic closure, the other side will not accept this. The democratization of South Korea and Taiwan since the 1980s, along with the increasing power of the people in the PRC, constitute a problem area Japan has had to confront.

Ties with mainland China were normalized in 1972 and Japan began providing development assistance in 1979. Vice Premier Deng Xiaoping, the promoter of "reform and opening-up" policies, posited the two faces of bilateral relations with Japan—history and economics—saying Japan was an economic mentor and yet the past must not be forgotten. Learn from Japan, he said, but don't forget history. During the 1980s, though, Japanese business ties and development assistance were so important that historical issues could be somewhat offset by economic cooperation.

By the 1990s Japan was economically weaker than China. Development assistance was curtailed, and Japan no longer had economic cards to play which could subdue historical narrative issues. That was all the more true in the early 2000s. Furthermore, the old mantras of "Japan-China friendship" and "repay evil with good" had become unusable because the friendship movement had waned in the course of social changes. By that point, the history aspect of the economics-and-history framework was increasingly prominent, and Japan-China relations came to be dominated by historical and territorial issues.

Bilateral affairs were then further roiled in the courtroom when the judiciary ruled that reparations from the Japanese government had been waived as part of the diplomatic normalization but that the right to seek reparations from the private sector had not been waived. With that, it became possible for a civilian plaintiff to prevail in a suit for reparations from a private party.

Then, in the early years of this century, the Tokyo High Court and even the Supreme Court handed down decisions saying the right to private reparations actually had been waived. That was a serious turn, because it signaled that the judiciary, which up to then had played a role in historical reconciliation, would no longer be as involved. What have been the consequences? There may not be a direct causal relationship, but the historical narrative issues came to be seen as political and social issues about the same time. The Japan-China Joint History Research Committee began its work in 2006, and dialogues were initiated in various other settings. At the same time, the Chinese judiciary got involved.

That is the story of how issues of historical narratives and reconciliation between Japan and China have been entangled in diplomatic maneuvering, economic relations, and various other shifting circumstances within the overall course of Japan-China relations. Some progress has actually been made toward reconciliation, as a result of dialogues and exchanges. Procedures to avoid the exacerbation of problems have worked to some extent, and there have been exchanges, dialogues, joint research, and other processes aimed at reconciliation. However, the measures that seemed to be in place to avoid exacerbation have gradually disappeared, bringing us to the current phase when the problems are escalating. Premier Wen Jiabao's address to the Diet on April 12, 2007, was a high-water mark for Japan-China reconciliation at the government level, but there have since been major changes in Chinese foreign policy. With the balance of power shifting in China's favor, historical issues have become ammunition for China to attack Japan in ways that are starting to illustrate the reality that China is eclipsing Japan in East Asia. It is imperative that we put our minds together and think about how to manage these issues.

HOSOYA: There are a number of points in there that we tend to overlook. Thank you. What have the last seven decades meant for Japan-Korea relations?

NISHINO: At the risk of oversimplification, let me say that basically the history involved has greatly evolved. During the twenty years from 1945 to 1965, there were no diplomatic relations. Negotiations began in 1951 concurrent with the conclusion of the San Francisco Peace Treaty, but the gulf opened by the different readings of history could not be bridged for fourteen long years, and it was only in 1965 that an equivocal settlement was reached. People studying Japan-Korea relations tend to think that this really happened for economic or Cold War reasons and that the historical narrative issue was put on a back burner.

From the Japanese perspective at that time, Korea's political and economic stability and development was essential to Japan's security. From the Korean perspective, economic development was the vital concern. So diplomatic relations were normalized in both countries' interests. That the economic objective was fully achieved is clear from the present state of the Korean economy. In addition, by the end of the 1980s, Korea had democratized, had become dynamic Korea, and attained what some have called "an excess of democracy." Hence the problem that Professor Kawashima spoke of, a problem brought about by the success of democracy, intruded on the relationship between Japan and Korea.

I mentioned earlier that the historical problems were put on a back burner, but I think Japan was sincerely working at this problem in the 1990s after entering the post–Cold War period. There was the Kōno Statement in 1993, the Murayama Statement in 1995, the establishment of the Asian Women's Fund also in 1995, and then, as a culmination of these efforts, the Japan–Republic of Korea Joint Declaration in 1998.

Going into the 2000s, historical issues became prominent again. From the Korean side the trigger was the annual visits to Yasukuni Shrine started by then–prime minister Koizumi Jun'ichirō in 2001. However, Japan also had Prime Minister Kan Naoto's thoughtful statement put out on the centennial of the Japan-Korea annexation treaty. This has not been much appreciated within Japan, but it was one of the major accomplishments of the Democratic Party administration in that it expressed Japan's feelings on colonial rule in depth.

At any rate, that is my understanding of the past seventy years in Japan-Korea relations, and I think there are many people in Japan who see things the same way, but mainstream opinion in Korea is different.

Korean democracy progressed in the 1990s, giving rise to the Kim Dae-jung administration in 1998 and then the Roh Moo-hyun administration in 2003. Until then there had been conservative administrations, but progressive governments then continued for two terms over ten years. Until then, only conservative thought and anticommunist ideology were allowed in Korean society, but with democratization, progressive thinking was gradually permitted. Korean society developed so that progressive thinking and conservative thinking each claim about half of society at present.

For example, if you look at the votes gained in the 2012 presidential elections, the conservative candidate, Park Geun-hye, got 51 percent and the progressive candidate, Moon Jae-in, got 48 percent, virtually splitting the vote. In the past, the progressive camp had not been able to speak out, but now they are able to raise their voices freely.

The core of the progressive camp is the people who had previously promoted democratization. Their basic thinking is that the 1965 normalization of diplomatic relations by the Park Chung-hee administration was flawed. At the time, Korea was weak and there was no alternative to what was done. But Korea has grown. The view has gathered strength in Korea that the Japan-Korea relationship should be reworked commensurate with Korea's present strength and international standing.

This not only is the view among the people at large but also is becoming the view within the legal establishment. Judicial thinking that the 1965 negotiations to normalize diplomatic relations need to be rethought is clearly evidenced in the Constitutional Court's August 2011 finding that the Korean government (executive) needs to do more to solve the comfort women issues and in the Supreme Court's May 2012 judgment recognizing that victims of forced labor have a right to seek individual compensation and referring a case back to a lower court. This pressure from Korean society and from the legal establishment places the Korean government in a very difficult position when it comes to respecting agreements reached with Japan at the governmental level.

Reconciliation Built on a Community of Interests

HOSOYA: The more I hear about this, the more difficult it sounds. Korea especially seems to involve a number of issues that make the relationship even more difficult than relations with China and the US are. And the passage of time may well have made these issues still more difficult to resolve. We seem to be entering an era in which it will be all the more important that people of good will put their collective heads together and devise realistic policies that are mutually satisfactory.

WATANABE: I think most people would agree that Japan-US relations overall have been good for the seventy years since the war. True, Japan has had anti-American leftists and right-wing nationalists, but we have muddled through and reached the necessary accommodations.

The G7 Summit was held at Schloss Elmau, Germany, in June 2015. Regarding maritime security, the Leaders Declaration says: "We are concerned by tensions in the East and South China Seas. . . . We strongly oppose the use of intimidation, coercion or force, as well as any unilateral actions that seek to change the status quo, such as large scale land reclamation." This statement clearly refers to China, and this wording was inserted by Japan and the US to reinforce global norms.

The same pattern shows up in Russia's exclusion from the March 2014 G8 meeting. That was decided by the leaders of the other seven nations in opposition to Russia's annexation of Crimea in Ukraine.

It is very much in the US interest to maintain the liberal world order, and the US provides strong support for that ideal, including force. Japan has a shared interest in the order maintained by the US, agrees with that ideal, and has consistently cooperated with the US since the end of the war. This actual convergence of interests supports fundamental reconciliation between the peoples of Japan and the US.

There have, however, been times when this was not true. When I was studying in New York in 1989, it was said among the local Japanese community that Japanese should refrain from going outside on December 7, which is the anniversary of the attack on Pearl Harbor. At that time, the Cold War had ended, Japan-US trade friction was intensifying, and Japan-US relations were worsening. The US had won the Cold War, the Soviet Union had collapsed, and the Berlin Wall had been demolished, but US economic power was on the wane while the economies of America's former enemies, Japan and Germany, were in peak condition. The Japan-as-outlier view of Japan emerged in reaction to that situation. The great misunderstanding that "Japan is not a true democracy; it is collectivist and unfair" was created and propagated by the media and academia. It was because I wanted to know the reason for this misunderstanding that I went to study in the US. I started studying political science in part to construct a theoretical foundation to refute this outlier-Japan thinking.

What I learned was that when the relations between countries themselves are bad, factors such as historical narrative differences and cultural differences are mobilized to demonize the other country. Conversely, when relations improve, the negative images are swept away. Hollywood movies are also made drawing upon and playing to those popular images. For example, the 1993 movie *Rising Sun* starring Sean Connery is a suspense film set in California about Japan-US economic friction during the early 1990s, when America was worried about Japanese companies acquiring US firms and invading the US market. The villain/murderer was the son of the CEO of a Japanese zaibatsu. Likewise, the villains were Nazis in World War II movies, Russians during the Cold War, and Arabs following September 11. The villains change depending upon how this or that country is perceived. But because the US is a democracy, "villain labeling" stops when the films do not do well or are found to be boring. This is one of democracy's strengths.

Yet democracy has its problems as well. For example, Korean Americans have taken the historical memory issue between Japan and South Korea to the US and are pushing their agenda there. This is taking place inside the US, so of course they are free to do this, but it causes problems for Japanese-Korean relations because people ask why South Korea is conducting anti-Japanese activities in the US. This demonstrates that there are also problematic aspects to American democracy's tolerance.

Even so, even given the negatives, American democracy is for the most part a positive thing, and we have to fully understand the basic American ideals of democracy and human rights. The historical memory issue is not a major problem between Japan and the US at present, but it should be carefully monitored because it could become a political issue depending upon the timing and the circumstances.

Hopes and Expectations for the Abe Statement

HOSOYA: Given what you have said about Japan-China, Japan-Korea, and Japan-US relations so far, my third and fourth questions to you are what the policy imperatives are—what Japan should do—for these three relationships, and then what you hope for or expect from the Abe Statement scheduled for next month.

KAWASHIMA: With the disclaimer that I am speaking within the scope allowed by the confidentiality agreements imposed by some organizations I work with, when the Cabinet Office ran a diplomacy public opinion survey in 2014 that included asking people what they thought of China, 80 percent said they "do not feel an affinity" with China. The proportion was even higher in Okinawa. Going the other way, about the same proportion of Chinese said they "do not feel an affinity" with Japan. So our national feelings toward each other are in rather poor shape. When the same survey was conducted in the 1980s, 70 percent or more of the Japanese respondents said they "feel an affinity." The corresponding figure was probably also high in China, where Japanese films were in vogue. The key moments in the souring of national sentiment on both sides have been the 1989 Tiananmen Square incident, the 1996 Taiwan Strait missile crisis, and the 2005 wave of anti-Japan demonstrations in China.

Yet when the Genron NPO conducted its Japan-China Public Opinion Poll, also in 2014, and asked about the importance of the other country, 70 percent of Japanese responded that the bilateral relationship is important. In a companion Chinese survey, 60 percent said the bilateral relationship is important.

Boiled down, the mutual public perception around Japan-China relations is, "I don't feel an affinity, but the bilateral relationship is important." This is not such a strange combination. For me personally, rather than yearning for the old "friendship" years and forced efforts to bring about a sense of closeness, it feels more natural to settle into a relationship where mutual trust is built up while coping with different kinds of strain, and firmly critical viewpoints are maintained while still recognizing how important the other country is.

China is Japan's top trading partner. There may be bilateral problems, but the current reality is that China is a key partner for the Japanese economy. China is definitely expanding, and it is undeniable that Chinese security and Chinese politics will be important for the future of Japan and the rest of the world. It is essential we watch developments closely and never look away. It is difficult to observe without prejudice, but China has become such a huge presence that there is no other choice.

One thing to remember is that Japan is a sensitive subject for the PRC. Several "anti-Japan dramas" are now running on television there, and they are riddled with historical inaccuracies. That helps explain why the Chinese public takes an even harsher view of Japan than the government does, and Chinese intellectuals have spoken out strongly against those TV programs. The Communist Party, which educated the country to be harsh on Japan, seems to be digging its own grave, but there is no doubt that Chinese public feelings toward Japan have soured somewhat; especially with the emergence of the discord over the Senkaku Islands and in the wake of the failure of Wen Jiabao's attempt to bring about reconciliation, Chinese policy toward Japan has grown more reactive since about 2009. There are positive attitudes about Japanese products and manga and so forth in the private sphere, but the public-sphere assessment of Japan is quite harsh. Meanwhile, political factions that prioritize economic development are stressing the importance of ties with Japan, while other factions emphasize the territorial issue. Such conflicting political agendas in China tend to have ramifications for Japan policy. So the Chinese stance toward Japan could shift depending upon the political situation there, and the government has to balance its international interests against domestic public opinion. Given all of this atmosphere, Japan is a difficult issue for the Chinese. The arrangement for the moment seems to be to discuss what can be discussed and avoid escalating conflict where possible. Over the last half-year, President Xi seems to have calibrated his responses to stop the pendulum from swinging too far.

What can we expect of the Abe Statement in August? I don't know. But if it can cover the three topics of how to view the period to 1945, how to view the seventy years since the war, and how to view the twenty-first century, then it should yield something different from the Murayama and Koizumi Statements. Both of those statements put more emphasis on the pre-1945 years, whereas I think the Abe Statement is likely to focus on the progress made in the postwar years, and the initiatives for reconciliation that have been attempted within the postwar bilateral relationship. I am hopeful there will be fresh ideas for moving forward in light of our critical introspection about the past and our determination of the facts.

Personally, in keeping with the fundamental approach I mentioned of closely watching what China does, I see several possibilities on the basis of Premier Wen Jiabao's April 12, 2007, address to the Diet.

One is the Peace, Friendship, and Exchange Initiative, which was initiated in 1994 with a statement by Prime Minister Murayama that differed from, but was part of the groundwork for, the 1995 Murayama Statement. Under the initiative, Japan budgeted a substantial sum to promote reconciliation at the grassroots level and related exchanges as a way of moving toward future reconciliation with the many European and Asian nations that Japan fought against in the war. I think that sort of effort should be continued in the future. Even toward a "forgive but not forget" nation, so long as there is no forgetting, Japan must continue to show that we have not forgotten the history either. All the more so toward a "never forgive, never forget" nation.

It is also important to get the facts out, not only about the prewar period but also about Japan's postwar initiatives for reconciliation. For example, the Japan Center for Asian Historical Records' website offers the convenience of free downloading of publicly available records held by national institutions—records located in the National Archives of Japan, the Foreign Ministry Diplomatic Archives, and the Defense Ministry's Center for Military History in the National Institute for Defense Studies. But for some reason, only the prewar records are available. If we want people to understand and appreciate Japan's postwar initiatives for reconciliation and our contributions to the global community, we have to take the lead in getting that information out. Additionally, there is the question of history education, especially more insightful study of the modern era. This is a domestic issue for Japan.

In closing, I will say one more thing. Taiwan worries me when I look at East Asia. We tend to think of Taiwan as pro-Japanese, but it is not that simple. A number of incidents have taken place in Taiwan signaling that they are very aware of and sensitive to history issues, and we should not take Taiwan for granted. Any change in the situation in Taiwan will bring corresponding change in Japan-China relations, Japan-US relations, and even the Okinawa situation. Now more than ever, we need to think seriously about reconciliation not only with the government but also with the people of Taiwan.

Doubly Humble and Doubly Appreciative

NISHINO: I have three main points to make. The first point is that, for Japan and Korea, relations are deteriorating on both sides. A recent Cabinet Office public opinion survey on diplomacy recorded the worst figures ever. In Japan, two out of three people said they "do not feel an affinity" with Korea. By way of contrast, until around 2009, two out of three people said they did feel an affinity with Korea. While the Korean view of Japan is very poor, at least it is consistent.

The main things that eroded Japanese feelings toward Korea were the visit by then President Lee Myung-bak to Takeshima Island in August 2012 and his remarks about the emperor. Japanese attitudes toward Korea have stayed down ever since. The leaders of the two countries would do well to take careful notice of this serious situation, and it is important that relations between the two countries be managed so they do not deteriorate further.

On a happier note, the leaders of the two countries attended receptions in Seoul and Tokyo on June 22, 2015, to commemorate the fiftieth anniversary of the normalization of diplomatic relations. They clearly hope to take the opportunity of this dynamic to somehow improve the bilateral relationship, and I am hopeful further progress can be made after the autumn trilateral summit among Japan, China, and Korea.

My second point is to highlight the importance of the two-track policy recently spoken of in Korea. This two-track policy refers to separating history problems and other issues so that the history problems do not poison other areas of the Japan-Korea relationship. However, it is also important that this not result in the historical issues being put aside. It is important a persistent effort be made to resolve the history problems. Both Korea and Japan have changed considerably since 1965. Both should grasp this reality and approach the question of what can be done carefully and determinedly in line with that realization.

There is one other thing I would like to say in this connection. The truth is that Japan-Korea exchanges and cooperation have been moving forward in areas other than the history questions—areas such as economics, culture, personnel exchanges, and recently security. But unfortunately, these areas have not received enough attention. Japan-Korea relations are multilayered and multifaceted, and while the history problems are important, they are only one part of the whole. I think we should make a greater effort to look at other areas and nurture the Japan-Korea connection.

My third point is two things I hope the Abe Statement will be and do. First is that I hope it will carry a message the international community can welcome. The Japan-China and Japan-Korea connections are important, and I hope this will be a statement that both countries welcome. From what Prime Minister Abe said at the leaders meeting at the sixtieth anniversary of the Asian-African Conference (Bandung Conference), his speech to the joint session of the Congress in Washington, and the discussions of the 21st Century Advisory Panel, it may well be difficult to win much praise from Korea. But I will be happy if Japan's past progress is understood, if a strong message about Japan's ongoing contributions to the international community is delivered, and if this is favorably received by the international community at large.

My second hope for this statement relates specifically to the relationship with Korea, where I hope the statement will be clear in telling Korea and the Korean people that the progress made so far in the bilateral relationship has been a joint effort by both countries. In that sense, it was clear in the June 2014 report on the Kōno Statement that the two governments have been making sincere efforts to work together on the history problems and the comfort women issue since the 1990s. Even though the report was heavily criticized in Korea and President Park Geun-hye has continued to insist that the Japanese side needs to show more good faith, I think the two sides need to hold further frank discussions about what more Japan should do and how the Korean side will reciprocate in good faith. Then, based on that, both governments should work to ratchet down the rhetoric on the history issues, especially the comfort women issue.

WATANABE: As you pointed out, it is important to remember that Japan-Korea relations can only work if the South Korean side is responsive. When German Chancellor Angela Merkel spoke in Tokyo in March 2015 regarding the postwar reconciliation between Germany and France, she said it was necessary for Germany to face up squarely to its past, but reconciliation still would not have been possible had it not been for the generous gestures of Germany's neighbors. This is a profoundly important message.

The US and Japan do not have many areas still requiring reconciliation. Nevertheless, if Japan cannot achieve reconciliation with its neighbors, Japan is less valuable as a US ally in Asia. Accordingly, improving Japan-US relations has to include not just sharing common values and interests in observing the international order and norms but also working for reconciliation with our neighbors.

Japan must first clarify what it wants to do in the international community and what sort of international order it seeks. It must then adopt policies consistent with this. In that sense, I am in favor of the proactive pacifism advocated by Prime Minister Abe. I think the fact that Japan is trying to loosen the legal restraints so it can contribute more to regional stability is a necessary step if Japan is to become a more mature nation. Unfortunately, this has not been explained very well to the citizenry, but it is essential the prime minister's August statement not contradict this policy. Self-righteous, backward-looking comments that deny the past should be avoided. So should a domestic-oriented stance. Looking at the debate on the security legislation, the antis strike me as inward-looking. They are afraid to make international-oriented contributions. I think Abe's statement should include how much Japan has contributed to the international community so far and pledge to strive to make even greater contributions in the future.

HOSOYA: If you will excuse a very mundane example, I sometimes find the human relations difficult in the courses I am teaching. But when we sometimes think we're carrying the whole load and the other people are just free-riding, it is important we discount our perception of how much we are doing by half and assume the other people are doing twice as much as we think they are. If we can do that, the results come out pretty close to the reality. If we can be doubly humble and doubly appreciative, we are less likely to exaggerate how much we are doing and less likely to underestimate the effort the other side is making. We are more likely to have a more realistic understanding of who is doing how much. It is all too easy to be critical of China, Korea, and the US, but we need first to be a little more humble and a little more critical about what we ourselves are doing or not doing, because that will make it easier to understand and appreciate what the other side is doing as well.

6

Historical Memory
and International Relations
in East Asia
The Abe Statement in Retrospect

Hosoya Yūichi, Kawashima Shin,
Nishino Jun'ya, and Watanabe Tsuneo

Just as Chapter 5 was an edited transcript of a panel discussion held in July 2015 before the Abe Statement was issued, this chapter is adapted from a panel discussion held in February 2016 subsequent to the August 2015 statement and looks at the reactions to the statement, both in Japan and overseas, and what impact it might have had. As such, it seeks both to elucidate the statement's significance and to look at how experts on China, Korea, the United States, and Europe see the statement in terms of history and international relations.

What Was the Abe Statement?

HOSOYA: I would like to start this discussion by looking at how the different national newspapers editorialized about the statement issued by Prime Minister Abe Shinzō on August 14, 2015. The paper that was most laudatory was the *Yomiuri Shimbun*. Their editorial was titled "Hansei to Owabi no Kimochi wo Shimeshita" (Expressing Remorse and Apologies) and the lead sentence was: "This statement deserves a thumbs-up for laying out a new path for Japan based upon full remorse for what happened during World War II."

Also on the positive side was the *Nihon Keizai Shimbun* (*Nikkei*), which titled its editorial "Nanajūnen Danwa wo Fumae, Nani wo Suruka da" (What Will Japan Do Based upon This Statement?) and then wrote in the body of the text that the statement is to be appreciated for having been generally very commonsensical. Especially noteworthy was that this *Nikkei* editorial rated the Abe Statement as better than the 1995 Murayama Statement. Whereas the Murayama Statement referred to the "mistaken national policy" pursued "during a certain period in the not too distant past" and was not explicit about what this referred to, the Abe Statement was "good in being more specific about what the cause of our remorse should be." The *Nikkei* liked the Abe Statement for being both longer and more explicit than the Murayama Statement. The *Nikkei* editorial then closed with something akin to an expression of popular sentiment: "The Prime Minister represents all of the people and should conduct his government taking into account the views of a broad range of society." If the Murayama Statement may be said to have exacerbated the left-right polarization over the historical memory issue and the Abe Statement may be said to have healed the divide, that is cause for a positive appraisal.

On the other side, the *Asahi Shimbun* was much more critical of the statement than the other papers were. Interestingly, the *Asahi* letters to the editor were overall favorable toward the Abe Statement, this in striking contrast to just a short time earlier when both the paper and the readers were strongly critical of Abe's efforts to reinterpret the rules so as to allow the Self-Defense Forces to take part in overseas combat operations.

Among the other papers, the *Sankei Shimbun* and the *Mainichi Shimbun* were on the critical side, albeit in a restrained way. It is noteworthy that the *Asahi, Sankei,* and *Mainichi* all called on the statement to be more clearly ideological. From its conservative standpoint, the *Sankei* wrote: "We keep having to apologize, and it is time to put an end to this apology-based foreign policy." It also said: "Abe should have been more forcefully Abe." In short, the *Sankei* seemed unhappy that the statement was not more ideological to the right. By contrast, the *Asahi* and *Mainichi* argued that the statement should have evidenced a more liberal ideology on the issue of historical memory. The *Yomiuri* and *Nikkei,* both of which saw the statement favorably, said that it should be a start to improving relations with Japan's immediate and nonimmediate neighbors and ventured that the statement will be useful in improving bilateral relations with the other countries in the region.

All of that said, what were the reactions in China, Korea, and the US? What significance do our experts here attach to the statement? To answer this question, I would like to hear first from Professor Kawashima, then Professor Nishino, and then Mr. Watanabe.

Four Key Aspects: Colonial Domination, Aggression, Sincere Remorse, and Apology

KAWASHIMA: Looking back at the mood during the months leading up to the Abe Statement, it had been fairly widely assumed that the government, like the prime minister himself, was on track to promote historical revisionism. That expectation of historical revisionism shifted immediately after Abe's April 2015 speech to a joint session of the US Congress. China and South Korea may not have changed their minds, but fewer people were calling Abe a revisionist in the West, especially in the US.

I think Japan got through 2015—the seventieth anniversary of the end of the war, the Abe Statement, and the Japan-Korea agreement on the comfort women issue as announced by the two foreign ministers—without any major missteps and managed to avoid heavy criticism, at least from the West, about government policies or the Abe administration.

The most important feature of the historical narrative in the Abe Statement is its recognition of the time around the 1931 Mukden Incident as a turning point. The Murayama and Koizumi Statements can be read as grouping everything before the war together. In contrast, taking the Mukden Incident of 1931 as a historical turning point was quite a big step. Of course, some read that as being positive about colonialism. I think South Korea would object to it, and plenty of others are not convinced. In terms of Japan-China relations, if 1931 is big, 1915 should also be called big. So why was 1931 taken as the turning point? There was discussion on that point by the Advisory Panel on the History of the 20th Century and on Japan's Role and the World Order in the 21st Century, of which I was a member, and I think it was something all of the assembled specialists could agree on. There will be arguments, but that view of history seems to have worked to some extent to make the discussion of the various conflicts and divergences of historical understanding palatable both in Japan and elsewhere.

The Abe Statement comprised four elements:

1. Naturally, it was based on the Murayama and Koizumi Statements, and used much of the same wording.
2. With those statements providing a draft manuscript, elements from speeches given by Prime Minister Abe during the past year were added, in ways that were not inconsistent.

3. Then material recommended by the 21st Century Advisory Panel was included.
4. Finally, some new content was slipped in, this new content including the line: "We must not let our children and grandchildren . . . be predestined to apologize," which reflected the thinking within the Kōmeitō and the LDP.

Public attention focused mainly on four terms that appear in the statement: colonial rule, aggression, deep remorse, and apology. The Abe Statement itself did not place that much emphasis on examining and explicating the history, instead emphasizing the postwar period and the future. Rather, it was the media that picked those four terms out and lined them up to be graded, like a report card. With the media setting the agenda like this, the four terms drew even stronger attention, because the Diet was in session when the statement was delivered and they became part of the debate on the security legislation. This in turn highlighted the importance of political considerations in drafting the statement and, judging from the media and public reactions, I suspect more care was taken with the wording than many of us first thought.

Aware of the overall atmosphere in Japan, China indicated that it was watching the media reactions closely and would be unable to credit any aspects of the statement that were heavily criticized in the Japanese media. As it turned out, most of the media viewed the statement positively, making it difficult for China to be strongly critical. In fact, Chinese objections went no further than to repeat statements of principle. These were given some media space, but on the whole there was no outright rejection of the Abe Statement. To put this in the context of the Japan-China relationship, in 2007 Premier Wen Jiabao spoke positively about the Murayama and Koizumi Statements in his address to the Diet. So far, China has not made any official comment on the Abe Statement. We will watch for a Chinese comment on the statement in the future, perhaps in an official bilateral document. The 1998 Japan-China Joint Declaration stated:

> The Japanese side observes the 1972 Joint Communiqué of the Government of Japan and the Government of the People's Republic of China and the 15 August 1995 Statement by former Prime Minister Tomiichi Murayama. The Japanese side is keenly conscious of the responsibility for the serious distress and damage that Japan caused to the Chinese people through its aggression against China during a certain period in the past and expressed deep remorse for this. The Chinese side hopes that the Japanese side will learn lessons from the

history and adhere to the path of peace and development. Based on this, both sides will develop long-standing relations of friendship.

Note the reference to the Murayama Statement of 1995. By 1998, Japan and China were already in accord that the Murayama Statement was a foundation for the relationship's further development. That is significant, and I suspect the assessment accorded the Abe Statement will be as important for the future of Japan-China relations as the assessments already accorded the Murayama and Koizumi Statements are.

Domestic Politics and International Relations

NISHINO: As someone specializing in Korea and the Korean Peninsula, I think Korea was wary from the start about the idea of Prime Minister Abe's issuing a statement. Personally, I think Abe's was a balanced statement, for several reasons. First is that it was drafted very much with an eye to both domestic and international politics. Here at home, for example, as Professor Kawashima indicated, it was very much part of the security legislation debate in the Diet.

Also, as Professor Hosoya pointed out, it seems to have struck a good balance among the different ideologies' positions on history, and the recommendations of the 21st Century Advisory Panel were clearly reflected here, making it a somewhat less conservative statement than it would have been had Prime Minister Abe's personal proclivities been more faithfully stated.

With regard to the international dimension, Prime Minister Abe's overseas speeches—his April 2015 Bandung Conference speech and his speech to the joint session of Congress in Washington, for example—were very important. These speeches were crafted thinking of the Japan-America and the Japan-Asia connections, and it was good to see them appropriately reflected in the August statement. Both international relations and domestic politics were clearly influential in the statement's writing.

The Abe Statement may just seem commonsensical here in Japan, but there are parts of that historical view that Korea would find difficult to accept. For example, Korea would take issue with the idea that Japan was a great power and was acting as a responsible member of the international community until 1931—that Japan only veered off onto this wrong path with the Mukden Incident and subsequent events.

Then again, there is Abe's statement that "the Japan-Russia War gave encouragement to many people under colonial rule from Asia to

Africa." This is diametrically opposed to the Korean view of history. As Korea sees it, the Russo-Japanese War was doubtless an important event, but it was an important event in Japan's long march to imperialism and the colonization of Korea. It strengthened Japan's hold on the Korean Peninsula, and the main loser in that war was not Russia but Korea. As such, the Korean people probably find the Abe Statement's version of history extremely difficult to accept.

But reading the Abe Statement, it looks as though these difficult Japan-Korea relations can be improved following the statement. There are, for example, two references to violations of women's human rights during the war, and I believe this is a message offered to Korea.

It is very interesting that President Park Geun-hye's National Liberation Day speech (one of the most important speeches for a Korean president) the next day commented favorably on Abe's statement. In her speech President Park said: "It is hard to deny that Prime Minister Abe Shinzō's statement of yesterday marking the 70th anniversary of the end of the war did not quite live up to our expectations." But she followed that with: "Notwithstanding, we take note of the message that was clearly conveyed to the international community; namely, that the position articulated by the previous Japanese cabinets, based on its apologies and remorse . . . will remain unshakable into the future" (official Korean translation).

Given that she focused on the idea that the position of previous cabinets will remain unshakable and said this is noteworthy, she seems to have viewed Abe's statement in a positive and forward-looking light. What I would like to speak to next is the question of whether President Park or the Korean government wants to improve Japan-Korea relations, and whether the Abe Statement was framed with that in mind.

Actually, and this is an instructive detail, President Park said at a Blue House conference on August 10 that she wants to see if the Abe Statement reaffirms the stance taken by successive cabinets. So in a way, Prime Minister Abe's statement was responding to President Park's concern. I may be reading too much into this, but I think this mention of the position articulated by the previous Japanese cabinets remaining unshakable is just as important as the four terms the media focused on, and I cannot help but feel this was scripted by the two governments.

For the Korean government, the Abe Statement was seen as very important for the development of its foreign policy in 2015, and the fact that the statement was open to multiple interpretations made it somewhat easier for them to approve of it and to move to improve Japan-Korea relations.

In terms of changing the relationship between Japan and Korea, the very fact that Abe's statement was equivocal can be seen as a positive. Also, the Abe Statement's "We must not let our children, grandchildren, and even further generations to come . . . be predestined to apologize" was, in fact, also spoken following the Japan-Korea agreement of December 28, 2015, and as Mr. Watanabe indicated, this phrasing was very much Abe being Abe. This was also noted and reported in Korea, and it seems to be seen as connected to Japan's concern that Korea is "moving the goal posts"—the idea that Korea has been escalating its demands and that this will have to stop. As such, this can be read as Prime Minister Abe asking how long Korea intends to continue demanding that successive generations apologize. It might not have been that explicit, but this is how it was seen in Korea.

Again, at the risk of reading too much into things, the paragraph preceding says: "Thanks to such manifestation of tolerance, Japan was able to return to the international community in the postwar era. Taking this opportunity of the 70th anniversary of the end of the war, Japan would like to express its heartfelt gratitude to all the nations and all the people who made every effort for reconciliation." The hidden message here might be taken as: "What about Japan-Korea relations? We very much hope Korea will be able to manifest that kind of tolerant spirit."

In the October 1998 Japan–Republic of Korea Joint Declaration, former prime minister Obuchi Keizō spoke of his "deep remorse and heartfelt apology." In response, President Kim Dae-jung expressed his appreciation for this and for the role that Japan has played for international peace and prosperity. The Abe Statement may well have been delivered in the hope that the two countries could return to the spirit of that 1998 joint declaration.

What Did the United States Think of the Abe Statement?

WATANABE: I would like to start with the US media reaction to the Abe Statement, because the Abe administration's understanding of history has come in for a great deal of criticism from both left and right in the media. Both the *New York Times* on the left and the *Wall Street Journal* on the right have long criticized the Abe administration's historical narrative. The criticism from the *New York Times* might be called ideological—that is to say, it was primarily criticism that the administration's historical narrative was not in line with liberal thinking. As such, it resembles the positions taken by the *Asahi* and *Mainichi* newspapers. In contrast, the criticism from the *Wall Street Journal* was not the kind of conservative ideological criticism you see in the *Sankei* but was rather criticism from the realist point of view—that Japan's failure to achieve reconciliation regarding history issues with South Korea is not consistent with the maintenance of regional stability, and hence not in US interests.

The turning point away from this critical view of Prime Minister Abe in the US was, as you have mentioned, his address to the joint session of Congress. Abe staged a reconciliation between Japan and America in that address, so at least as far as the US is concerned, he eliminated suspicions that he might be a historical revisionist. While this is open to debate, you might say he affirmed that he has no intention of rethinking the San Francisco Peace Treaty arrangements.

The US sees the comfort women issue as a litmus test of Japan's historical narrative, because it is being positioned as a women's issue and as a human rights issue, and the protection of women's human rights is a fundamental value for American democracy. It is only natural that the liberal *New York Times* is very interested in this issue, and the US liberal media were very harsh toward Japan, and especially the Abe administration, prior to the Abe Statement. The US conservative media also champion respect for human rights and very much desire improved Japan–South Korea relations to counter North Korea and China in line with US national security interests, so they were also harsh on Japan. These demands from both left and right in the US doubtless affected the Abe administration and the Liberal Democratic Party.

This was reflected in the substance of Prime Minister Abe's address to the joint session of Congress, and the negative view in the US was greatly mitigated by that speech. His speech emphasized the reconciliation between Japan and the US following the Second World War, and he highlighted this reconciliation by inviting Japanese Diet member Shindō Yoshitaka, a member of the Japanese House of Representatives and the grandson of Iwo Jima garrison commander Kuribayashi Tadamichi, and Lieutenant-General Lawrence Snowden, an American veteran who fought on Iwo Jima, to Washington for his address. I think that Korea and Korean Americans must have been very unhappy with this. US representative and House Foreign Affairs Committee chairman Ed Royce, who has many Korean American constituents and supporters, was absent when Prime Minister Abe addressed Congress, because he was attending a relative's funeral, but he later released a statement criticizing the speech for not including reconciliation with Asia. Royce especially stressed the lack of any apology for the military comfort women. True, Prime Minister Abe's speech made little mention of the military comfort women. Instead, Abe made deeply reflective comments regarding the military comfort women at a joint press conference with President Obama after the Japan-US summit meeting. I think he struck a balance here. While Congressman Royce came down hard on Abe, the liberal media, who certainly also heard Prime Minister Abe's press conference, did not react that harshly. On the contrary, they ran comparatively favorable articles. The success of Abe's address to Congress also had an effect within South Korea and caused the Park administration's foreign policy team to recognize that excessive Japan bashing could alienate the US. I think this was a positive thing, and I suspect China is also well aware of this point. Abe's speech was probably another step in the reconciliation process between Japan and the US and laid the foundations for a favorable reaction to the Abe Statement on the seventieth anniversary of the end of the war.

One very interesting reaction to the Abe Statement in the US was that of the *New York Times*. Until then, this liberal newspaper had been so strongly anti-Abe that it habitually used the epithet "outspoken nationalist" every time it wrote about him, but this time the editorial page did not even mention the Abe Statement. I do not know why, but the paper apparently decided that the statement was not worth praising but also not worth criticizing. I think this is a sign that it was received positively in the US, as is clear from the editorial in the *Washington Post,* which is also a liberal newspaper. The editorial was not aggressively negative and could even be termed relatively positive. Regarding the Abe Statement, it said: "Mr. Abe notes that Japan 'has repeatedly expressed the feelings of deep remorse and heartfelt apology,' a position he says 'will remain unshakable into the future,'" but continues, "Sadly, he couldn't bring himself to repeat that apology." Perhaps the *Washington Post* was troubled by Abe's typically conservative statement that "we must not let our children, grandchildren, and even further generations to come, who have nothing to do with that war, be predestined to apologize." But the editorial also praises Abe, saying: "He acknowledges the 'immeasurable damage and suffering' Japan inflicted on innocent people in neighboring countries," and continues, "On balance, though, Mr. Abe's statement is far more conciliatory and less nationalistic than his critics feared it would be."

Politically, the *Washington Post* takes liberal positions, but it dispassionately observes the Abe administration within the reality of international relations in Asia. The editorial touches on the Chinese "striking double standard" of feeling free to pass judgment on Japan's historical narrative while not facing up to its own past, including the many victims of the Cultural Revolution, and notes the difficulty all countries have facing the ugliness in their past. It also stresses support for Japan's changing its interpretation of its constitution and actively cooperating with security efforts in Asia. The editorial closes by noting that it is important that Japan not attempt to rewrite its prewar history and cause unnecessary concern among its neighbors. This is close to the Obama administration's position and reflects the Washington consensus among people knowledgeable about conditions in Asia. So I think the Abe Statement was rather well received there.

Looking at the comments from US Asian experts, the more critical they had been of the Abe administration before, the more appreciative they were of the Abe Statement. More than being directly angry about the Abe administration's version of history, these experts fear that the consequent worsening of Japan-Korea and Japan-China relations might undercut US influence in Asia. The Abe Statement was important in mitigating those concerns. I have continued to monitor the US media, and the perception is that relations between Japan and China and between Japan and Korea, particularly relations with South Korea, have been improving since the Abe Statement. Criticism and concern regarding Prime Minister Abe's reading of history have settled down, and I think we have reached the stage where they will not erupt again unless something extraordinary happens.

How the Abe Statement Differs from Past Statements by Other Prime Ministers

Hᴏsᴏʏᴀ: Another very important issue here is understanding how the Abe Statement differs from, or is the same as, the earlier Murayama Statement. I mentioned the *Asahi* editorial a bit earlier. Basically, the *Asahi,* and Murayama himself, for that matter, felt that the Murayama Statement was far better in substance than the Abe Statement was. From there, the *Asahi* went on to ask why Abe went to the trouble of issuing this inadequate statement. Yet given today's international climate, it is unlikely that simply repeating or reaffirming the Murayama Statement would suffice to improve relations with China and Korea or to induce a positive turn in relations with the US. After all, Prime Minister Abe had already said, in his New Year's address to the nation in January 2015, that he was in accord with the Murayama Statement and the positions expressed by past administrations. So there would not be much point in simply affirming the Murayama Statement again, and he obviously needed to include additional wording taking account of the current international climate.

That said, it is no easy task to understand how the Abe Statement is consistent with the Murayama Statement, how the two statements are connected, and why they have been received differently, not least because Abe himself has been critical of the Murayama Statement. Looking at the Murayama Statement and the Abe Statement as a pair, let me ask each of you to comment briefly on the significance of the two statements' continuities and discontinuities.

Was the Abe Statement in the Tradition of Past Statements?

KAWASHIMA: Aside from the Murayama and Koizumi Statements, there have been other statements by other prime ministers including Prime Minister Miyazawa and, on a joint occasion with South Korea, Prime Minister Kan. This time, Prime Minister Abe made the statement in the most formal style, which is a clear indication that it is a successor which builds on previous statements. That intention was made clear in advance, when the speech was billed as "the prime minister's statement" rather than "a statement by the prime minister." Moreover, the statement itself said clearly: "The position articulated by the previous cabinets will remain unshakable into the future." And it did in fact use the same format as the Murayama and Koizumi Statements. In that sense, there is continuity with the previous statements.

Yet I see four differences that distinguish the Abe Statement from the previous statements. First, the Abe Statement presented a larger historical viewpoint. The style of the earlier statements was to posit that Japan was reborn after the war—that is, that modern history is split into prewar and postwar and the postwar part is affirmed. In contrast, the Abe Statement speaks to the prewar period and says Japan took the wrong road from the late 1920s or 1931. In other words, the Abe Statement expressed the historical viewpoint that Japan was on the right track from the Meiji Restoration on but strayed significantly from that course during the late 1920s up to the Mukden Incident. This will likely be criticized by South Korea and neighboring countries on the grounds that Japan invaded other countries and had colonies starting in the Meiji period, but it is still a big departure from the previous statements.

Second, the Abe Statement strongly reflects the recent international situation and the Abe administration's policy on security, especially in the reference near the end to "the past, when Japan ended up becoming a challenger to the international order." The Abe Statement expresses regret that Japan, which had been in sync with and a contributor to the international order, at some point became "a challenger to the new international order," and it stresses that Japan again became a contributor without being a challenger in the postwar period.

This is a major point. Obviously it is an assertion, against the backdrop of recent major changes in the international situation, that Japan attaches great importance to the existing global order, with an explanation in historical terms that Japan will never again be such a challenger. At the same time, it implicitly criticizes any country that does or might challenge the postwar international order. There are two references in the Abe Statement to the formation of economic blocs. These serve to strongly emphasize that Japan itself upholds the economic rules that underpin free trade, and they were obviously included with an eye to the Trans-Pacific Partnership (TPP)—another policy priority for the current administration. Regarding nuclear and other military force, there is the sentence: "Japan will continue to firmly uphold the principle that any disputes must be settled peacefully and diplomatically based on the respect for the rule of law and not through the use of force," which also seems to be there in support of the current administration's security proposals. These points can be read as declaring, with security policy and the TPP in mind, that Japan will never deviate from the path it has consistently followed since the war. These aspects were not in the Murayama Statement.

The third thing, and this could also be termed a similarity, has to do with reconciliation. The Murayama Statement also spoke of reconciliation, but the Abe Statement goes further and says: "We must not let our children, grandchildren, and even further generations to come, who have nothing to do with that war, be predestined to apologize." That sentence was widely picked up by the media in Japan and elsewhere as condoning war amnesia. Yet the two sentences that immediately follow it give it a very different meaning: "Still, even so, we Japanese, across generations, must squarely face the history of the past. We have the responsibility to inherit the past, in all humbleness, and pass it on to the future." This is the concept of eventual resolution, as the statement quite properly calls for coming to grips with the past, transmitting history to future generations, and, mentioned twice, being grateful for the tolerance shown by neighboring countries. There we can see a basis for reconciliation. Thus the Abe Statement does not just talk about reconciliation but fully lays out the substance of this reconciliation, which in that context means more than apologies. Indeed, the Abe Statement is distinctive in focusing on not just the idea but also the potential for reconciliation.

The fourth difference is a bit of a worry. The 1995 Murayama Statement is the document that is famous, while Prime Minister Murayama's 1994 statement on Japan-China relations is hardly known. Yet it was based on that 1994 statement that the Peace, Friendship, and Exchange Initiative was developed as an attempt to reach actual reconciliation, a substantial budget was allocated for the initiative, and it was somewhat successful.

The 21st Century Advisory Panel report of 2015 included recommendations linked to the Peace, Friendship, and Exchange Initiative. It is impossible to know how much longer Abe will be prime minister, but it is important to watch and see what he does in terms of funding actual exchange and reconciliation programs at the national and local citizen levels.

And if I might add a fifth difference, it would be linguistic. The Murayama Statement was delivered in Japanese, and even though it was put into English afterward, there was a strong sense that it was rooted in Japanese. For the Abe Statement, the planning included full recognition of the linguistic subtleties, and English, Korean, and Chinese versions were simultaneously released. Notably, the Korean and Chinese versions were released by the Japanese embassies in Seoul and Beijing. This rather effectively ensured three things: first, that there would not be conflicting translations in circulation; second, that the foreign-language versions of the Abe Statement would be prepared in Japan; and third, that foreigners would understand what Japan meant to say. That awareness of public diplomacy is a change from the Murayama Statement.

HOSOYA: Yes, it is clear that the Abe Statement was a very tight-knit document. And it is equally clear that it is important to analyze the elaborate logic woven in there. If relations with China and Korea are better as a result of this Abe Statement, we can probably conclude that the logic that Professor Kawashima pointed out was accepted by the Chinese and Korean governments. I wonder if Professor Nishino would agree with this.

From Being Directed at Asia to Being Directed at the International Community at Large

NISHINO: Professor Kawashima provided some very important guidelines as to how to interpret the Abe Statement, and I would like to make a few follow-up remarks. Professor Kawashima touched first on the difference in historical views and second on the international order. Keeping these points in mind and giving thought to the context of Japan-Korea relations, I think the difference between the Abe Statement and the previous statements was their target audiences—who the intended listener was.

The Abe Statement was given with a strong awareness of first the US and then the international community as a whole, whereas the Murayama and Koizumi Statements were basically directed at Asia. The reception the statement gets and the sense that is read into it very much depend on the target audience. On Korea, the Abe Statement differed from past statements in portraying Japan before the Mukden Incident as acting appropriately and playing a constructive role within the prevailing international norms, but this head-on conflicts with the Imperial Japan view that Koreans have of that history. That is to say, it brought the different historical views out more clearly. These different readings are closely linked to how the two countries view the Russo-Japanese War.

Another point of difference from the previous prime ministers' statements that bears mentioning is the call to proactive pacifism. The Koizumi Statement mentioned taking pride in Japan's contributions to the international community, but I think Prime Minister Abe wanted to use his signature "proactive contribution to peace" in the statement.

Then there is the issue that Professor Kawashima indicated is a concern. I agree with him on this question as to whether the Abe Statement will be accompanied by realistic follow-through. Unfortunately, there has not been much in the way of practical measures following the statement. The report of the 21st Century Advisory Panel, in a part where I think Professor Kawashima made a contribution, states the importance of history education, joint history studies, youth exchange projects, and the like. Happily, the Korean side has also indicated it wants to do joint history research. There are many ways this can be done. Japan and Korea could do it together, for example, or bring in researchers from other countries and make it a larger international study. I believe good follow-through measures and policies could make the Abe Statement even more significant.

The Regional Order and the Importance of Balance

WATANABE: Concerning the proactive pacifism that Professor Nishino referred to earlier, I think it embodies a realism that was lacking in the Murayama Statement but is present in the Abe Statement. The Abe Statement recognizes realism, especially a regard for regional balance and regional order, as important. I think that is incorporated in the Abe Statement, specifically in his words: "Incident, aggression, war— we shall never again resort to any form of the threat or use of force as a means of settling international disputes." It is important this refers not only to Japan but to all nations. In the end, as Professor Kawashima pointed out earlier, it is not Japan that is challenging the current order. On the contrary, as a US ally, Japan is on the side of maintaining the international order together with the US, its allies, and other cooperating countries. This is the fundamental structure of the current international community, and this is what underlies Abe's proactive pacifism. While maintaining its basic stance of an exclusively defensive capability, Japan is cooperating constructively for regional stability. Japan is, for example, collaborating with the US and other countries in the region for capacity building in Southeast Asia and for providing the public good of regional maritime security. This is all proactive pacifism. I think the biggest difference is that the Abe Statement clearly laid out how Japan will be a player in the international order in the Asia Pacific region.

Given the emotions involved, it is not easy for South Korea to accept Japan's proactive pacifism. After the First World War, Japan was on the side of maintaining the international order as a permanent member of the Council of the League of Nations from 1920 to 1933. Japan had annexed Korea ten years earlier, in 1910, and this annexation was recognized by the other countries there as one means of maintaining international order in line with the prevailing international norms. This would not be allowed under the current rules, and the Korean people find this history intolerable. It is thus essential, especially considering the importance of relations with South Korea, that Japan be cautious about historical memory in the proactive pacifism context. I agree with Professor Nishino on the difficulty and the importance of the South Korean side's accepting Japan's apology. When German Chancellor Angela Merkel gave a speech in Japan the other day, someone asked her how Japan should resolve the historical memory issue with its neighbors. In reply, Chancellor Merkel noted that Germany was able to achieve reconciliation in Europe only because its neighbors generously accepted its apologies. Korea and China may see Germany's contrition as a model case for Japan's apology and remorse, but Chancellor Merkel reminded us that the other side's willingness to accept the apology is just as important, and her answer-that-was-not-an-answer pointed out the need for Korea to take this difficult step. More than Japan, which is apologizing, Korea has the difficult problem of calming national sensitivities and accepting the apology.

Understanding Historical Memory in the Overall Context of International Relations

Japanese and Asian Historical Narratives as Seen from Europe

HOSOYA: Mr. Watanabe raised some very important points there. First was the idea—and this is something we have been talking about—that the international community dealt with Japan in the spirit of tolerance. This was very clearly hinted at in German Chancellor Angela Merkel's remarks in Tokyo. One mainstream contention has long been that Japan has much to learn from Germany in facing its history, but Chancellor Merkel seemed to be saying that Germany was accepted by the international community largely due to the hand of reconciliation that Germany's neighbors extended it. Of course, she also reminded us that Germany faced up to its history forthrightly, but the point was that both were essential to Germany's being accepted. Japan's recognizing its historical responsibilities and atoning are not alone sufficient for Japan to be reaccepted in the international community.

In that sense, the two conditions that the chancellor noted as necessary for historical reconciliation—that Japan face up to its history forthrightly and that its neighbors be willing to extend the hand of reconciliation—are both touched upon in the Abe Statement. So in that sense, I feel the remarks that the chancellor delivered in Tokyo had an important impact on the Abe Statement. This showed up in the Abe speech to the joint session of Congress in the US in April and the August Abe Statement, both of which expressed appreciation and gratitude for the forgiving spirit evidenced by the United States, the UK, Australia, and others moving toward historical reconciliation.

In seeking to understand Germany's historic reconciliation with the rest of Europe, it is important to consider that there were three different aspects to this. These are distinct aspects, and it only complicates the issue of historical memory to mix them together and talk about them as different parts of a comprehensive single aspect. The first aspect is that of human rights, the second that of responsibility for the war, and the third that of colonialism. Of the three, the human rights aspect was the most important in postwar Europe.

What was it that Germany apologized for and expressed remorse over after the war? It was the affront to human rights and dignity. It was the history of the Holocaust. This Holocaust—an unprecedented transgression against human rights—was the most important and heaviest burden Germany bore after the war. Roughly two-thirds of the approximately 9 million Jews living in Europe were caught up and killed in the Holocaust. Thus, in achieving reconciliation despite this gruesome history, the first thing Germany had to do was to make peace with Israel, and second was to reconcile with Poland, where the most famous death camp—Auschwitz—was located. Of course, Germany did not invade Israel or even go to war with Israel, so if it were just a question of Germany's apologizing for starting and waging the war, the people to apologize to would be the British, the Soviets, and the United States—the countries that Germany actually fought against. Logically, any apology for the war per se should have been directed to the Allied countries, but it was the Holocaust that demanded the most attention and sincerest contrition.

Were this simply a question of war crimes, Germany also had a case against the Allied powers. The Allied bombing of Dresden, for example, inflicted massive damage and left an estimated 130,000 dead. Similarly, Japan would have had a case against the United States given the estimated 300,000 who perished in the fire-bombing of Tokyo. It is true that Germany not only apologized for the transgression against humanity but also apologized for the aggression, invasion, occupation, and other wartime deeds; but the two issues were separate, and the crimes against humanity were far more serious.

On the issue of colonialism, Germany had no colonies to speak of, and this was not a major issue. Indeed, if anyone should have apologized for colonial occupation and colonialism, it would have been Britain and France with their extensive overseas colonies. However, Britain and France were on the winning side, so there was no need for them to apologize and appear contrite for their possession and domination of colonies. Instead, even after the war's end, there were major differences between the United States, which championed anti-colonialism and self-determination, and Britain and France, which continued to hold on to and to try to justify their overseas colonies.

Thus the United States and Britain clashed, for example, over the nondiscrimination language in the fourth clause of the Atlantic Charter (which implied abandonment of the British principle of imperial preference with regard to tariffs). In fact, this question of maintaining or dismantling empires was the most divisive issue for the Allied powers and ended up being separated from the question of Korea's postwar independence from Japan.

It should thus be understood that incorporating the "colonialism is evil" idea into the "universal values" championed since the war was not something that could be easily done or resolved, given the British and French histories of colonial domination. Colonialism remains a serious and divisive issue in Britain and France, and it is one of the issues that right and left are most sharply divided on. Indeed, this relates directly to the questions raised by the flow of refugees and immigrants into the European Union countries today. The question of colonialism is far more sensitive and far more difficult for the international community to deal with than are the other two questions (crimes against humanity and responsibility for the war).

There has been widespread sympathy for the Korean case on the comfort women as an issue involving transgressions against women. Similarly, there is a considerable body of opinion saying that Japan should be more apologetic and remorseful about its responsibility for the war in Asia, including everything from the 1931 Mukden Incident and all the rest of the aggression in violation of the League of Nations Covenant, the Kellogg-Briand Pact, and the other efforts to outlaw war. By contrast, the very scathing argument made in Korea that Japan's victory in the Russo-Japanese War marked the start of Japan's colonization of the Korean Peninsula has not gotten much traction in Europe—which makes sense, given that the European powers were themselves fighting to expand their colonial empires at the time and do not think it obvious that anyone should have to apologize for having had colonies. Conversely, there are those who argue that the Russo-Japanese War was instrumental in freeing many Asian peoples from the yoke of European colonial rule. Indeed, many in Turkey, Africa, and elsewhere have applauded Japan's victory in the Russo-Japanese War. This position, however, could easily draw European criticism if Japan pointed it out, since it could be seen as Japan using Asianism to justify Japanese actions and, by extension, painting the US and Europe as enemies of an Asia defined by race. Because such a position could be seen as strikingly similar to the Asianism that Japan professed before the war, it is a most difficult argument for Japan to make. While Japan tends to see European and Asian civilizations as distinct and separate, the Asian countries that were colonized tend not to see that much difference among the United States, the European powers, and Japan when all of them sought to gain and maintain colonial domination. To them, their independence is the overriding issue.

Of the issues cited—the human rights issue, the wartime responsibility issue, and the colonization issue—it is colonization that is the most difficult for the international community to resolve, for all of the reasons mentioned. Thus, while there are definitely issues between Japan and Korea over how they remember and assess the wartime years of colonization and domination, it should be noted that this is not a unique situation and that this has been a difficult issue throughout human history. All three of these issues have to be dealt with while taking into consideration people's feelings, but the issue of colonial rule is perhaps the most sensitive of the three and the issue over which differences and discord are most likely to arise.

Mr. Watanabe has pointed out that the Murayama Statement seemed divorced from reality but the Abe Statement seemed connected to the real world. Professor Nishino has noted the reference to what Abe called Japan's proactive contribution to peace, and pointed out that the two statements seem directed at different audiences.

Writing in *Tōa* [East Asia, a monthly journal published by the Kazankai Foundation and devoted to the evolving situation in Asia], Kyoto University professor Nakanishi Hiroshi has suggested that the Abe Statement was written primarily for readers in the United States, Europe, and Australia while the Murayama Statement envisioned a primarily Asian readership, and he has gone on to say we need a statement that is crafted for both audiences. I think this is a very important point. Given the different audiences they were written for, he says, it is only natural that the Murayama Statement and the Abe Statement should say different things in different ways, yet there is neither anyone thinking Japan should just try to make peace with the West and ignore Asia nor anyone saying Japan should pursue reconciliation only with Asia and ignore the West. Japan clearly needs to find reconciliation with both audiences. This rings very true to me.

In that sense, we should understand that the Abe Statement attracted the attention it did because historical memory has become a major point of contention throughout the international community. International relations expert Kōsaka Masataka wrote in *Kokusai Seiji* [International Relations], his book recently reissued by Chūkō Shinsho, that "every state has its own systems of power, interests, and values." He then followed up by adding: "Justice comes in many flavors in the international community, such that in discussing justice, we have to realize we are talking about justice in this or that specific instance. It is not at all unusual that one country could consider something entirely fair and another could consider the same thing grossly unfair. This is also a cause of tension and strife." I suspect this perspective is the key to understanding why the historical memory issue is so difficult.

Because the state is also a values system, the values that it holds dear and expounds are intricately linked to the state's identity, which means that issues of history and issues of values are important questions of state and not to be taken lightly. Scholars have traditionally discussed international politics within the realism paradigm assuming power and interests to be central, but we have to add the issue of values and put it on our radar. In international relations theory, this comes out as constructivism, and such scholars as Boston University's Thomas Berger and Cornell's Peter Katzenstein have discussed Japan's Asian security policies with special attention to the issue of cultural norms. In short, it seems obvious that the wartime experience, the issue of how people remember this history, and cultural norms are all closely tied to Japan's postwar Asian security policy. Given that, it is easy to understand why history issues and the question of historical narratives have come to be seen as important from an international relations perspective as well. In view of all of this, what can we expect in the wake of the Abe Statement? What is the outlook for Japan-China, Japan-Korea, and Japan-US relations?

The Values Structure to Which China Aspires

KAWASHIMA: China is certainly pushing forward on all three fronts: power structures, interest structures, and value structures. Power and interests go without saying. As for values, China itself is talking about Asia and is asserting Chinese values. China has specifically articulated such ideas as the New Security Concept for Asia and Chinese leadership in shaping the future of Asia. At the same time, China's representatives are careful to emphasize that this Chinese Asia will not run counter to the existing global order. That was signified by China's September 3, 2015, Victory Day military parade marking the seventieth anniversary of the end of the war with Japan. On the one hand, the parade was certainly meant to show off Chinese power, but at the same time, it emphasized the idea that China has stood with the victors on the side of the global order since World War II. The Chinese power and interest structures were naturally involved, and it is just recently that they have turned their attention to value systems. Going forward, China wants to seize the initiative in Asia, and it has repeatedly stressed both its desire to lead the way and the fact that it contributes to the global order. History is also being mobilized in this cause. In the global arena, China talks about great power cooperation, trotting out stories of the US and China fighting together against Japan and of China being allied with the Soviet Union and the Russian Federation, while in East Asia, China is quick to criticize Japan on historical issues and to emphasize China's superiority.

Second, and for exactly those reasons, historical narrative issues are more and more conspicuous on the global stage. The UNESCO World Heritage Sites and Memory of the World Register issues are not necessarily rooted in the year 2015, as projects nurtured in Nanjing and elsewhere have been emerging gradually since before the turn of the century. Looking ahead, we should expect China to continue creating such "facts" on the international scene. They continue to play the systems at UNESCO and other institutions to obtain international endorsement of what they call historical facts. It would not surprise me if they next tried to upgrade from Memory of the World Register status to World Cultural Heritage Site status, and they may well be lobbying for that right now in Paris or elsewhere. That trend is not going to stop, even if bilateral relations settle down, and even if historical perception issues among Japan, China, and South Korea are to some extent resolved. These Chinese actions are being taken to address the whole world, as well as to align with Chinese domestic history education and history-related propaganda efforts. Relations with Japan are by no means the only concern. Since this is being coordinated with history education and domestic propaganda in general, it is unlikely to change any time soon.

Third, summit-level relations between Japan and China went into hiatus after the Noda administration purchased (which was seen as "nationalized") the Senkakus in 2012. There were no summit meetings during the first year of the second Abe administration, and relations chilled further at the end of 2013 when Abe visited the Yasukuni Shrine. Summit meetings only resumed in the fall of 2014. Japan-China relations are admittedly difficult in some respects, yet there is a potential opening for reconciliation, as was clearly indicated in the Abe Statement. The words "We must not let our children . . . be predestined to apologize" were followed with: "Still, even so, we Japanese, across generations, must squarely face the history of the past. We have the responsibility to inherit the past, in all humbleness, and pass it on to the future." This looks very much like a rephrasing of what the Chinese are always telling Japan to do, which is: "Take history as a mirror and face forward to the future." That wording can be taken as an opening for Japan and China to come together to some extent and find common ground. Yet even if bilateral relations improve, it is difficult to imagine China not caring about history issues in either the East Asian or the global arena, so closely have the historical issues become linked with government legitimacy and the territorial issue. Not only have history issues become value issues bound up with the party's legitimacy and territorial claims; they have also become integral to China's relations with its neighbors. Originally, the power and interest structures were the big areas and the values were subordinate. Lately, however, history issues have emerged and the value issues, which are deeply related to history, are beginning to grow more important for China and could conceivably become independent variables. In that sense, even if Japan-China relations were settled in the traditional spheres of power and interests, the values component would still be left and the history issues could possibly become huge, not only in Japan-China relations but for all of East Asia and the world.

What Are the Shared Interests in Japan-Korea Relations?

NISHINO: As Professor Hosoya said, taking the three different European issues of human rights, responsibility for war, and colonization, basically Korea has been most concerned with the issue of colonial rule. The comfort women problem is closely connected with human rights, and I think that the strong emphasis developing on this is really a new phenomenon. Korea has made a strong appeal to the international community in connection with the comfort women issue as an issue of the human rights of women during wartime.

As seen in terms of power, interests, and values as explained by Professor Kōsaka Masataka, Korea has long seen itself as basically powerless and so it has concentrated so far on pursuing economic development for financial gain. Recently, however, Korea has begun to make a strong values pitch—a human rights pitch—to the international community. This is why, for example, the comfort women issue has become a more prominent element in Korean diplomacy over the past few years. That said, I am very curious what will happen in light of the Japan-Korea agreement announced on December 28, 2015.

I think there were three important points to this agreement. The first is legal responsibility, which is closely connected to the issue of human rights in time of war and which has long been a Korean concern. On this issue, I personally feel that Japan has tended to move toward the Korean position. Specifically, the announcement of the agreement offered an apology including the words "The Government of Japan is painfully aware of responsibilities" and expressing anew Abe's most sincere apologies as prime minister of Japan. I feel this was quite a compromise. The second point relates to the idea of "moving the goalposts," and states that this announcement means "this issue is resolved finally and irreversibly." The word "irreversibly" also is used in relation to the North Korean nuclear issue, so it drew a strong reaction from Koreans who said it is not the sort of term that should be used between friendly countries such as Japan and Korea. However, I suspect the Abe administration insisted on it. Finally, the third point relates to the values issue, where there was agreement to refrain from accusing or criticizing each other regarding this issue in the international community. This is very significant, and it deserves abundant appreciation. I think the fact that the Japanese and Korean governments could reach this agreement shows they share a common determination to move forward. The relationship will be built on maintaining this agreement, continuing the Japan-Korea connection, and going on in both sides' best interests.

What these mutual interests are for Japan and Korea, however, is a difficult question. In the short term, North Korea is an extremely important common problem for both Japan and Korea, and cooperating to manage it is an important issue for the relationship. But beyond that, what are the medium- to long-term interests the two countries share? This is a major issue for Japan-Korea relations. I think there are two possibilities here. One is that, as the two most developed democracies in East Asia, we should cooperate in taking the lead in the regional order. It would be very desirable, even ideal, if we could cooperate in this area. At present Japan is committed to the Trans-Pacific Partnership (TPP) and Korea is committed to the Asian Infrastructure Investment Bank (AIIB). These are two different regional economic orders. Korea says it wants to join the TPP, but this area of Japan-Korea cooperation will not be easy. Tellingly, the Abe administration's *Diplomatic Blue Book* has dropped the part about Japan and Korea sharing common values.

The second point is how Japan and Korea can cooperate in view of the relationship between the US and China. Korea is very conscious of the idea that China and America might form a G2 (Group of

Two), but the idea of a Sino-American G2 does not seem to be on the Japanese radar. The two countries obviously have a very different sense of Sino-American relations and of how the international order is developing in East Asia. The two countries' different perceptions of the international order and how they can cooperate in this region is clearly a major question mark over Japan-Korea relations. Happily, I think that the short-term Japan-Korea relationship is going well now that we have this agreement on the comfort women issue, but, given the present reality of North Korean nuclear and missile tests, there are more basic problems still to be worked out.

A Stable Japan-US Relationship

WATANABE: The US will have a presidential election in November 2016, and there will be a change of administration. With all due respects to Professor Nishino, Japan has long been concerned that the US and China might team up to form a G2, and this may also emerge in the US as criticism of the Obama administration. But I think the Obama administration will calmly continue to maintain a balance. That is, I think the US will continue to both collaborate with China in areas where this is possible, such as countering global warming, and to restrain China in areas that do not lend themselves to compromise, such as cyber-security and territorial rights in the South China Sea. Because Japan may become anxious about America's ambiguous stance, it will probably try to contribute positively with its proactive pacifism where it can and lobby the US to continue maintaining its military presence to restrain China. Because the Abe administration's security legislation was not very well received in Japan, the Abe administration has been cautious about actively implementing policies based on the new legislation prior to the House of Councilors election in the summer of 2016. Japan may not be able to soon deliver what the US expects. However, the US understands the political situation here. And for the US, the urgent foreign policy issues are to end the Syrian civil war and to implement the nuclear agreement with Iran. This means the US wants to avoid completely alienating Russia and China. While restraining China in such areas as the South China Sea and cyber-security, the US is cooperating with China on the Iranian nuclear agreement and the Syria issue and in implementing the 2015 United Nations Climate Change Conference Paris Agreement to halt global warming. In short, while the US and China are at loggerheads over the South China Sea and cyber-security, they are also acting like a G2 in some areas, which is causing continued concern in Japan and South Korea.

One of the reasons for this complex situation is what may be called an identity crisis in US foreign policy. Both Democratic and Republican voters are dissatisfied with what they call the establishment. These people feel ambivalent, as they are critical of the Obama administration and the deterioration in America's international standing and also hate the negative legacy of Bush's Iraq War for global involvement and intervention. I think Jeb Bush is doing so poorly in the Republican primaries because there is a strong-rooted awareness that his brother, President George W. Bush, started the Iraq War and that the military and fiscal burden of that war are linked to the present decline in US influence. The reason candidate Hillary Clinton is having an unexpectedly difficult battle in the Democratic primaries may be criticism that the timid Obama diplomacy she oversaw as secretary of state has weakened US influence internationally. I see the debate over foreign policy as having a major impact on the 2016 US presidential election, but even if the debate in the US shakes the foreign policy establishment, the Obama administration will continue to view the Japan-US alliance as important and will continue to restrain China while also cooperating with China where it can. Considering this US position, it seems fair to say that Japan-US relations are back to stable now that Japan has alleviated concerns regarding the historical narrative issue with its Asian neighbors and we have greater trust in and expectations of Japan's role in security cooperation.

The Postwar Global Order and International Politics Going Forward

HOSOYA: In looking ahead at what the future might hold, it is important to realize, as has already come up in our discussion, that the issue of conflicting historical narratives is not one that can be resolved separate and apart from everything else but has to be seen as inexorably linked to the questions of the international order and Japan's foreign policy in the years ahead. Changes in the international situation may well impact the question of historical narratives, and vice versa.

There are, after all, several unaddressed areas in the current international order, mainly because the current global order was formed around the basic Cold War structures. During the Cold War, both China and Korea were seen as divided countries; neither took part in the San Francisco Peace Conference, and neither played a significant role in structuring the postwar Asia Pacific order. So you have three countries—Japan, which lost the war; Korea, which gained its independence from Japan but was unable to participate in the San Francisco Peace Conference as an independent country; and China, which had tense-at-best relations with the United States for some time after the war and did not have diplomatic relations with Japan or the US for a few decades—that harbor dissatisfaction with the current postwar order in this region.

Prime Minister Abe has long spoken of his desire to restructure the postwar international order. Likewise, China is also engaged in a grand endeavor to alter the international order that the Western powers created, as with its AIIB project. And even the United States has expressed a desire to rethink the current international order in which it alone is responsible for maintaining order in the Asia Pacific region and has to devote immense resources to this task.

None of the major countries in the region is really happy with the international order as it currently stands, and they all seem to want to make some changes. We seem to have two parallel tracks, one wanting to maintain the international order and the other wanting to transform the international order. So let me ask each of you, in reference to the San Francisco Peace Conference, what norms the international order in this region should be based upon, how the international order should be maintained, and how it should be altered.

What China Wants from History

KAWASHIMA: First, about the framework of peace that has grown out of the San Francisco Peace Treaty. The San Francisco Peace Treaty was a product of the Cold War era, and the June 22, 1965, Treaty on Basic Relations between Japan and the Republic of Korea was based on it; yet not just on it, as the treaty states the two countries have resolved to conclude the treaty "Recalling the relevant provisions of the Treaty of Peace with Japan signed at the city of San Francisco on September 8, 1951, and the Resolution 195 (III) adopted by the United Nations General Assembly on December 12, 1948." The same is true of the Treaty of Peace between Japan and the Republic of China of April 28, 1952. The 1972 joint communiqué between Japan and the PRC does not mention the San Francisco Peace Treaty, yet it is clearly based on it. This pattern has been maintained through the four basic Japan-PRC declarations. As I noted earlier, the 1998 Joint Declaration on Building Partnership explicitly states: "The Japanese side observes the 1972 Joint Communiqué of the Government of Japan and the Government of the People's Republic of China and the 15 August 1995 Statement by former Prime Minister Tomiichi Murayama." Thus the bottom line in the bilateral relationship has not changed significantly. Because the

Abe Statement, even though issued by an administration widely regarded as conservative, conformed to previous statements, I do not see any major deviation from this bottom line in the relationship. As to modifying the San Francisco Peace Treaty system, China has not indicated any desire for major changes so far. If it did, China would likely try to impose its interpretations on the significance of and preconditions for the treaty.

I fully agree with Professor Hosoya's comments about the great importance of the domestic and international political situations. Whatever China itself does concerning history will end up having global and regional political ramifications quite apart from any impact it might have on the bilateral relationship, and there is the danger that these ramifications could come back to haunt the bilateral relationship. So in assessing relations with China, Japan needs to take a global perspective. Even today, the Chinese government is moving to strengthen its control over not only history education but also historical research. The Communist Party, with its monopoly on power, is moving to narrow the scope of allowable historical views, in effect to prohibit plural interpretations. Within China, the party is encouraging monolithic interpretations in history classes and academic history studies, and it is bolstering the publication of propaganda pieces about history for foreign consumption. While there is still a bottom line in place to keep history issues from completely poisoning Japan-China relations, rather delicate policy coordination will be needed to keep this bottom line intact.

In the longer-run context, if there are significant changes in the global order and China's position changes significantly, it will likely try to modify the bottom line. China's style of expression in its relations toward Japan and the world will also change with further democratization and diversification in Chinese thinking, but it remains to be seen how this will play out.

The San Francisco Peace Treaty System and Japan-US Relations

WATANABE: I do not think the historical narrative issue will become a problem between Japan and the US over the long term unless there is some very major development such as a change in the San Francisco Peace Treaty system. The Japan-US Security Treaty was concluded the same year as the San Francisco Peace Treaty and was incorporated into the San Francisco Peace Treaty arrangements. Japan and the US subsequently expanded the range of cooperation in the Guidelines for Japan-US Defense Cooperation in 1978 and 1997. The recent 2015

revision of the guidelines saw a further strengthening of this cooperation for regional stability. Japan and the US have a solid agreement and
shared interests on security cooperation in Asia. Japan understands that
the US military presence is the key to stability in the Asia Pacific
region, and our position is one of supporting and cooperating with that
presence. Meanwhile, the US considers Asia Pacific stability—maintained in multilateral, multitiered cooperation with Japan, Australia,
South Korea, India, and other allies and cooperating countries—a
means of encouraging China to become a cooperative player. I think
China realizes that it does not have sufficient power to challenge this
head-on. China is gradually acting to expand its influence in the region
and may intend to challenge US hegemony at some point in the future
if circumstances permit, but for now at least China does not think it
can replace the US as the regional hegemon.

International politics is always changing, and the history issue will
continue to be influenced by such changes. Japan must be careful its
historical narrative does not become an impediment to the maintenance
and exercise of Japanese and US power for regional stability. For this
reason as well, it is important that Japan be careful with its relations not
only with the US but also with the European and Asian countries. South
Korea and China are particularly important. Whether Japan can respond
calmly and pragmatically on diplomatic and security policy issues—as
well as on history issues—is the crucial question. Elsewhere, the US
has dynamically developed its foreign policy, but there is currently a
strong inward orientation in its domestic politics. Those candidates who
are oriented toward domestic issues are the ones getting public support
in the current presidential election. Nevertheless, because US national
interests would ultimately be harmed if the US became isolationist, you
have a conflict between the establishment types who recognize that
and the people who are inward-oriented and support anti-establishment
candidates. Yet not even those who advocate an inward-looking policy would go so far as to try to alter the San Francisco Peace Treaty
arrangements that are so much to the US's advantage. I expect Japan
will associate with the other Asian countries, while carefully watching
where the US is going as shown by the presidential election.

The Tottering 1965 Structure

NISHINO: The Japan-Korea relationship is basically the same as Professor Kawashima said the Japan-China relationship is. Because the
1965 Japan-Korea Treaty on Basic Relations and its attached agree-

ments were drawn up in consideration of the San Francisco Peace Treaty, there will be overall support for them.

It might seem that the 1965 structure is now faltering within Korea, or at least that more voices are being heard objecting to the 1965 structure. The Constitutional Court's August 2011 decision in relation to the comfort women and the Korean High Court May 2012 decision on forced labor are typical. In 2005, when Roh Moo-hyun was president, the Japan-Korea negotiating documents were all made public and a Korean joint public-private committee of researchers that studied these documents concluded that Japan had residual legal responsibility in areas including the comfort women issue. That is the Korean government's present position. Given the circumstances of the 2015 Japan-Korea joint agreement, the 1965 structure has been basically maintained and could even be said to have been reinforced. In addition, the apology and deep remorse that were absent in 1965 were made explicit in the Japan-Korea joint statement of 1998. The 1965 structure has been augmented over the years.

China is another factor that has become more important to the Japan-Korea relationship, and the question of how Korea will cooperate with China in response to the North Korean problem is an extremely important one for the relationship. In addition to the San Francisco Peace Treaty arrangements, which are the foundation of the East Asia regional order, the Armistice Agreement arrangements put in place following the Korean War are equally important for Korea. In the long term, it is essential the parties concerned move to replace the armistice agreement and move toward reunification. For Korea, the major issues are how the San Francisco arrangements and the armistice arrangements can evolve compatibly. China is extremely important to the reunification process because it is, along with the United Nations forces led by the US, a signatory to the armistice agreement, as is North Korea. Korea's relations with China are inevitably and intrinsically different from Korea's relations with Japan, both geographically and with regard to the arrangements defining them. Japanese and Korean views of China, and the Chinese attitudes that each of them will have to deal with, are different now and may well not overlap in the future. However, I think it is important Japan and Korea understand the nature of each other's relations with China and take this into account in looking at how they can cooperate.

Japanese and Korean views of China are unlikely to fully converge, but I still think Japan and Korea will be able to cooperate sufficiently from the overall regional perspective. Indeed, we have already seen some of this kind of cooperation in the Japan-Korea relationship following the 1998 Japan-Korea joint statement. Cooperation in the East Asia region has made considerable progress, thanks in large part to initiatives taken by President Kim Dae-jung since the Japan-Korea joint statement was issued. There has also been some evolutionary progress among the three countries of Japan, China, and Korea, and I think this is a good thing for Japan and Korea. Looking ahead, it is important the Japanese side and the Korean side both move toward strengthening this kind of cooperation in fuller awareness of its significance.

Hosoya: Thank you for raising that important point. Indeed, each country has its own history and its own historical narratives, and we have to start by being cognizant of and understanding of these different narratives. Rather than criticizing others and trying to force our own ideas of what is just and what is unjust on them, we have to think about what each country considers just and why, and have to make the effort to understand how this sense of justice is rooted in their historical experience. If we can develop a deeper understanding of the political situation within each country, as well as the international situation as it impacts that country, it might well be possible to understand the different historical narratives the different countries cling to. Of course, this process will demand considerable mutual understanding as well as willingness to compromise.

Conservatives and liberals alike tend to see their own version of justice as the one and only true version of justice, which is both a cause of domestic discord and a cause of international disputes. It is very important we be able to understand and respect the other person's thinking, and it is also important to be able to identify possible points of compromise therein. Now more than ever, this should not be just a question of power and interests but should also be a question of values and historical narratives and a most careful search for mutually satisfactory compromises and for positions that can be accepted both domestically and internationally.

All of Asia is beset with fierce conflict, but there is still considerable room for looking for compromise, adjusting positions in the name of reconciliation, and working to avoid outright clashes. The current peace is a very fragile thing, a temporary truce as it were, and Asia's future hinges on whether or not we can turn our attentions to shoring up and strengthening today's tentative peace.

7

Historical Memory and International History
A Guide for Further Reading

Hosoya Yūichi

In 2015, the seventieth anniversary of the end of World
War II, both the Japanese government and the Abe administration
were watched closely to see what historical narrative they would
promote. In his January 1 New Year's Reflections, Prime Minister
Abe said:

> This year we mark the milestone of the seventieth anniversary of
> the end of World War II. Throughout its postwar history, Japan
> has, based on feelings of deep remorse regarding World War II,
> walked the path of a free and democratic nation and of a consis-
> tently peace-loving nation, while contributing to global peace and
> prosperity. As we reflect on the past in heading towards the eight-
> ieth, ninetieth, and hundredth anniversaries to come, what kind of
> nation will Japan be and what kinds of contributions will we
> make to the world? Taking this opportunity, I wish to make this
> a year in which we send out to the world a message about the
> kind of country we aim to be and get off to a dynamic start
> towards building a "new Japan." (provisional translation by the
> prime minister's office)

Asked about his reading of history at his New Year's press conference on January 5, the prime minister followed up:

> As I have been saying all along, the Abe Cabinet upholds the posi-
> tion on the recognition outlined by the previous administrations in
> its entirety, including the Murayama Statement. Moreover, we will

uphold this position. Over the seventy years since the end of
World War II, Japan has built up a free and democratic nation that
upholds human rights and respects the rule of law, has advanced
along the path of a peace-loving nation, and has made major contributions to the peace, development, democratization, and so on,
of the Asia-Pacific region and the world. As we come to this
milestone of the 70th anniversary since the end of the war, I
intend to consolidate wisdom when considering what the Abe
administration can send out as a message to the world concerning Japan's remorse over World War II, the path we have walked
since the war as a peace-loving nation, and how Japan will contribute further to benefit the Asia Pacific region and the world,
and then incorporate that into a new statement. (provisional translation by the prime minister's office)

As seen in his response at the January 5 press conference, there
are three aspects that Abe intends to bring together and synthesize in
his administration's policy toward the historical memory issue. The
first is remorse over World War II, the second is the path Japan has
taken since the war as a peace-loving nation, and the third is the wish
to contribute to further peace and prosperity based upon what he has
elsewhere termed "proactive contribution to peace."

In effect, this is an effort to synthesize past, present, and future,
and the three aspects are naturally interrelated. Only by looking sincerely at its past can Japan gain the trust of the international community for its present and future foreign policies and other national
security policies. Japan's postwar stance as a peace-loving nation
has been maintained and should be acknowledged as grounded in
remorse and revulsion at the wartime experience. The issue of historical memory is not simply a question of understanding the past
but is also irrevocably linked to today's foreign policy and provides
a lodestone for defining tomorrow's policy efforts.

In fact, Prime Minister Abe said much the same thing in framing
this issue as a three-tier construct at the inaugural session of the
Advisory Panel on the History of the 20th Century and on Japan's
Role and the World Order in the 21st Century held at the prime minister's office on February 25. The issue of historical memory will
have a profound impact and will be one of the defining issues in
Japanese foreign policy in 2015. At the same time, how Japan faces
the many foreign policy issues before it will have a major impact on
the prime minister's seventieth-anniversary statement in August. It is
thus worth briefly introducing some of the literature that has been
published recently on the issue of historical memory.

Centennial of the Start of World War I

World War I broke out in 1914, and the past few years have seen a vast outpouring of books on the subject in both Japanese and English. The historian Eric Hobsbawm has characterized World War I as the start of what he termed "the short 20th century."[1] Raising the curtain on the world as we now know it, World War I was a most significant turning point and a key starting point for the issue of historical memory. This makes it important that we understand the research being done on the war and how the war is being recorded and remembered a century later.[2]

In English, Yale University professor Jay Winter has edited the three-volume *Cambridge History of the First World War,* which is the latest research we have to date on that war.[3] In keeping with the trend in historical studies, the essays in this collection tend to look not so much at the military and diplomatic history as at the war's social and cultural impact. Some of the many chapters that touch on historical memory include Bruno Cabanes's "1919: Aftermath" in the first volume and John Horne's "The Great War at Its Centenary" in the third volume. Joy Damousi's "Mourning Practices" in the third volume goes a bit further and looks at how the dead were memorialized, individually and collectively, in the war's wake. While Guoqi Xu's "Asia" in the second volume does look specifically at the situation in Asia, it is somewhat disappointing that there are no Japanese authors in any of the three volumes. World War I engendered major political upheaval, friction, and discord in East Asia, yet no comprehensive treatment of these events has yet been written, which stems at least in part from the fact that the dispute over historical memory is so deep-rooted in the region.

The editor of the three volumes, Jay Winter, is himself an expert in the memories and memorializations of World War I and has produced several noteworthy volumes on this subject, among them *Sites of Memory, Sites of Mourning: The Great War in European Cultural History* (Cambridge University Press, 1995), *War and Remembrance in the Twentieth Century* (coedited with Emmanuel Sivan, Cambridge University Press, 2000), and *The Great War in History: Debates and Controversies, 1914 to the Present* (coedited with Antoine Prost, Cambridge University Press, 2005).

This is not to say there are no works focusing on the military and diplomatic aspects: *The Oxford Illustrated History of the First World War* (new edition edited by Hew Strachan, Oxford University Press, 2014) is an excellent collection of outstanding papers on this subject.

Specifically, Modris Eksteins's chapter "Memory and the Great War" looks at how the war was remembered. Having taken a massive toll in suffering and damage on a global scale, the war also had a major impact on the worlds of literature and cinema, and numerous steles have been erected around the globe to commemorate the dead.

In *The Long Shadow: The Great War and the Twentieth Century* (Simon and Schuster, 2013), the celebrated Cambridge University professor David Reynolds, while noting that recent scholarship on World War I has tended to take a cultural turn, has tried to present a comprehensive overview with more attention paid to the diplomatic and military sides. Acknowledging that the war's impact and significance differed for the UK, France, Germany, and the United States, Reynolds's work looks specifically at the impact on British foreign policy and society from the longer-term historical perspective.

In Japanese, 2014 saw the publication of four volumes of essays on World War I from the faculty of the Kyoto University Institute for Research in Humanities.[4] While these four volumes are more slanted toward the literary and philosophical than the Cambridge set is, it is noteworthy that there are many chapters focusing on Japan and Asia. The series characterized as "Gendai no Kiten" (Origins of the Present), volume four includes such thought-provoking chapters as Endō Ken's "Yōroppa Tōgō e Mukete: Kiten to shite no Daiichiji Sekai Taisen" (World War I as the Starting Point for European Integration), Itō Junji's "Teikoku Soren no Seiritsu: Minami Kōkasasu ni okeru Roshiateikoku no Hōkai to Saitōgō" (The Rise of the Soviet Empire: The Russian Empire's Implosion and Reunification in Southern Caucasus), and Nakano Kōtarō's "Amerika no Seiki no Shidō (The Start of the American Century). Recounting the remembrances of the war and the way historical memory and recollection take place with more focus on Japan and the rest of Asia would have imparted additional depth to the essays. Looking at World War I in military history terms, the publication of *Daiichiji Sekai Taisen to sono Eikyō* (The First World War and Its Ramifications) (Kinseisha, 2015) by the Military History Society of Japan is a welcome addition to the literature.

The scholarship is not yet settled even on World War I, which was a full century ago, and new research keeps coming out year after year. How countries and peoples remember the war differs from country to country, and it is not easy to achieve an objective understanding of these different narratives. All the more difficult is it, then, to achieve a single shared narrative for the history of World War II, which was more recent and is still within living memory for many people.

Issues in Historical Memory

Of late, not only historians but also political scientists, international relations experts, and others have pointed to the importance of historical remembrance and historical memory. Jan-Werner Müller, fellow at Oxford University's All Souls College and an authority on German history, has written that "despite the intense focus on memory in history, sociology and cultural studies, the memory-power nexus remains curiously unexamined."[5] We still very much tend to see issues of historical remembrance and historical memory as simple issues of sensitivity or sincerity, but as noted, it is imperative we take this as a more political issue and avail ourselves of the full range of resources to examine dispassionately how memory is used in power terms. This is essential if we are to move the issue of historical memory from the realm of fable to the realm of fact.

A number of researchers have been examining the issues of historical remembrance and historical memory from this perspective. Jennifer Lind, for example, has looked at the questions of historical remembrance and historical reconciliation from her standpoint as an international political scientist. Her *Sorry States: Apologies in International Politics* (Cornell University Press, 2008) is a groundbreaking work dealing with Japan and the question of East Asian reconciliation. Boston University's Thomas Berger is an international political scientist who draws upon constructivist theory in dealing with this issue and who has published research comparing the Japanese and German postwar experiences.[6]

Ruptured Histories: War, Memory, and the Post–Cold War in Asia (coedited by Sheila Miyoshi Jager and Rana Mitter, Harvard University Press, 2007) is a good work on historical memory issues authored primarily by American researchers who specialize in modern Japanese history and East Asian history and have contributed essays on the comfort women, Yasukuni Shrine, the Vietnam War, and other contentious historical memory issues. Similarly, *Echoes of Empire: Memory, Identity, and Colonial Legacies* (coedited by Kalypso Nicolaidis, Berny Sebe, and Gabrielle Maas, Tauris, 2015) features essays by a wide range of scholars on memory and identity issues in the wake of an empire's losing its colonies. As the different authors deal with different empires (e.g., the Ottoman Empire, the Spanish Empire, the Japanese Empire, and the Soviet Union) in different situations leaving different legacies, this is a useful comparative work. With contributions by historians and political scientists alike, it provides interesting perspectives on empire's many aspects.

Finally, *East Asia's Haunted Present: Historical Memories and the Resurgence of Nationalism* (coedited by Hasegawa Tsuyoshi and Tōgō Kazuhiko, Praeger Security International, 2008) has a range of American, Japanese, Chinese, and Korean researchers writing on historical memory issues from a political science perspective and shows how the two issues of nationalism and historical memory are tightly intertwined in East Asia.

Anglo-Japanese Historical Reconciliation

Relations between Japan and the UK are often cited as a success story in Japan's efforts for postwar reconciliation. Moving swiftly after the attack on Pearl Harbor, Japanese forces quickly occupied Singapore and the Malay Peninsula, taking large numbers of British citizens prisoner in the process. Following the war, relations were strained at best as British veterans were harshly unforgiving on the treatment of British prisoners of war (POWs), the many deaths that accompanied the building of the Burma Railway, and other grievances. However, major progress was achieved on historical reconciliation starting in the 1980s as the two governments made a serious effort to come to terms with these issues, citizen groups promoted better relations, and more. Much of this history is detailed in Kosuge Nobuko's *Sengo Wakai: Nihon wa "Kako" kara Tokihanatareru no ka* (Postwar Reconciliation: Can Japan Disentangle Itself from Its Past?) (Chūōkōron Shinsha, 2005) and *Popī to Sakura: Nichiei Wakai wo Tsumuginaosu* (Poppies and Cherry Blossoms: Spinning the Bitter Memories into British-Japanese Reconciliation) (Iwanami Shoten, 2008). Although it is not much talked about, there was a long period during which Japanese-Anglo relations were contentious over their historical narratives concerning the war, and understanding how the two countries moved from rancor to reconciliation should prove instructive for understanding the issues Japan faces today. In this, it is clear that reconciliation can be achieved only if both sides make the requisite effort.

In addition to the two works just noted, there are several other outstanding works on Japanese-Anglo reconciliation. Both *Sensō to Wakai no Nichiei Kankei-shi* (Japan and Britain at War and Peace) (coedited by Kosuge Nobuko and Hugo Dobson, Hōsei University

Press, 2011) and *Sensō no Kioku to Horyo Mondai* (War Memories
and POW Issues) (coedited by Kibata Yōichi, Kosuge Nobuko, and
Phillip Towle, University of Tokyo Press, 2003), for example, provide
a good understanding of the issues and travails involved in this difficult reconciliation. Unlike the situations with China and Korea, the
reconciliation process with Britain included a complex mix of racial
and religious issues and even different understandings of international
law. All of these issues and more are dealt with from a variety of
angles in these two volumes.

The European Experience and
the Asian Experience

Because Europe and Asia are so very different in their essential historical memory issues, the international environments in which they
find themselves, and the conditions required for reconciliation, it is
possible that trying to make the difficult linkages between them might
well further confuse the complex issues and make them still more
intractable. Nonetheless, it is worth looking at them, not for facile
analogies but for academically sound comparisons. *Rekishi to Wakai*
(History and Reconciliation) (coedited by Kurosawa Fumitaka and Ian
Nish, University of Tokyo Press, 2011) is one such straightforward
academic contribution. In this work, a bevy of respected historians
examine and compare the historical reconciliations between Germany
and France, Britain and Ireland, France and Algeria, and other com-
binations, and then go from there to look at Japan's issues with China
and Korea. Even just looking at the range of case studies presented,
this is clearly one of the most comprehensive, layered studies of historical reconciliation available. Also interesting is *Yomigaeru "Kokka"
to "Rekishi": Posuto Reisen 20nen no Ōshū* (Looking Back at State
and History: Europe 20 Years After the End of the Cold War) (Fuyō
Shobō Shuppan, 2009) by Miyoshi Norihide, a staff writer for the
Yomiuri newspaper who takes up the historical reconciliation issues
between Russia and Estonia, Germany and Poland, and others that
have previously not received much attention or discussion in Japan.
Although Europe is often cited as an example for Asian reconciliation,
the overlapping of World War II historical issues and Cold War historical issues has worked to complicate reconciliation in practice.

   In his *Kioku no Seiji: Yōroppa no Rekishi Ninshiki Funsō* (The
Politics of Memory: Europe's Historical Memory Disputes) (Iwanami

Shoten, 2016), Kwansei Gakuin University professor of Russian history Hashimoto Nobuya has provided a detailed recounting of the historical memory issues that Russia faces, with special attention to Russia's relations with the Baltic states. Russia's reconciliation with its neighbors is all the more complex and all the more difficult in that relations with the Baltic states and the countries of East Europe have undergone vast upheavals of historic proportions in World War II, the Cold War, and then the collapse of the Soviet Union. Indeed, the end of the Cold War was like the melting of a vast glacier allowing all manner of previously submerged issues to surface.

The Historical Memory Issue in East Asia

As might be expected, a large library of research has already been published on historical memory in East Asia, the region where it seems most difficult and the region of most intense interest for Japanese scholars. Two of the earlier works examining and explicating this issue's importance are *Ima Rekishi Mondai ni dō Torikumuka* (How to Deal with the History Issue Now) (Iwanami Shoten, 2001), edited by Funabashi Yōichi, and Funabashi's *Rekishi Wakai no Tabi: Tairitsu no Kako kara Kyōsei no Mirai e* (The History Reconciliation Journey: From a Past of Confrontation to a Future of Cooperation) (Asahi Shimbun, 2004). The historical memory question was already recognized as a critical issue putting a damper on both Japan-Korea and Japan-China relations when the Kōno Statement on the comfort women question was issued in 1993, and again when the Murayama Statement on war responsibility was issued in 1995, and the two Funabashi texts are significant in pulling together the scholarly research on the issues involved from a very comprehensive and overall perspective.

Another nonacademic who was among the first to show interest in these issues is Wakamiya Yoshibumi, whose *Sengo Hoshū no Ajia-kan* (Asahi Shimbun, 1995; published in English by LTCB International Library Foundation in 1999 as *The Postwar Conservative View of Asia*) looks at how the conservative Liberal Democratic Party Diet members understood the historical memory issue. This work has since been updated, reissued as *Sengo 70nen: Hoshū no Ajia-kan* (Conservatives' Views of Asia 70 Years After the War's End), and is still read. A more recent work is *Higashi Ajia no Rekishi Masatsu to Wakai Kanōsei: Reisengo no Kokusai Chitsujo to Rekishi Ninshiki wo meguru Shomondai* (Historical Friction in East Asia and the Possibility of Reconciliation: The Post–Cold War International Order and the Historical Memory Issue) (Gaifūsha, 2011), edited by Kan Hideki, which brings together the research of a range of Japanese, American, British, Chinese, and Korean international relations experts and historians. This work is significant in that the research focus is not on journalistic issues for general readership but is clearly on history aspects as understood by historians.

Japan's Postwar Path

With the opening of Japanese postwar foreign policy archives, the contributions from oral history, and other research resources, it has been possible for the academic research to achieve better-grounded results, and a number of outstanding works have been published. Among them University of Tsukuba professor emeritus Hatano Sumio, who once served as a Ministry of Foreign Affairs officer and was a long-term editorial board member for the diplomatic archives of the ministry (*Gaikō Bunsho,* Documents on Japanese Foreign Policy), has authored *Kokka to Rekishi: Sengo Nihon no Rekishi Mondai* (State and History: History Issues in Postwar Japan) (Chūōkōron Shinsha, 2011), which is indispensable reading on this issue even today. Starting with the issue of reparations, he covers a wide range of issues including the history textbooks, the Yasukuni Shrine controversy, the comfort women, and collaborative history research, many of which issues he was at the table for, providing a balanced grounding for objective discussion. Also informative is Hattori Ryūji's *Gaikō Dokyumento: Rekishi Ninshiki* (Diplomacy Documents: Historical Perception) (Iwanami Shoten, 2015), in which the author draws upon a wide range of oral histories as well as material ferreted out by freedom-of-information requests to cover areas that had not previously been in the public eye and includes the latest research findings to substantiate his discussion. These two works by outstanding historians are untainted by ideology, personal feelings, political considerations, and the like, and look at the essential issues with the good historian's dispassionate gaze.

Historical memory in the Japan-China context is expertly treated by two Seton Hall University political science professors, Wang Zheng and He Yinan. In his acclaimed *Never Forget National Humiliation: Historical Memory in Chinese Politics and Foreign Relations* (Columbia University Press, 2014; Japanese translation published the same year), Wang zeros in on the frequently invoked Chinese slogan "Wu wang guo chi" (Never forget national humiliation) and discusses how Chinese politics and foreign policy have been shaped by the historical memory issue. Complementing this, He Yinan's *The Search for Reconciliation: Sino-Japanese and German-Polish Relations Since World War II* (Cambridge University Press, 2009) provides a well-balanced comparison of the different paths to Japan-China and Germany-Poland reconciliation. Both works provide vivid descriptions of how the Chinese government mobilized patriotism and nationalism to further national unity and legitimize Chinese Communist Party rule.

Looking at the historical memory issue between Japan and Korea, Kimura Kan's *Nikkan Rekishi Ninshiki Mondai towa Nanika: Rekishi Kyōkasho, Ianfu, Popyulizumu* (What Are the Historical Memory Issues Between Japan and Korea: History Textbooks, Comfort Women, and Populism) (Minerva Shobō, 2014) is particularly outstanding. A professor at Kobe University, where he teaches Korean politics, Kimura draws upon a broad range of statistical data, media reports, and more to eloquently describe how the historical memory issue became so prominent in Korea. As in the Chinese case, domestic political considerations were a major factor propelling the historical memory issue to the forefront, which means that it will be extremely difficult to resolve this issue by diplomacy alone so long as domestic political calculations play such an important role.

Conclusion

The most perplexing historical memory issues currently confronting Japan are those with China and Korea. The comfort women issue is especially vexing, and relations were so strained that it was impossible to even hold a Japan-Korea summit meeting prior to the bilateral agreement of December 2015. It was not even easy to research these issues calmly in Korea, as illustrated by the furor that accompanied the publication of Park Yu-ha's *Teikoku no Ianfu: Shokuminchi Shihai to Kioku no Tatakai* (Comfort Women of the Empire: Colonial Rule and the Clash of Memory) (Asahi Shimbun, 2014). It is similarly difficult to research the comfort woman issue, the Nanjing Massacre, and a few other issues in Japan.

As E. H. Carr has famously said, "We can view the past, and achieve our understanding of the past, only through the eyes of the present."[7] In other words, understanding Chinese politics, Korean politics, and Japanese politics is essential to understanding Japan's historical memory issues with China and Korea. Why have such issues arisen? Why are they so intractable? Answering these questions demands more than just understanding the historical facts and more than just searching through the historical record. Nonjudgmentally understanding the past, the present, and how the two are intertwined are all prerequisite to developing an appropriate approach to resolving the issue of historical memory.

Notes

1. Eric Hobsbawm, *Interesting Times: A Twentieth-Century Life* (London: Allen Lane, 2002).

2. Naraoka Sōchi's "Daiichiji Sekai Taisen to Nihon" (World War I and Japan), *Asuteion* (Asteion) 84 (2016), is a particularly good review of recent research on World War I from a Japanese perspective.

3. Jay Winter, ed., *The Cambridge History of the First World War*, vol. 1, *Global War*, and vol. 2, *The State* (Cambridge: Cambridge University Press, 2014).

4. Yamamuro Shin'ichi, Okada Akeo, Koseki Takashi, and Fujihara Tatsushi, eds., *Daiichiji Sekai Taisen* (World War I), vol. 1, *Sekai Sensō* (Global War), vol. 2, *Sōryokusen* (Total War), vol. 3, *Seishin no Henyō* (Psychological Impact), and vol. 4, *Isan* (Legacy) (Tokyo: Iwanami Shoten, 2014).

5. Jan-Werner Müller, "Introduction: The Power of Memory, the Memory of Power, and the Power over Memory," in Jan-Werner Müller, ed., *Memory and Power in Post-War Europe: Studies in the Presence of the Past* (Cambridge: Cambridge University Press, 2002), p. 2.

6. Thomas Berger, *War, Guilt, and World Politics After World War II* (Cambridge: Cambridge University Press, 2012).

7. E. H. Carr, *What Is History,* Japanese translation (*Rekishi towa Nani ka*) by Shimizu Ikutarō (Tokyo: Iwanami Shoten, 1962), p. 31.

8

Key Sources
on the Postwar Era

Komiya Kazuo

In the years since World War II ended, the field of postwar
studies has broadened out from its focus on near-real-time political science and economics to encompass the total range of history concerns.

Research into the history of the occupation was pioneered by,
notably among others, Takemae Eiji, whose first solo work on the
period was *Amerika Tainichi Rōdō Seisaku no Kenkyū* (A Study of
US Labor Policy for Japan) published by Nippon Hyōronsha in 1970,
a quarter of a century after the war. During the 1980s, occupation
studies gained wide acceptance among historians with the publication
of such works as the two-volume *Beikoku no Nihon Senryō Seisaku:
Sengo Nihon no Sekkeizu* (US Policy for the Occupation of Japan:
The Blueprint for Postwar Japan) by Iokibe Makoto (Chūōkōronsha,
1985); *San Furanshisuko Kōwa e no Michi* (The Road to the San
Francisco Peace Treaty) by Hosoya Chihiro (Chūōkōronsha, 1984);
and *San Furanshisuko Kōwa* (The San Francisco Peace Treaty)
coedited by Watanabe Akio and Miyazato Seigen (University of
Tokyo Press, 1986).

The year 1989 was a turning point both on the international scene,
with the Cold War ending late in the year, and on the Japanese scene,
with the passing of the emperor early in the year to close out the
Shōwa period. In the 1990s, there was increasing research, and recognition of research, on the period following the recovery of independence. Much of this work focused on, for example, the conclusion and

amendment of the Japan–United States Mutual Security Treaty, the reversion of Okinawa, the post-1955 political structure, and what was called the economic miracle. In 1995, half a century after the war, Kitaoka Shin'ichi, who had previously done groundbreaking work on the Imperial Japanese Army's Asia policy, published *Jimintō: Seikentō no 38nen* (The LDP: 38 Years in Power) (Yomiuri Shimbunsha), which firmly established post-independence Japan and the political structure that locked into place in 1955 as fit subjects for historical study.

The first decade of the twenty-first century saw a succession of publications about postwar Japanese diplomacy and politics by younger researchers who had begun working in the 1990s after the end of the Cold War. Some of these works have been reviewed on the Tokyo Foundation for Policy Research website.

Today, seven decades after the war, an overview of historical research on postwar Japan with particular attention to politics and foreign policy reveals a substantial library in diplomatic history, where striking progress has been made, as opposed to a thinness of accumulated knowledge in political history. This disparity is largely attributable to the wealth of the diplomatic record, which has been opened to the public earlier than the domestic political archives. Today, the 1970s are recognized as a legitimate subject of study, and scholars are moving to widen their focus to include the 1980s and 1990s.

Having started as near-current events studies, research on the postwar period has now become history as history, as the scope of the research has broadened and the literature has flowered over the past seventy years. That said, different people have approached and seen the postwar period differently, and there has been little scholarly consensus. In the two-volume *Sengo towa Nanika: Seijigaku to Rekishigaku no Taiwa* (What Does Postwar Mean? Dialogue Between Political Science and History) edited by Fukunaga Fumio and Kōno Yasuko (Maruzen, 2014), Watanabe Akio, Iokibe Makoto, Katō Yōko, Makihara Izuru, and other first-rank researchers illuminate postwar Japan from various perspectives. This lively collection awakens the reader to the diversity of ways the period can be perceived depending upon the researcher's values and approach, as well as generational differences. These two volumes are replete with useful hints for thinking about the postwar era, and they may be profitably dipped into whatever the reader's particular area of interest.

This chapter introduces a range of documents (books, articles, reviews, and more) that are informative about potential points of contention in thinking about the seven decades since the war. Given the space limitations and the author's specialization, it is inevitably focused on politics and foreign policy. That said, the nonspecialist reader has been kept very much in mind and priority has been given to surveys and works available in mass-market editions.

Postwar History Overviews and Chronological Divisions

For a general overview of postwar history with the emphasis on politics and diplomacy, the sixth, seventh, and eighth volumes of the *Nihon no Kindai* (Modern Japan) series from Chūōkōron Shinsha run from the end of the war to present times. They are: *Sensō, Sengo, Fukkō 1941–1955* (War, Postwar, and Recovery, 1941–1955) by Iokibe Makoto (2001); *Keizai Seichō no Kajitsu 1955–1972* (Fruits of Economic Growth, 1955–1972) by Inoki Takenori (2000); and *Taikoku Nihon no Yuragi* (Great Power Japan at Risk) by Watanabe Akio (2000). Iokibe lays out a groundbreaking chronological division for early postwar history, beginning not with the war's end but in 1941 at the start of the Pacific War and going through the occupation period to the 1955 conservative merger that created the Liberal Democratic Party (LDP).

A perspective that includes economics as well as politics and foreign policy is found in Kōno Yasuko's *Sengo to Kōdo Seichō no Shūen* (The End of the Postwar Rapid Economic Growth), issued as the twenty-fourth volume in Kōdansha's twenty-six-volume *Nihon no Rekishi* (History of Japan) series (2002). Given the advances made in this field, it is increasingly difficult for a single author to pen a proper general history of the entire period from 1945 into the early twenty-first century. Indeed, such broad coverage was already difficult when Kōno wrote, and hers is an amazing work summarizing the first fifty postwar years.

Yoshikawa Kōbunkan has recently published the *Gendai Nihon Seiji-shi* (History of Modern Japanese Politics) series on the postwar period including works by Sadō Akihiro, the preeminent historian of postwar defense policy, and younger researchers in five volumes: *Senryō kara Dokuritsu e 1945–1952* (From Occupation to Independence, 1945–1952) by Kusonoki Ayako (2013); *Dokuritsu Kansei e no Kutō 1952–1960* (The Struggle for Complete Independence, 1952–1960) by Ikeda Shintarō (2011); *Kōdo Seichō to Okinawa Henkan 1960–1972*

(Rapid Economic Growth and Okinawa's Reversion, 1960–1972) by Nakashima Takuma (2012); *Taikoku Nihon no Seiji Shidō 1972–1989* (Great Power Japan's Political Leadership, 1972–1989) by Wakatsuki Hidekazu (2012); and *Kaikaku Seiji no Konmei 1989–* (The Turmoil of Reform Politics, 1989–) by Sadō Akihiro (2012).

Where should we locate the delineations in postwar history? If the focus is on the international environment and Japanese foreign policy, possible critical junctures are the recovery of independence, the Anpo revision, internationalization, and the end of the Cold War. If domestic politics is the focus, possible milestones might be the long Yoshida administration, the conservative-party merger to form the 1955 structure, the conservative/reformist equilibrium, the conservative revival, and the 1993 power turnover and coalition government. Yet a third possibility is to focus on economic conditions, in which case they could be economic recovery, the rapid-growth period, the slow-growth period, stable growth and the bubble economy, and the postbubble deflation.

There being no firm chronological divisions that hold across the social sciences, postwar delineations will vary depending on the specialist and the field. Nevertheless, a nebulous consensus is coalescing and future debate will likely focus on identifying where the "postwar" as essentially distinct from the prewar began. Indeed, Fukunaga and Kōno's *Sengo towa Nanika* has already laid the groundwork for this discussion.

The Asia Pacific War and Japanese Colonial Rule

The Tokyo Trials

Higurashi Yoshinobu's *Tokyo Saiban* (The Tokyo Trials) (Kōdansha, 2008)—an abridgment of his *Tokyo Saiban no Kokusai Kankei: Kokusai Seiji ni okeru Kenryoku to Kihan* (International Aspects of the Tokyo Trials: Authority and Criteria in International Politics) (Bokutakusha, 2002)—offers a full treatment of the International Military Tribunal for the Far East in one volume. While Higurashi emphasizes the international political context, Ushimura Kei emphasizes the civilizational (ideological) aspects in *Bunmei no Sabaki wo koete: Tainichi Senpan Saiban Dokkai no Kokoromi* (Chūōkōron Shinsha, 2001), translated as *Beyond the Judgment of Civilization: The Intellectual Legacy of the Japanese War Crimes Trials, 1946–49* (International House of Japan, 2003) and in *Shōsha no Sabaki ni Mukiatte: Tokyo Saiban wo Yominaosu* (Facing Victors' Justice: Reconsidering the Tokyo Trials) (Chikuma Shobō, 2004). A good book sorting out the controversies about the trials is *Tokyo Saiban wo Tadashiku Yomu* (Correctly Reading the Tokyo Trials) (Bungeishunjū, 2008) coauthored by Higurashi and Ushimura.

For a detailed treatment of the historical facts, turn to *Saiban e no Michi* (Path to the Tokyo Trials) (Kōdansha, 2006). The Nuremberg Trials are an indispensable reference in understanding the Tokyo Trials, and the latest reliable study is *Nyurunberuku Saiban* (The Nuremberg Trials) by Shiba Kensuke (Iwanami Shoten, 2015).

Memories of the War

Japan signed the Instrument of Surrender on September 2, 1945. However, it is customary in Japan to assume that August 15, the day the emperor made his radio broadcast announcing the acceptance of the Potsdam Declaration, marks the end of the war. How that came to be is elucidated by Satō Takumi in *Hachigatsu Jūgonichi no Shinwa: Shūsen Kinenbi no Mediagaku* (A Study of the Media and the Mythical August 15 Anniversary of the End of the War) (Chikuma Shobō, 2005; expanded edition, 2014). Similarly, *Higashi Ajia no Shūsen Kinenbi: Haiboku to Shōri no Aida* (End-of-the-War Anniversaries in East Asia: Between Defeat and Victory) (Chikuma Shobō, 2007) edited by Satō Takumi and Son An Suk is a good introduction to the discrepancies between when Japan and China and other neighboring countries mark the war's end.

How do postwar Japanese perceive the Second Sino-Japanese War and the Asia Pacific War, and how have perceptions been changing? Yoshida Yutaka's *Nihonjin no Sensōkan: Sengo-shi no naka no Hen'yō* (Japanese Views on the War: The Changes During Postwar History) (Iwanami Shoten, 1995) is an insightful volume worth perusing.

There has also been a flourish of studies on the social history of war recently, and there is strong interest in how memories were formed about the war in China and the Pacific in the 1930s and 1940s. One outstanding work to come out of this research is *Sensō Taiken no Sengo-shi: Katarareta Taiken, Shōgen, Kioku* (Postwar Histories of Wartime Experience: Recounted Experiences, Testimonies, and Memories) by Narita Ryūichi (in Iwanami Shoten's 2010 *Sensō no Keiken wo Tou* [Asking About Wartime Experiences] series).

Along with the flourishing of social history and cultural studies, the atomic-bombing question has come to be discussed not only in terms of Japan's views on peace and nuclear weapons but also in terms of collective memory. One outstanding example is *Genbaku no Kioku: Hiroshima: Nagasaki no Shisō* (Memories of the Atomic Bomb: The Ideology of Hiroshima and Nagasaki) by Okuda Hiroko (Keiō University Press, 2010).

Postwar Responsibility

There are numerous works about Japan's postwar responsibility. Debate on this issue was sparked by Takahashi Tetsuya's *Sengo Sekininron* (On Postwar Responsibility) (Kōdansha, 1999). More recently, attention has been turning to the concept of postwar responsibility in response to the views of Asian nations where Japan was the aggressor. Two examples are *Sengo Sekinin: Ajia no Manazashi ni Kotaete* (Postwar Responsibility: Meeting Asia's Gaze) by Utsumi Aiko, Ōnuma Yasuaki, Tanaka Hiroshi, and Katō Yōko (Iwanami Shoten, 2014) and *Shokuminchi Sekininron: Datsushokuminchi no Hikakushi* (On Colonial Responsibility: A Comparative History of Decolonization) edited by Nagahara Yōko (Aoki Shoten, 2009).

Historical Awareness

The historical awareness issues that have arisen between Japan and China and between Japan and South Korea starting in the 1980s are very much diplomatic issues. Two essential explorations of the problem by frontline Japanese postwar diplomatic history researchers are *Kokka to Rekishi: Sengo Nihon no Rekishi Mondai* (The State and History: Postwar Japan's History Issues) by Hatano Sumio (Chūōkōron Shinsha, 2011) and *Gaikō Dokyumento: Rekishi Ninshiki* (Diplomacy Documents: Historical Awareness) by Hattori Ryūji (Iwanami Shoten, 2015). Hatano's discussion extends to historical awareness issues at the political and foreign policy levels up through the 1970s.

On Japan–South Korea historical perception issues, the definitive work as of this time is Kimura Kan's *Nikkan Rekishi Ninshiki Mondai to wa Nanika: Rekishi Kyōkasho, Ianfu, Popyurizumu* (What Is the Japanese-Korean Historical Awareness Problem? History Textbooks, Comfort Women, and Populism) (Minerva Shobō, 2014).

Yasukuni

It is impossible to discuss memorializing and consoling the spirits of Japan's war-dead without mentioning Yasukuni Shrine. A solid volume tracing the postwar Yasukuni problem is *Yasukuni Jinja: Semegiau Senbotsusha Tsuitō no Yukue* (Yasukuni Shrine: Conflicting Futures for Memorializing the War-Dead) by Akazawa Shirō (Iwanami Shoten, 2005). Akazawa has also presented his more recent findings in *Senbotsusha Gōshi to Yasukuni Jinja* (Yasukuni Shrine and Collective Enshrinement of the War-Dead) (Yoshikawa Kōbunkan, 2015). Another must-read text that covers the vicissitudes of the postwar Yasukuni problem and concisely summarizes the issues is "Sengo Nihon no Seiji to Irei" (Politics and the Consoling of Departed Spirits in Postwar Japan) by Murai Ryōta, in *Kokkyō wo Koeru Rekishi Ninshiki: Nicchu Taiwa no Kokoromi* edited by Liu Jie, Mitani Hiroshi, and Yang Daqing (University of Tokyo Press, 2006) and translated as *Toward a History Beyond Borders: Contentious Issues in Sino-Japanese Relations* (Harvard University Asia Center, 2012). Although it has not caught the public eye, *Shinpen Yasukuni Jinja Mondai Shiryōshū* (New Compilation of Records on the Yasukuni Shrine Problem) (2007) from the Research and Legislative Reference Bureau of the National Diet Library is a valuable resource for frank discussion of the Yasukuni problem.

Demobilization and Repatriation, Detainees in Siberia, and Recovery of Remains

Demobilization and repatriation have yet to garner sufficient attention, although the research has recently started to pick up as more historical records have become available. One example is Katō Yōko's chapter "Haisha no Kikan: Chūgoku kara no Haisha no Fukuin-hikiage Mondai no Tenkai" (Return of the Defeated: The Evolving Issue of Demobilization and Repatriation of Defeated Soldiers from China) in her *Sensō no Ronri: Nichiro Sensō kara Taiheiyō Sensō made* (The Logic of War: From the Russo-Japanese War to the Pacific War) (Keisō Shobō, 2005). Another is Katō Kiyofumi's chapter "Dainippon Teikoku no Hōkai to Zanryū Nihonjin Hikiage Mondai: Kokusai Kankei no naka no Kaigai Hikiage" (Repatriating Left-Behind Japanese After the Empire's Collapse: Repatriation as an International Relations Issue), in *Dainippon Teikoku no Hōkai to Hikiage-fukuin* (Demobilization and Repatriation

After the Empire's Collapse) edited by Masuda Hiroshi (Keiō University Press, 2012).

It is impossible to examine the issue of Japanese detainees in Siberia without resource to Soviet archives. Tomita Takeshi, a specialist in twentieth-century Russian history, presents valuable findings in *Shiberia Yokoryūshatachi no Sensō: Reisenka no Yoron to Undō 1945–1956* (The Siberian Detainees' War: Public Opinion and Campaigns During the Cold War, 1945–1956) (Jinbun Shoin, 2013) and *Shiberia Yokuryū: Sutārin Dokusaika, Shūyōjo Guntō no Jitsuzō* (Siberian Detention: Conditions in the Gulag Under Stalin) (Chūōkōron Shinsha, 2016).

Hamai Kazufumi draws on diplomatic records to analyze the recovery of remains and the memorialization of soldiers who died overseas in *Kaigai Senbotsusha no Sengo-shi: Ikotsu Henkan to Irei* (Postwar History of the Overseas War-Dead: Recovery of Remains and Consolation of Spirits) (Yoshikawa Kōbunkan, 2014). As with demobilization and repatriation, the return of military remains from overseas was part of the "postwar process," which is to say it was a foreign policy issue.

The Occupation Reforms and Japan's Postwar Reboot

What Was the Occupation Period?

Fukunaga Fumio's *Nihon Senryō-shi 1945–1952: Tokyo-Washinton-Okinawa* (History of the Occupation of Japan, 1945–1952: Tokyo, Washington, and Okinawa) (Chūōkōron Shinsha, 2014) is a very recent, very credible overview of the occupation period, and it is enhanced by his devoting space to developments in Okinawa during the occupation. This question of how to include Okinawa, and hence how to depict Japan in its entirety, is a key concern to be addressed in future postwar histories.

For readers wishing to learn about the differing levels of Japanese and American enthusiasm for the key occupation reforms, including women's suffrage and land reform, there is "Senryō Kaikaku no Sanruikei" (The Three Patterns in Occupation Reforms) by Iokibe Makoto, the leading researcher on US Japan policy during the occupation, in *Leviathan* no. 6 (1990). Providing a different perspective, Itō Takashi and Amemiya Shōichi draw attention to the postwar influence of the reformist groups who advocated a centrally controlled economy during the prewar Shōwa and wartime years and emphasize how the postwar political-economic system inherited personal networks and systems from the prewar Shōwa period. The standout overview of the occupation years here is Amemiya's *Senryō to Kaikaku* (Occupation and Reform), the seventh volume in the Iwanami Shoten *Nihon Kingendai-shi* (Modern Japanese History) series (2008).

Birth of the Constitution and the Role of the Media

Koseki Shōichi's account of the constitution's drafting and promulgation in *Shinkenpō no Tanjō* (The Birth of the New Constitution) (Chūōkōronsha, 1989; revised edition *Nihonkoku Kenpō no Tanjō* [The Birth of the Japanese Constitution], Iwanami Shoten, 2009), translated as *The Birth of Japan's Postwar Constitution* (Westview Press, 1998), is a classic in the field. Also worth reading is Nishi Osamu's *Nihonkoku Kenpō wa Kōshite Umareta* (How the Japanese Constitution Was Born) (Chūōkōron Shinsha, 2000), a tour de force based on a painstaking review of available resources.

In *Sengo-shi no Naka no Kenpō to Jānarizumu* (The Constitution and Journalism in Postwar History) (Kashiwa Shobō, 1998), Ariyama Teruo traces how the press, which had supported the war and fanned public fervor, viewed the new constitution favorably and took a leading role in promoting democracy postwar.

The People Experience the Occupation

In looking back at postwar Japan's course, one unavoidable issue is that of how the people experienced the occupation. The realities of life for ordinary people under the occupation are portrayed from many angles, drawing on immense amounts of material, in *Embracing Defeat: Japan in the Wake of World War II* by John W. Dower (Norton, 1999), and Yoshimi Yoshiaki's two-volume *Yakeato kara no Demokurashī: Kusanone no Senryōki Taiken* (Democracy from the Ruins: The Grassroots Occupation Experience) (Iwanami Shoten, 2014).

Fresh Starts for the Vanquished

Comparisons with Germany, which also recovered from defeat to become one of the world's leading economic powers, offer a wealth of hints for understanding Japan's postwar trajectory. Ōtake Hideo was among the first to use the comparative politics methodology on Japan and Germany in *Adenauā to Yoshida Shigeru* (Adenauer and Yoshida Shigeru) (Chūōkōronsha, 1988) and *Futatsu no Sengo: Doitsu to Nihon* (Two Postwars: Germany and Japan) (NHK, 1992), the latter providing an overview of the two countries' experiences. A trustworthy work on Konrad Adenauer and the rebuilding of West Germany is the compact and lucid *Adenauā: Gendai Doitsu wo Tsukutta Seijika* (Adenauer: The Politician Who Built Today's Germany) by Itabashi Takumi (Chūōkōron Shinsha, 2014). That said, it would also be interesting if someone would write a good book comparing Adenauer and Kishi Nobusuke.

There are far fewer studies comparing the Japanese and Italian postwar experiences than there are comparing Japan and Germany. Ishida Ken has broken the ice with *Haisen kara Kenpō e: Nichi-Doku-I Kenpō Seitei no Hikakuseiji-shi* (From Defeat to Constitution: A Comparative Political History of Constitution Enactment in Japan, Germany, and Italy) (Iwanami Shoten, 2009). Bringing Italy into the discussion is a welcome development in deepening our understanding of postwar Japan.

The Paths of Japanese Diplomacy and Security

Overviews of Postwar Diplomacy

The definitive work so far on Japan's postwar diplomatic history is the third, expanded edition of *Sengo Nihon Gaikō-shi* edited by Iokibe Makoto (Yūhikaku, 2014). (The second edition was translated by Robert D. Eldridge as *The Diplomatic History of Postwar Japan* and published by Routledge in 2011.) In addition, such first-rate authors as Kitaoka Shin'ichi, Nakanishi Hiroshi, and Watanabe Akio have published essays considering diplomatic history from long-term, macroscopic perspectives. See, for example, Kitaoka's "Kokusai Kyōchō no Jōken: Senkanki no Nihon to Sengo no Nihon" (The Conditions for International Harmony: Japan Between Wars and After the War) in the magazine *Kokusai Mondai* (International Affairs) (published by the Japan Institute of International Affairs; vol. 423, 1995); Nakanishi's "Nijūsseiki no Nihongaikō" (Japanese Diplomacy in the 20th Century) in *Kokusai Mondai* (vol. 489, 2000); Nakanishi's "Sekai Chitsujo no Hen'yō to Nihongaikō no Kiseki" (The World Order in Transition and the Path of Japanese Diplomacy) in *Kokusai*

Mondai (vol. 578, 2009); and Watanabe's "Nichibei Dōmei no Gojū-nen no Kiseki to Nijūisseiki e no tenbō" (The Japan-US Alliance: The First 50 Years and Prospects for the 21st Century) in *Kokusai Mondai* (vol. 490, 2001). These essays, along with Iokibe's previously mentioned *Sengo Nihon Gaikō-shi,* provide a good overview of postwar Japanese foreign policy.

Unfortunately, *Sengo Nihon Gaikō-shi* does not include a full treatment of the post–Cold War period. Fortunately, that need was fulfilled by Miyagi Taizō in *Gendai Nihon Gaikō-shi: Reisengo no Mosaku, Shushōtachi no Ketsudan* (Modern Japan's Foreign Policy: Leadership Decisions in the Post–Cold War Fog) (Chūōkōron Shinsha, 2016).

The Cold War

Understanding the Cold War is indispensable to understanding postwar Japanese foreign policy, and a wide array of excellent works are available. For the nonspecialist reader seeking a quick overview, the best choice is *Reisen* (Cold War) (Yūhikaku, 2011) by Sasaki Takuya, the preeminent Japanese historian of postwar US foreign policy.

How the Cold War was carried over and played out in Asia is a crucial aspect. Here the generalist reader would do well to start with Shimotomai Nobuo's *Ajia Reisen-shi* (History of the Cold War in Asia) (Chūōkōron Shinsha, 2004) and progress to Nagai Yōnosuke's *Reisen no Kigen: Sengo Ajia no Kokusai Kankyō* (Origins of the Cold War: The International Environment in Postwar Asia), originally published by Chūōkōronsha in 1978 and now available in two volumes from Chūōkōron Shinsha (2013).

The San Francisco Peace Treaty

The 1951 peace treaty, which was the starting line for Japan's reentry to the international community, is a key element not to be neglected in looking back on the postwar years. The classic works on the treaty are the previously mentioned *San Furanshisuko Kōwa e no Michi* (The Road to the San Francisco Peace Treaty) (Chūōkōronsha, 1984) by Hosoya Chihiro; and *San Furanshisuko Kōwa* (The San Francisco Peace Treaty) (University of Tokyo Press, 1986) edited by Watanabe Akio and Miyazato Seigen. There is also the two-volume *Yoshida Shigeru to San Furanshisuko Kōwa* (Yoshida Shigeru and the San Francisco Peace Treaty) by Miura Yōichi (Ōtsuki Shoten, 1996), which is the most recent scholarly treatment of the treaty.

For a quick understanding of how very important the treaty was for Japan, it would be hard to do better than Watanabe Akio's "Kōwa Mondai to Nihon no Sentaku" (The Treaty Issue and Japan's Choices) in the just-cited *San Furanshisuko Kōwa;* Hatano Sumio's "San Furanshisuko Kōwa Taisei" (The San Francisco Peace Treaty System) in *Nihon no Gaikō Dainikan: Gaikō-shi Sengohen* (Japanese Diplomacy: Postwar Diplomatic History) (Iwanami Shoten, 2013); and Miyagi Taizō's "San Furanshisuko Kōwa to Yoshida Rosen no Sentaku" (The San Francisco Peace Treaty and the Yoshida Line Policy Choices) in *Kokusai Mondai* (vol. 638, 2015).

Japan-US Security Arrangements

Fully utilizing a tremendous amount of material from the US side, Sakamoto Kazuya has written an essential work on the 1960 battle over the revision of the Japan–United States Mutual Security Treaty, *Nichibei Domei no Kizuna: Anpo Jōyaku to Sōgosei no Mosaku* (The United States–Japan Bonds of Alliance: Groping for Reciprocity in the Anpo Treaty) (Yūhikaku, 2000). More recently, who can forget the recent uproar over reports that the treaty carried a number of secret protocols? How they took shape is detailed by Hatano Sumio, who is deeply conversant with Japan's foreign policy record, in *Rekishi toshite no Nichibei Anpo Jōyaku: Kimitsu Gaikō Kiroku ga Akasu Mitsuyaku no Kyojitsu* (The Japan–United States Anpo Treaty as History: The Truth About the Secret Agreements as Revealed in Confidential Diplomatic Records) (Iwanami Shoten, 2010).

Other thought-provoking essays about the Japan–United States alliance in the post–Cold War era include Watanabe Akio's "Reisen no Shūketsu to Nichibei Anpo no Saiteigi: Okinawa Mondai wo Fukumete" (Redefining the Japan–United States Security Agreement After the Cold War, Including the Okinawa Question) in *Kokusai Mondai* (vol. 594, 2010) and Sakamoto Kazuya's "Nichibei Dōmei no Kadai: Anpo Kaitei Gojūnen no Shiten kara" (Issues in the Japan–United States Alliance, Fifty Years After the Anpo Treaty Revision) in *Kokusai Mondai* (vol. 588, 2010).

Japan's Three Nonnuclear Principles and Nonproliferation

Kurosaki Akira details the US sense of hyper-alarm in the 1960s and 1970s about the possibility that Japan might go nuclear, as well as

Japan's thinking about nuclear weapons during that period (including its ratification of the Nuclear Nonproliferation Treaty and the adoption of the three nonnuclear principles (no possession, no introduction, and no transit allowed), in *Kakuheiki to Nichibei Kankei: Amerika no Kakufukakusan Gaikō to Nihon no Sentaku 1960–1976* (Nuclear Weapons and Japan–United States Relations: American Nuclear Nonproliferation Diplomacy and Japan's Choices, 1960–1976) (Yūshisha, 2006).

Rearmament, Civilian Control, and the Self-Defense Forces

Ōtake Hideo portrays the rearmament question as the fork in the road where conservatives and reformists part ways in *Saigunbi to Nashonarizumu: Hoshu, Riberaru, Shakaiminshushugi no Bōeikan* (The Rearmament Question and Nationalism: The Conservatives, Liberals, and Social Democrats' Views on Defense) (Chūōkōronsha, 1988; reissued by Kōdansha in 2005 under the title *Saigunbi to Nashyonarizumu: Sengo Nihon no Bōeikan* [The Rearmament Question and Nationalism: Postwar Japanese Views on Defense]). Masuda Hiroshi's survey of the circumstances of the creation of the land, sea, and air forces, *Jieitai no Tanjō: Nihon no Saigunbi to Amerika* (The Birth of the Self-Defense Forces: Japanese Rearmament and America) (Chūōkōron Shinsha, 2004), is especially valuable for its third section on the little-researched founding of the Air Self-Defense Force.

Sadō Akihiro has written several surveys of defense policy and civilian control from the creation of the Self-Defense Forces to the present time. Notable among them for lay readers are *Sengo Seiji to Jieitai* (Postwar Politics and the Self-Defense Forces) (Yoshikawa Kōbunkan, 2006), which is available in translation under the title *The Self-Defense Forces and Postwar Politics in Japan* (Japan Publishing Industry Foundation for Culture, 2017), and *Jieitai-shi: Bōei Seisaku no Nanajūnen* (History of the Self-Defense Forces: Defense Policy at Seventy) (Chikuma Shobō, 2015). For more specialist readers, he has *Sengo Nihon no Bōei to Seiji* (Defense and Politics in Postwar Japan) (Yoshikawa Kōbunkan, 2003) and *Jieitaishiron: Sei-kan-gun-min no Rokujūnen* (On the History of the Self-Defense Forces: Sixty Years of Interaction among Politicians, Bureaucrats, Soldiers, and Citizens) (Yoshikawa Kōbunkan, 2015).

Nakajima Shingo provides a detailed look at the development of the principle of civilian control, which characterizes postwar civilian-military relations in Japan, in *Sengo Nihon no Bōei Seisaku: Yoshida Rosen wo Meguru Seiji-Gaikō-Gunji* (Postwar Japanese Military Policy: Political, Diplomatic, and Military Aspects of the Yoshida Line) (Keiō University Press, 2006).

Reconciling with Asia and Building New Relationships

One of the main issues in postwar Japanese diplomacy was that of how to get back into the international community's good graces and be a responsible member of society in Asia. The 1955 Bandung Conference was the first international meeting attended by Japan as an independent nation after the war. Essential reading for understanding its significance is Miyagi Taizō's *Bandon Kaigi to Nihon no Ajia Fukki: Amerika to Ajia no Hazama de* (The Bandung Conference and Japan's Return to Asia: Between America and Asia) (Sōshisha, 2001). With the Chinese mainland under communist rule, Japan found avenues open to it in maritime Southeast Asia. This was a time of turbulence in Southeast Asia, but how Japan viewed the region and built new relationships is shown in Miyagi's *"Kaiyō Kokka" Nihon no Sengo-shi* (A Postwar History of Maritime Japan) (Chikuma Shobō, 2008), translated by Hanabusa Midori as *Japan's Quest for Stability in Southeast Asia: Navigating the Turning Points in Postwar Asia* (Routledge, 2018). Miyagi delves deeper into this issue in his *Sengo Ajia Chitsujo no Mosaku to Nihon: Umi no Ajia no Sengo-shi 1957–1966* (Japan and the Search for a Postwar Asian Order: Maritime Asia's Postwar, 1957–1966) (Sōbunsha, 2004).

The question of reparations for the former colonies and now newly independent Southeast Asian nations was a serious diplomatic issue for postwar Japan. Although we have yet to have a satisfactory book-length treatment of the question from the international relations viewpoint, the chapter on the political dynamics of the reparations question in Kitaoka Shin'ichi's *Monko Kaihō Seisaku to Nihon* (The Open-Door Policy and Japan) (University of Tokyo Press, 2015) is logical, readable, and understandable for the lay reader, despite being a somewhat academic treatment.

The regionalism concept had arisen in the 1930s and was carried over in the postwar era. In Japan, its chief manifestation was Pan-Asianism. Although historians have done considerable work on regionalism, their findings have yet to be popularized for the general reader. Nevertheless, those interested in looking at regionalism and how it figured in Japanese foreign policy should turn to a pair of articles by Hatano Sumio: "Sengo Ajia Gaikō no Rinen Keisei: Chiikishugi to Tōzai no Kakehashi" (The Formation of Diplomatic Ideals in Postwar Asia: Regionalism and Bridging East and West) in *Kokusai Mondai* (vol. 546, 2005) and "Chiikishugi wo Meguru Nihon Gaikō to Ajia" (Regionalism-Centered Japanese Diplomacy and Asia) also in *Kokusai Mondai* (vol. 578, 2009). For more on Japanese foreign policy in Asia, see *Gendai Nihon no Tōnan Ajia Seisaku 1950–2005* (Japan's Southeast Asia Policy Today, 1950–2005) by Hatano Sumio and Satō Susumu (Waseda University Press, 2007) and *Sengo Nihon no Ajia Gaikō* (Postwar Japanese Asia Foreign Policy) by Miyagi Taizō (Minerva Shobō, 2015).

The New Asia Pacific Order

Watanabe Akio was a preeminent international relations scholar and an early advocate of viewing Asia and Oceania as a single region. Many of his ideas were picked up and incorporated in the Pacific Basin community concept put forward by Prime Minister Ōhira Masayoshi, which came to fruition with the establishment of the Pacific Basin cooperation concept in 1989. While the presence of the Asia Pacific Economic Cooperation (APEC) form is waning in the twenty-first century, the concept of an East Asian and Pacific Basin regional organization still holds great potential, as hinted at and elucidated in much of Watanabe's work, including "Tōron: Taiheiyō no Jidai no Rekishiteki Igi" (Discussion: The Historical Significance of the Pacific Era), a roundtable with Hosoya Chihiro and Nagai Yōnosuke in *Kokusai Mondai* (vol. 301, 1985); his book *Ajia-taiheiyō no Kokusai Kankei to Nihon* (Asia Pacific International Relations and Japan) (University of Tokyo Press, 1992); and two essay collections he edited, *Ajia Taiheiyō Rentai Kōsō* (The Asia Pacific Solidarity Concept) (NTT, 2005) and *Ajia Taiheiyō to Atarashii Chiikishugi no Tenkai* (Asia Pacific and the Development of a New Regionalism) (Chikura Shobō, 2010).

Reconciliation with China and South Korea

The multivolume *Nikkan Kokkō Seijōka Mondai Shiryō* (Documents on the Normalization of Japan–South Korea Relations) edited by Asano Toyomi and colleagues was published by Gendai Shiryō Shuppan starting with the first volume in 2010. Other recent academic research on this topic has appeared in *Rekishi toshite no*

Nikkan Kokkō Seijōka (History of Japan-Korea Normalization of
Diplomatic Relations), volumes 1, *Higashiajia reisen Hen* (The East
Asia Cold War) and 2, *Datsushokuminchika Hen* (Decolonization),
both edited by Lee Jong Wong, Kimiya Tadashi, and Asano Toyomi
(Hōsei University Press, 2011). See also the essays on the Japanese
and Korean assertions that complicated the normalization process in
the first section of *Sengo Nihon no Baishō Mondai to Highashiajia
Chiiki Saihen: Seikyūken to Rekishi Ninshiki Mondai no Kigen* (The
Japanese War Reparations Question and East Asian Realignment:
Origins of the Claims and Historical Awareness Issues) edited by
Asano Toyomi (Jigakusha, 2013).

On the normalization of relations with China, Hattori Ryūji drew
upon oral accounts by former diplomats in *Nitchū Kokkō Seijōka:
Tanaka Kakuei, Ōhira Masayoshi, Kanryōtachi no Chōsen* (Normal-
ization of Japan-China Relations: The Challenges Tanaka Kakuei,
Ōhira Masayoshi, and Government Officials Faced) (Chūōkōron
Shinsha, 2011). Another informative work is *Nitchu Kokkō Seijōka
no Seijishi* (A Political History of Japan-China Normalization) by
Inoue Masaya (University of Nagoya Press, 2010).

The Reversion of Okinawa and the Base Problem

Vast expanses of land throughout Okinawa were requisitioned for US
military bases while Okinawa was under US occupation. A good
starting point for understanding the complexities of the resultant economic reliance on the bases amid widespread popular resistance to
their presence is Taira Yoshitoshi's *Sengo Okinawa to Beigun Kichi:
Juyō Tokyozetsu no Hazama de 1945–1972* (Postwar Okinawa and
US Military Bases: Between Acceptance and Rejection, 1945–1972)
(Hōsei University Press, 2012).

A key aspect of Okinawan reversion is that, even though the San
Francisco Peace Treaty placed Okinawa under US trusteeship, it
acknowledged Japan's residual sovereignty. The run-up to that
arrangement is detailed by Robert D. Eldridge in *The Origins of the
Bilateral Okinawa Problem: Okinawa in Postwar US-Japan Relations, 1945–1952* (Routledge-Garland, 2001).

Watanabe Akio conveys the atmosphere that prevailed when the
Okinawan reversion was ongoing in *Sengo Nihon no Seiji to Gaikō:
Okinawa Mondai wo Meguru Seiji Katei* (Postwar Japanese Politics
and Foreign Policy: Political Process in Okinawan Reversion) (Fuku-
mura Shuppan, 1970). Like Watanabe, Kōno Yasuko sheds new light

on the importance of the reversion within Japan–United States relations in *Okinawa Henkan wo Meguru Seiji to Gaikō: Nichibei Kankei-shi no Bunmyaku* (The Politics and Diplomacy of Okinawa's Reversion: Okinawa in the Context of Japan–United States Relations) (University of Tokyo Press, 1994). It should be noted that they were forced to rely on US resources as their principal primary sources because the bulk of Japanese postwar diplomatic records were yet to be opened.

The later release of further Japanese archival records and a series of interviews with former diplomats enabled Nakashima Takuma to flesh out the record in *Okinawa Henkan to Nichibei Anpo Taisei* (Okinawa's Reversion and the Japan–United States Security Alliance) (Yūhikaku, 2012). This is the best recent work examining reversion within the security framework.

Diplomatic historians are turning their attention to the problems with US bases post-reversion. In *Okinawa Henkango no Nichibei Anpo: Beigun Kichi wo Meguru Sōkoku* (The Japan–United States Security Alliance After the Reversion of Okinawa: Conflict over US Military Bases) (Yoshikawa Kōbunkan, 2016), for example, Nozoe Fumiaki examines the little-researched area of post-reversion Japan–United States relations in light of there having been no base reduction since reversion.

On the relations between post-reversion Okinawa and the government in Tokyo, Sadō Akihiro presents the prefectural "international city" initiative to get rid of the military bases and develop Okinawa's industrial and ecological potential as an example of the tension between regional development and US bases in *Okinawa Gendai Seiji-shi: Jiritsu wo Meguru Kōbō* (A Political History of Today's Okinawa: The Battle over Autonomy) (Yoshida Shoten, 2014). This compelling book also examines other recent political developments in Okinawa, including the Yonaguni economic development plan and the controversy over opening a new base for Japan's Self-Defense Forces on Yonaguni.

Omnidirectional Diplomacy

With the 1970s détente, Japan sought to build friendly relations not only with the Western bloc but also with all nations, pursuing what was called omnidirectional diplomacy for peace. The primary achievement was the Fukuda Doctrine—the three principles of Southeast Asia policy—enunciated in August 1977. The ups and downs of this omnidirectional approach are traced by Wakatsuki

Hidekazu in *Zenhōi Gaikō no Jidai: Reisen Henyōki no Nihon to Ajia 1971–80* (The Era of Omnidirectional Diplomacy: Japan and Asia During the Cold War Transformation, 1971–80) (Nihon Keizai Hyōronsha, 2006), a valuable book for anyone considering Japan's foreign policy possibilities.

Peacekeeping Operations

Self-Defense Forces participation in UN peacekeeping operations in Cambodia and elsewhere, and in reconstruction in Iraq, is a showcase example of Japan's post–Cold War international contributions. Shōji Takayuki, a younger historian who has focused on this topic, has produced *Jieitai Kaigai Haken to Nihon Gaikō: Reisengo ni okeru Jinteki Kōken no Mosaku* (Self-Defense Forces Overseas Secondment and Japanese Foreign Policy: Looking for Ways to Contribute Human Skills post–Cold War) (Nihon Keizai Hyōronsha, 2015).

Japanese participation in peacekeeping operations was in fact considered during the Kishi, Ikeda, and Satō administrations soon after the peace treaty was signed and Japan regained its independence—a bit of history that is important to understanding the post–Cold War situation. For more on this, see "Yoshida Rosen to PKO Sanka Mondai" (The Yoshida Line and the Question of Participating in Peacekeeping Operations) by Murakami Tomoaki in *Kokusai Seiji* (vol. 151, 2008).

Conclusion

As promised in the introductory section, this chapter has presented a bibliography of instructive works, mainly in the areas of politics and foreign policy, about the potential points of contention in thinking about the seven decades since the war. Though only a few drops in the ocean of literature about postwar Japan, they are a good start for readers wishing to look back on the historical trajectories.

In 2018 Japan will celebrate the 150th anniversary of the Meiji Restoration. On the 100th anniversary, in 1968, Japan's economy had surpassed West Germany's to become the second largest in terms of gross domestic product in the world. The "rich country, strong army" policy proclaimed by the Meiji oligarchs had suffused prewar Japan. With defeat in 1945 and the adoption of the no-war constitution, the "strong army" half fell by the wayside and only the "rich country" half remained. Nevertheless, as the subsequent rapid growth made Japan one of the world's leading economic powers, this determination to be a "rich country" was well and truly achieved. Moreover, as liberal democracy became firmly established in the postwar era, the popular demand for political democracy, nurtured through the prewar era from the time of the freedom and democracy movement, has also been achieved.

In his August 14, 2015, statement commemorating the seventieth anniversary of the war's end, Prime Minister Abe said: "We have created a free and democratic country, abided by the rule of law, and consistently upheld that pledge never to wage a war again. While taking silent pride in the path we have walked as a peace-loving nation for as long as seventy years, we remain determined never to deviate from this steadfast course."

Recognition that postwar Japan has "walked as a peace-loving nation" is well established in Japan and around the world. Yet in comparison to Japan's record as a "peace-loving nation," there has not been sufficient recognition, either inside or outside of Japan, of Japan having "abided by the rule of law" and having "created a free and democratic country," heir to the prewar constitutionalist tradition on the basis of deep reflection about the war. We thus hope to see more research and studies taking this perspective and being shared with the world at large.

What is needed now is more dialogue linking the 70th anniversary of the war's end and the 150th anniversary of the Restoration. When the underlying principles connecting those two events are discovered, we will have attained a historical awareness sufficient unto Japan's 150 years of modernity.

Postscript

Miyagi Taizō

Historical memory is a monumentally difficult issue to resolve in large part because achieving shared understandings of historical events is an essential part of bringing people together and forging a national identity. For national unity purposes it is important that the citizenry share common memories both of events they actually experienced and of historical events that they have experienced only vicariously through education and folklore. In a way, it is only natural that different citizenries should perceive their different histories differently. Yet when neighboring countries/citizenries have sharply conflicting recollections and interpretations of shared historical events, friction ensues—and this friction grows worse and can lead to diplomatic tensions if it is not addressed but rather blithely dismissed because "there's no way everyone can agree on all aspects of historical memory."

This is especially so in the aftermath of conflict, with one side asking how many times the same old accusations are going to be dragged up and the other side not feeling any sense of justice or closure despite the legalistic settlements that may have been reached. Because the two countries' populations are so involved and invested in the same event, passions are extremely difficult to contain and are easily set afire.

The old adage admonishes us to learn from history. Knowing history is an essential first step to avoiding or resolving such bilateral acrimony, and in this case the history has to be the history of our and others' historical memories. Much of the pertinent historical narrative in Japan starts in the mid–nineteenth century leading up to and including the Meiji Restoration, goes up to and through World War II, and then continues on with the postwar period of reconstruction and rebuilding, including Japan's becoming one of the leading economic powers in the 1980s. It is only when we can see this transformation and the factors that contributed to it that we can understand the current era and the significant features of our historical narrative. That is what this book has set out to do, starting with an introduction to the prewar history and how it figures in the popular memory and then jumping to the different postwar eras and the three important historical memory statements (Murayama in 1995, Koizumi in 2005, and Abe in 2015).

Insights are to be found throughout the chapters on the three era-defining politicians: Yoshida Shigeru, who accepted the Allied forces' reading of history and met their "good loser" expectations while showing little interest in Asian nationalism; Satō Eisaku, who understood the important role that political parties can play in molding national consensus on historical memory; and Nakasone Yasuhiro, who recognized the importance of alleviating historical memory discord over the short to medium term and acted accordingly, even if it went against his own personal preferences.

At the same time, we would be remiss were we to omit mention of Okinawa and the different path it took—or was forced to take—within the Japanese context. Indeed, it would be impossible to draw a complete picture of Japan's postwar self-image without including the Okinawan experience, Okinawa being where the imperative of national unification and the burden of the Japan–United States Mutual Security Treaty clash most explicitly. Building upon these specifics, the two panel discussions provided a wealth of intriguing comments, including Watanabe's observation that historical narrative and cultural differences tend to be trotted out to demonize the other side when bilateral relations turn sour, and Professor Hosoya's reminder that we cannot abandon the effort for historical reconciliation just because it is difficult but rather need to find ways to achieve real reconciliation with minimum adverse impact.

One thing that I hope this book has brought into clearer focus is the very important role politics plays here. The historical memory issue is obviously not the sole purview of politics or politicians, and one of its distinguishing characteristics is the way it is the total sum of the citizenry's emotions and aspirations. Another may be the way it is possible, when politicians are immobilized by politics, to put the historical memory issue into perspective by promoting an array of cultural and economic exchanges. Yet when historical memory friction flares up, it generates bursts of negative energy that overwhelm citizen-level economic and cultural exchanges and tends to be viewed as a top-level issue. The issue has to be addressed, but concentrating exclusively on easing the tensions and improving the relationship risks alienating your own electorate and rupturing the national consensus. For better or worse, the ideological alignments during the Cold War provided a bedrock lodestone that could define policy. Now that the Cold War is over, that certainty has been lost, and the question of historical recollection and historical narratives demands the most adroit political helmsmanship, both internationally and domestically.

Reconciliation is by no means easy, but to abandon the effort is to invite disaster. Undespairing, unassuming, and unwavering crisis management is really the only choice. Even if reconciliation-for-all-time cannot be attained, none would deny the need for attentive crisis management. Patience and perseverance are the foundations of the everyday crisis management that is needed to defuse, if not resolve, historical narrative differences.

We have tried in this book to look at historical memory in a broad range of different circumstances, and it would be wrong to try to draw a single conclusion from these varied studies. That said, I suspect that the need for this day-in-day-out crisis management mindset and everyday attention has been a common thread running through all of the discussion.

Appendix 1

Statement by
Prime Minister Murayama Tomiichi:
"On the Occasion of the 50th Anniversary
of the War's End"

August 15, 1995

The world has seen fifty years elapse since the war came to an end. Now, when I remember the many people both at home and abroad who fell victim to war, my heart is overwhelmed by a flood of emotions.

The peace and prosperity of today were built as Japan overcame great difficulty to arise from a devastated land after defeat in the war. That achievement is something of which we are proud, and let me herein express my heartfelt admiration for the wisdom and untiring effort of each and every one of our citizens. Let me also express once again my profound gratitude for the indispensable support and assistance extended to Japan by the countries of the world, beginning with the United States of America. I am also delighted that we have been able to build the friendly relations which we enjoy today with the neighboring countries of the Asia-Pacific region, the United States and the countries of Europe.

Now that Japan has come to enjoy peace and abundance, we tend to overlook the pricelessness and blessings of peace. Our task is to convey to younger generations the horrors of war, so that we never repeat the errors in our history. I believe that, as we join hands, especially with the peoples of neighboring countries, to ensure true peace in the Asia-Pacific region—indeed, in the entire world—it is necessary, more than anything else, that we foster relations with all countries based on deep understanding and trust. Guided by this conviction, the

Government has launched the Peace, Friendship and Exchange Initiative, which consists of two parts promoting: support for historical research into relations in the modern era between Japan and the neighboring countries of Asia and elsewhere; and rapid expansion of exchanges with those countries. Furthermore, I will continue in all sincerity to do my utmost in efforts being made on the issues arisen from the war, in order to further strengthen the relations of trust between Japan and those countries.

Now, upon this historic occasion of the 50th anniversary of the war's end, we should bear in mind that we must look into the past to learn from the lessons of history, and ensure that we do not stray from the path to the peace and prosperity of human society in the future.

During a certain period in the not too distant past, Japan, following a mistaken national policy, advanced along the road to war, only to ensnare the Japanese people in a fateful crisis, and, through its colonial rule and aggression, caused tremendous damage and suffering to the people of many countries, particularly to those of Asian nations. In the hope that no such mistake be made in the future, I regard, in a spirit of humility, these irrefutable facts of history, and express here once again my feelings of deep remorse and state my heartfelt apology. Allow me also to express my feelings of profound mourning for all victims, both at home and abroad, of that history.

Building from our deep remorse on this occasion of the 50th anniversary of the end of the war, Japan must eliminate self-righteous nationalism, promote international coordination as a responsible member of the international community and, thereby, advance the principles of peace and democracy. At the same time, as the only country to have experienced the devastation of atomic bombing, Japan, with a view to the ultimate elimination of nuclear weapons, must actively strive to further global disarmament in areas such as the strengthening of the nuclear non-proliferation regime. It is my conviction that in this way alone can Japan atone for its past and lay to rest the spirits of those who perished.

It is said that one can rely on good faith. And so, at this time of remembrance, I declare to the people of Japan and abroad my intention to make good faith the foundation of our Government policy, and this is my vow.

Appendix 2

Statement by
Prime Minister Koizumi Junichirō
August 15, 2005

On the sixtieth anniversary of the end of the war, I reaffirm my determination that Japan must never again take the path to war, reflecting that the peace and prosperity we enjoy today are founded on the ultimate sacrifices of those who lost their lives for the war against their will.

More than three million compatriots died in the war—in the battlefield thinking about their homeland and worrying about their families, while others perished amidst the destruction of war, or after the war in remote foreign countries.

In the past, Japan, through its colonial rule and aggression, caused tremendous damage and suffering to the people of many countries, particularly to those of Asian nations. Sincerely facing these facts of history, I once again express my feelings of deep remorse and heartfelt apology, and also express the feelings of mourning for all victims, both at home and abroad, in the war. I am determined not to allow the lessons of that horrible war to erode, and to contribute to the peace and prosperity of the world without ever again waging a war.

After the war, Japan rebuilt itself from a devastated land owing to the ceaseless efforts of its people and the assistance extended by many countries, and accepted the San Francisco Peace Treaty, being the first step of its reversion to the international community. Japan has resolutely maintained its principle of resolving all matters by peaceful means and not by force, and proactively extended material and personnel assistance for the sake of the peace and prosperity of the world through official development assistance (ODA) and United Nations peacekeeping operations.

Japan's postwar history has indeed been six decades of manifesting its remorse on the war through actions.

The postwar generations now exceed 70 percent of Japan's population. Each and every Japanese, through his or her own experience and peace-oriented education, sincerely seeks international peace. Today, many Japanese are actively engaged in activities for peace and humanitarian assistance around the world, through such organizations as the Japan Overseas Cooperation Volunteers, and have been receiving much trust and high appreciation from the local people. Exchange with Asian countries in a wide variety of areas, such as economy and culture, has also increased on an unprecedented scale. I believe it is necessary to work hand in hand with other Asian countries, especially with China and the Republic of Korea, which are Japan's neighboring countries separated only by a strip of water, to maintain peace and pursue the development of the region. Through squarely facing the past and rightly recognizing the history, I intend to build a future-oriented cooperative relationship based on mutual understanding and trust with Asian countries.

The international community is now faced with more complex and difficult challenges than ever imagined before: progress of the developing countries, alleviation of poverty, conservation of the global environment, nonproliferation of weapons of mass destruction, and the prevention and eradication of terrorism. In order to contribute to world peace, Japan will proactively fulfill its role as a responsible member of the international community, upholding its pledge not to engage in war and based on its experience as the only nation to have suffered from the atomic bombings and the path it has followed over the sixty years after war.

On this occasion marking the sixtieth anniversary of the war's end, Japan, as a peace-loving nation, expresses here again that it will work to achieve peace and prosperity of all humankind with all its resources, together with all the nations of shared aspiration.

Appendix 3

Statement by
Prime Minister Abe Shinzō

August 14, 2015

Cabinet Decision

On the 70th anniversary of the end of the war, we must calmly reflect upon the road to war, the path we have taken since it ended, and the era of the 20th century. We must learn from the lessons of history the wisdom for our future.

More than one hundred years ago, vast colonies possessed mainly by the Western powers stretched out across the world. With their overwhelming supremacy in technology, waves of colonial rule surged toward Asia in the 19th century. There is no doubt that the resultant sense of crisis drove Japan forward to achieve modernization. Japan built a constitutional government earlier than any other nation in Asia. The country preserved its independence throughout. The Japan-Russia War gave encouragement to many people under colonial rule from Asia to Africa.

After World War I, which embroiled the world, the movement for self-determination gained momentum and put brakes on colonization that had been underway. It was a horrible war that claimed as many as ten million lives. With a strong desire for peace stirred in them, people founded the League of Nations and brought forth the General Treaty for Renunciation of War. There emerged in the international community a new tide of outlawing war itself.

At the beginning, Japan, too, kept steps with other nations. However, with the Great Depression setting in and the Western countries launching economic blocs by involving colonial economies, Japan's economy suffered a major blow. In such circumstances, Japan's sense of isolation deepened and it attempted to overcome its diplomatic and economic deadlock through the use of force. Its domestic political system could not serve as a brake to stop such attempts. In this way, Japan lost sight of the overall trends in the world.

With the Manchurian Incident, followed by the withdrawal from the League of Nations, Japan gradually transformed itself into a challenger to the new international order that the international community sought to establish after tremendous sacrifices. Japan took the wrong course and advanced along the road to war.

And, seventy years ago, Japan was defeated.

On the 70th anniversary of the end of the war, I bow my head deeply before the souls of all those who perished both at home and abroad. I express my feelings of profound grief and my eternal, sincere condolences.

More than three million of our compatriots lost their lives during the war: on the battlefields worrying about the future of their homeland and wishing for the happiness of their families; in remote foreign countries after the war, in extreme cold or heat, suffering from starvation and disease. The atomic bombings of Hiroshima and Nagasaki, the air raids on Tokyo and other cities, and the ground battles in Okinawa, among others, took a heavy toll among ordinary citizens without mercy.

Also in countries that fought against Japan, countless lives were lost among young people with promising futures. In China, Southeast Asia, the Pacific islands and elsewhere that became the battlefields, numerous innocent citizens suffered and fell victim to battles as well as hardships such as severe deprivation of food. We must never forget that there were women behind the battlefields whose honour and dignity were severely injured.

Upon the innocent people did our country inflict immeasurable damage and suffering. History is harsh. What is done cannot be undone. Each and every one of them had his or her life, dream, and beloved family. When I squarely contemplate this obvious fact, even now, I find myself speechless and my heart is rent with the utmost grief.

The peace we enjoy today exists only upon such precious sacrifices. And therein lies the origin of postwar Japan.

We must never again repeat the devastation of war.

Incident, aggression, war—we shall never again resort to any form of the threat or use of force as a means of settling international disputes. We shall abandon colonial rule forever and respect the right of self-determination of all peoples throughout the world.

With deep repentance for the war, Japan made that pledge. Upon it, we have created a free and democratic country, abided by the rule of law, and consistently upheld that pledge never to wage a war again. While taking silent pride in the path we have walked as a peace-loving nation for as long as seventy years, we remain determined never to deviate from this steadfast course.

Japan has repeatedly expressed the feelings of deep remorse and heartfelt apology for its actions during the war. In order to manifest such feelings through concrete actions, we have engraved in our hearts the histories of suffering of the people in Asia as our neighbours: those in Southeast Asian countries such as Indonesia and the Philippines, and Taiwan, the Republic of Korea and China, among others; and we have consistently devoted ourselves to the peace and prosperity of the region since the end of the war.

Such position articulated by the previous cabinets will remain unshakable into the future.

However, no matter what kind of efforts we may make, the sorrows of those who lost their family members and the painful memories of those who underwent immense sufferings by the destruction of war will never be healed.

Thus, we must take to heart the following.

The fact that more than six million Japanese repatriates managed to come home safely after the war from various parts of the Asia-Pacific and became the driving force behind Japan's postwar reconstruction; the fact that nearly three thousand Japanese children left behind in China were able to grow up there and set foot on the soil of their homeland again; and the fact that former POWs of the United States, the United Kingdom, the Netherlands, Australia, and other nations have visited Japan for many years to continue praying for the souls of the war-dead on both sides.

How much emotional struggle must have existed and what great efforts must have been necessary for the Chinese people who underwent all the sufferings of the war and for the former POWs who experienced unbearable sufferings caused by the Japanese military in order for them to be so tolerant nevertheless?

That is what we must turn our thoughts to reflect upon.

Thanks to such manifestation of tolerance, Japan was able to return to the international community in the postwar era. Taking this opportunity of the 70th anniversary of the end of the war, Japan would like to express its heartfelt gratitude to all the nations and all the people who made every effort for reconciliation.

In Japan, the postwar generations now exceed eighty percent of its population. We must not let our children, grandchildren, and even further generations to come, who have nothing to do with that war, be predestined to apologize. Still, even so, we Japanese, across generations, must squarely face the history of the past. We have the responsibility to inherit the past, in all humbleness, and pass it on to the future.

Our parents' and grandparents' generations were able to survive in a devastated land in sheer poverty after the war. The future they brought about is the one our current generation inherited and the one we will hand down to the next generation. Together with the tireless efforts of our predecessors, this has only been possible through the goodwill and assistance extended to us that transcended hatred by a truly large number of countries, such as the United States, Australia, and European nations, which Japan had fiercely fought against as enemies.

We must pass this down from generation to generation into the future. We have the great responsibility to take the lessons of history deeply into our hearts, to carve out a better future, and to make all possible efforts for the peace and prosperity of Asia and the world.

We will engrave in our hearts the past, when Japan attempted to break its deadlock with force. Upon this reflection, Japan will continue to firmly uphold the principle that any disputes must be settled peacefully and diplomatically based on the respect for the rule of law and not through the use of force, and to reach out to other countries in the world to do the same. As the only country to have ever suffered the devastation of atomic bombings during war, Japan will fulfill its responsibility in the international community, aiming at the non-proliferation and ultimate abolition of nuclear weapons.

We will engrave in our hearts the past, when the dignity and honour of many women were severely injured during wars in the 20th century. Upon this reflection, Japan wishes to be a country always at the side of such women's injured hearts. Japan will lead the world in making the 21st century an era in which women's human rights are not infringed upon.

We will engrave in our hearts the past, when forming economic blocs made the seeds of conflict thrive. Upon this reflection, Japan will continue to develop a free, fair, and open international economic system that will not be influenced by the arbitrary intentions of any nation. We will strengthen assistance for developing countries, and lead the world toward further prosperity. Prosperity is the very foundation for peace. Japan will make even greater efforts to fight against poverty, which also serves as a hotbed of violence, and to provide opportunities for medical services, education, and self-reliance to all the people in the world.

We will engrave in our hearts the past, when Japan ended up becoming a challenger to the international order. Upon this reflection, Japan will firmly uphold basic values such as freedom, democracy, and human rights as unyielding values and, by working hand in hand with countries that share such values, hoist the flag of "Proactive Contribution to Peace," and contribute to the peace and prosperity of the world more than ever before.

Heading toward the 80th, the 90th, and the centennial anniversary of the end of the war, we are determined to create such a Japan together with the Japanese people.

Appendix 4
Postwar Prime Ministers

NAME	TERM IN OFFICE
Suzuki Kantarō	April 7, 1945–August 17, 1945
Higashikuni Naruhiko	August 17, 1945–October 9, 1945
Shidehara Kijūrō	October 9, 1945–May 22, 1946
Yoshida Shigeru	May 22, 1946–May 24, 1947
Katayama Tetsu	May 24, 1947–March 10, 1948
Ashida Hitoshi	March 10, 1948–October 15, 1948
Yoshida Shigeru	October 15, 1948–December 10, 1954
Hatoyama Ichirō	December 10, 1954–December 23, 1956
Ishibashi Tanzan	December 23, 1956–February 25, 1957
Kishi Shinsuke	February 25, 1957–July 19, 1960
Ikeda Hayato	July 19, 1960–November 9, 1964
Satō Eisaku	November 9, 1964–July 7, 1972
Tanaka Kakuei	July 7, 1972–December 9, 1974
Miki Takeo	December 9, 1974–December 24, 1976
Fukuda Takeo	December 24, 1976–December 7, 1978
Ōhira Masayoshi	December 7, 1978–June 12, 1980
Itō Masayoshi (acting prime minister)	June 12, 1980–July 17, 1980
Suzuki Zenkō	July 17, 1980–November 27, 1982
Nakasone Yasuhiro	November 27, 1982–November 6, 1987
Takeshita Noboru	November 6, 1987–June 3, 1989
Uno Sōsuke	June 3, 1989–August 10, 1989

NAME	TERM IN OFFICE
Kaifu Toshiaki	August 10, 1989–November 5, 1991
Miyazawa Kiichi	November 5, 1991–August 9, 1993
Hosokawa Morihiro	August 9, 1993–April 28, 1994
Hata Tsutomu	April 28, 1994–June 30, 1994
Murayama Tomiichi	June 30, 1994–January 11, 1996
Hashimoto Ryūtarō	January 11, 1996–July 30, 1998
Obuchi Keizō	July 30, 1998–April 5, 2000
Mori Yoshirō	April 5, 2000–April 26, 2001
Kozumi Jun'ichirō	April 26, 2001–September 26, 2006
Abe Shinzō	September 26, 2006–September 26, 2007
Fukuda Yasuo	September 26, 2007–September 24, 2008
Asō Tarō	September 24, 2008–September 16, 2009
Hatoyama Yukio	September 16, 2009–June 8, 2010
Kan Naoto	June 8, 2010–September 2, 2011
Noda Yoshihiko	September 2, 2011–December 26, 2012
Abe Shinzō	December 26, 2012–present

Bibliography

Akazawa Shirō. *Yasukuni Jinja: Semegiau Senbotsusha Tsuitō no Yukue* (Yasukuni Shrine: The Future of Conflicted War Memorials). Tokyo: Iwanami Shoten, 2005.

America-Japan Society. "Iwo Jima Fairu" (The Iwo Jima Files). Archive. Tokyo.

Asano Toyomi. *Teikoku Nihon no Shokuminchi Hōsei: Hōiki Tōgō to Teikoku Chitsujo* (Law Enforcement in the Japanese Colonies: The Integration of Jurisdiction and Imperial Order). Nagoya: University of Nagoya Press, 2008.

Aso Kazuko. "Musume no Tachiba kara" (A Daughter's Perspective). In *Yoshida Shigeru 10nen Kaisō* (A Decade's Recollections of Yoshida Shigeru), vol. 4. Tokyo: Chūōkōron-sha, 1998.

Etō Naoko. *Chūgoku Nashonarizumu no Naka no Nihon: Aikokushugi no Henyō to Rekishi Ninshiki Mondai* (Japan in Chinese Nationalism: Changes in Patriotism and the Problem of Historical Memory). Tokyo: Keisō Shobō, 2014.

Fukunaga Fumio and Kōno Yasuko. *Sengo towa Nanika: Seijigaku to Rekishigaku no Taiwa* (What Does Postwar Mean? Dialogue Between Political Science and History). Vols. 1–2. Tokyo: Maruzen, 2014.

Gekkan Shakaitō Editorial Board. *Nihon Shakaitō no 30nen* (JSP 30-Year History). Vol. 3. Tokyo: Shakai Shimpō, 1975.

Gotōda Masaharu. *Jō to Ri* (Sentiment and Reason). Vol. 2. Tokyo: Kōdansha, 1998.

Hasegawa Kazutoshi. *Shushō Hishokan ga Kataru Nakasone Gaikō no Butai-ura* (Secretary to the Prime Minister Talks About the Background to Nakasone Foreign Policy). Tokyo: Asahi Shimbun, 2014.

Hasumi Yoshihiro. "Tennō go Hōchū no Kaisō: Ano Netsuretsu Kangeiburi ga Natsukashii" (Remembering the Emperor's Visit to China: Fond

197

Memories of That Enthusiastic Welcome). *Asia Information Forum,* August 4, 2013. http://asiainfo.or.jp/column/20130804.

Hata Ikuhiko. *Yasukuni Jinja no Saijin-tachi* (The Enshrined at Yasukuni Shrine). Tokyo: Shinchōsha, 2010.

Hatano Sumio. *Kokka to Rekishi: Sengo Nihon no Rekishi Mondai* (The State and History: Postwar Japan's History Issues). Tokyo: Chūōkōron-Shinsha, 2011.

Hattori Ryūji. *Gaikō Dokyumento: Rekishi Ninshiki* (Diplomacy Documents: Historical Awareness). Tokyo: Iwanami Shoten, 2015.

———. *Nitchū Kokkō Seijō-ka* (Normalization of Relations with China). Tokyo: Chūōkōron-Shinsha, 2011.

Hayashi Fusao. *Dai-Tōa Sensō Kōteiron* (A Positive View of the Greater East Asia War). Tokyo: Chūōkōron-Shinsha, 2014.

Honda Katsuichi. *Chūgoku no Tabi* (Travels in China). Tokyo: Asahi Shimbun, 1972.

Hosokawa Morihiro. *Naishō Roku: Hosokawa Morihiro Sōri Daijin Nikki* (Record of Internal Conflict: The Diary of Prime Minister Hosokawa Morihiro). Tokyo: Nikkei, 2010.

Ichitani Kazuo. "Yasukuni Jinja Sanpai Mondai" (The Yasukuni Shrine Controversy). In *Kiro ni Tatsu Nicchū Kankei* (Sino-Japanese Relations at a Crossroads), edited by Iechika Ryōko et al. Tokyo: Kōyō Shobō, 2007.

Ienaga Saburō. *Taiheiyō Sensō* (The Pacific War). Tokyo: Iwanami Shoten, 1968. Translated as *The Pacific War, 1931–1945* (New York: Pantheon, 1978).

Ikeda Naotaka. "Shingapōru Kessai Mondai to Nihon no Taiō" (The Singapore Blood Debt Problem and the Japanese Response). *Kokugakuin University Institute for Japanese Culture and Classics Annual* 94 (September 2004).

Iokibe Kaoru. "Uso no Meiji-shi: Fukuchi Ōchi no Chōsen" (Journalist Fukuchi Ōchi's Challenge to Meiji Lies). *Asuteion* (Asteion) 84 (May 2016).

———. "Uso no Meiji-shi: Junkan no Kannen Nitsuite" (Lies of Meiji History: On the Concept of Cycles). *Asuteion* (Asteion) 85 (November 2016).

Ishihara Shintarō. *Rekishi no Jūjiro ni Tatte* (Standing at the Crossroads of History). Kyoto: PHP Institute, 2015.

Itō Tomonaga. *Ki wo Terawazu: Rikugun Shō Kōkyū Fukkan Miyama Yōzō no Shōwa* (Shōwa War Department Adjutant General Yōzō Miyama: An Ordinary Man). Tokyo: Kōdansha, 2009.

Japan Association of International Relations, Division for Research into the Causes of the Pacific War, ed. *Taiheiyō Sensō e no Michi* (Japan's Road to the Pacific War). 7 vols. plus a volume of appendixes. Tokyo: Asahi Shimbun, 1962–1963. Selections are available in English in the five-volume *Japan's Road to the Pacific War* (New York: Columbia University Press, 1976–1994). The final volume, dealing with the period under discussion, is *The Final Confrontation: Japan's Negotiations with the United States, 1941,* edited by James William Morley and translated by David A. Titus (New York: Columbia University Press, 1994).

Japan Socialist Party Policy Council, ed. *Nihon Shakaitō Seisaku Shiryō Shūsei* (Collected JSP Policy Documents). Tokyo, 1990.

Jiyū Minshu-tō Okinawa-kenren-shi Hensan Iinkai (Federation of Okinawa Prefecture LDP Branches History Compilation Committee), ed. *Sengo Rokujūnen Okinawa no Seijō: Jiyū Minshu-tō Okinawa-kenren-shi* (Political Conditions in Okinawa Sixty Years After the War: History of Federation of Okinawa Prefecture LDP Branches). Naha: Federation of Okinawa Prefecture LDP Branches, 2005.

Kimiya Tadashi and Lee Won-deog, eds. *Nikkan Kankei-shi 1965–2015* (History of Japan-Korea Relations, 1965–2015). Vol. 1, *Seiji* (Politics). Tokyo: University of Tokyo Press, 2015.

Kimizuka Naotaka. *Joō Heika no Burūribon: Eikoku Kunshō Gaikō-shi* (Her Majesty's Blue Ribbon UK Decoration Diplomacy). Tokyo: Chūōkōron-Shinsha, 2014.

Kimura Kan. *Nikkan Rekishi Ninshiki Mondai to wa Nanika: Rekishi Kyōkasho, Ianfu, Popyulizumu* (What Are the Historical Memory Issues Between Japan and Korea? History Textbooks, Comfort Women, and Populism). Kyoto: Minerva Shobō, 2014.

Kitaoka Shin'ichi. *Kanryōsei toshiteno Nihon Rikugun* (The Japanese Imperial Army as Bureaucracy). Tokyo: Chikuma Shobō, 2012.

———. *Monko Kaihō Seisaku to Nihon* (The Open-Door Policy and Japan). Tokyo: University of Tokyo Press, 2015.

Kōno Yasuko and Taira Yoshitoshi, eds. *Taiwa Okinawa no Sengo: Seiji, Rekishi, Shikō* (Conversation About Postwar Okinawa: Politics, History, and Thought). Tokyo: Yoshida Shoten, 2017.

Kurashi-no-techō Editorial Department, ed. *Sensō-chū no Kurashi no Kiroku, Hozonban* (Life During the War, Special Issue). Tokyo: Kurashi-no-techō, 1969.

Lee Jong Wong, Kimiya Tadashi, and Asano Toyomi, eds. *Rekishi toshiteno Nikkan Kokkō Seijōka* (History of Japan-Korea Normalization of Diplomatic Relations). Vols. 1–2. Tokyo: Hōsei University Press, 2011.

Lee Kuan Yew. *The Singapore Story: Memoirs of Lee Kuan Yew.* Japanese translation. Tokyo: Nikkei, 2000.

Mainichi Shimbun Yasukuni Reporting Group, ed. *Yasukuni Sengo Hishi: A-Kyū Senpan wo Gōshishita Otoko* (Yasukuni's Secret Postwar History: The Man Who Enshrined the Class A War Criminals). Tokyo: Kadokawa, 2015.

Masuo Chisako. *Chūgoku Seiji Gaikō no Tenkanten* (Turning Points in Chinese Politics and Diplomacy). Tokyo: University of Tokyo Press, 2010.

Matsuzawa Yūsaku. *Jiyū-minken Undō: Demokurashii no Yume to Zasetsu* (The Freedom and Democracy Movement: Democracy's Hopes and Disillusionment). Tokyo: Iwanami Shinsho, 2016.

Mikuriya Takashi. *Kingendai Nihon wo Shiryō de Yomu: Ōkubo Toshimichi nikki kara Tomita Memo made* (Readings in Modern Japanese History: From Ōkubo Toshimichi's Diary to the Tomita Memo). Tokyo: Chūōkōron-Shinsha, 2011.

Mikuriya Takashi and Nakamura Takafusa. *Kikigaki: Miyazawa Kiichi Kaiko Roku* (As He Told It: Miyazawa Kiichi Memoirs). Tokyo: Iwanami Shoten, 2005.

Miyagi Taizō. *Kaiyō Kokka Nihon no Sengo-shi* (Japan's Quest for Stability in Southeast Asia). Tokyo: Chikuma Shobō, 2008.

Miyagi Taizō and Watanabe Tsuyoshi. *Futenma, Henoko: Yugamerareta Nijūnen* (Futenma and Henoko: Twenty Years of Distortion). Tokyo: Shūeisha, 2016.

Murai Ryōta. "1970nen no Nihon no Kōsō: Aratana Nihon e no Toikake ni Kotaete" (Japanese Thought in the 1970s: Answering Questions for a New Japan). In *Daini no Sengo no Keisei Katei* (Japan's Second Postwar Restart), edited by Fukunaga Fumio. Tokyo: Yuhikaku, 2015.

———. "Sengo Nihon no Seiji to Irei" (Politics and Memorial in Postwar Japan). In *Kokkyō wo Koeru Rekishi Ninshiki: Nitchū Taiwa no Kokoromi* (History Across Borders: Attempting a Japan-China Dialogue), edited by Liu Jie, Mitani Hiroshi, and Yang Daqing. Tokyo: University of Tokyo Press, 2006.

Nakae Yōsuke. *Ajia Gaikō: Dō to Sei* (Asian Diplomacy: Dynamism and Stasis). Tokyo: Sōtensha, 2010.

Nakasone Yasuhiro. *Nakasone Yasuhiro ga Kataru Sengo Nihon Gaikō* (Nakasone Yasuhiro Talks About Postwar Japanese Foreign Policy). Tokyo: Shinchōsha, 2012.

———. *Tenchi Ujō* (The Sentient World). Tokyo: Bungeishunjūsha, 1996.

Nakasone Yasuhiro and Ishihara Shintarō. *Eien Nare, Nippon* (Viva Japan). Kyoto: PHP Institute, 2003.

Naraoka Sochi. *Taika Nijūichikajō Yōkyū toha Nan Dattanoka: Daiichiji Sekaitaisen to Nitchū Tairitsu no Genten* (What Were Japan's 21 Demands of China: World War I and the Origins of the Japan-China Conflict). Nagoya: Nagoya University Press, 2015.

National Diet Library Research and Legislative Reference Bureau. *Shinhen Yasukuni Jinja Mondai Shiryō Shū* (Yasukuni Shrine Problem Archives). New ed. Tokyo: National Diet Library, 2007.

———. *Yasukuni Jinja Mondai Shiryō Shū* (Yasukuni Shrine Problem Archives). Tokyo: National Diet Library, 1976.

Ōhira Masayoshi. *Ōhira Masayoshi Zen Chosaku-shū* (The Complete Works of Ōhira Masayoshi). Vol. 2. Edited by Fukunaga Fumio. Tokyo: Kōdansha, 2010.

Okinawa Taimusu-sha, ed. *Okinawa wo Kataru 1: Jidai e no Dengon* (Talking About Okinawa 1: Message to Future Generations). Naha: Okinawa Times, 2016.

Okinawa-ken Sokoku Fukki Tōsō-shi Hensan Iinkai (Committee for the Compilation of the History of the Struggle for Okinawa's Reversion to the Motherland). *Okinawa-ken Sokoku Fukki Tōsō-shi: Shiryō-hen* (History of the Struggle for Okinawa's Reversion to the Motherland: Source Material). Naha: Okinawa Jiji, 1982.

Onaga Takeshi. *Tatakau Min'i* (The People's Will to Fight). Tokyo: Kadokawa, 2015.

Ōnuma Yasuaki and Egawa Shōko. *Rekishi Ninshiki to wa Nanika* (What Is Historical Memory?). Tokyo: Chūōkōron-Shinsha, 2015.

Prime Minister's Office. *Satō Naikaku Sōri Daijin Enzetsu Shū* (Collected Speeches of Prime Minister Satō Eisaku). Tokyo, 1970.

Reischauer, Edwin. *Nihon Kindai no Atarashii Mikata* (A New View of Modern Japan). Tokyo: Kōdansha, 1965.

Sakai Tetsuya, ed. *Heiwa Kokka no Aidentitī* (Identifying as a Nation of Peace). Tokyo: Iwanami Shoten, 2016.

Sakurazawa Makoto. *Okinawa Gendaishi: Beikoku Tōchi, Hondo Fukki kara Oru Okinawa made* (Contemporary Okinawa History: From US Rule and Reversion to All-Okinawa). Tokyo: Chūōkōron Shinsha, 2015.

Satō Eisaku. *Kyō wa Asu no Zenjitsu* (Today Is the Day Before Tomorrow). Tokyo: Face, 1964.

Satō Susumu. "Tai-Shingapōru/Marēshia Kessai Mondai to Sono Kaiketsu" (Resolving the Blood-Debt Issue with Singapore and Malaysia). *Journal of East Asian Studies* (Nishōgakusha University) 38 (March 2008).

Shiina Etsusaburō Tsuitō-roku Kankō-kai (Shiina Etsusaburō Memorial Record Publication Society), ed. *Kiroku Shiina Etsusaburō* (The Shiina Etsusaburō Record). Vol. 2. Tokyo, 1982.

Taira Yoshitoshi. "Beigun Kichi Mondai wa Nihon Zentai no Mondai Da: Dōjō ya Hihan ni Todomaranai Chōsen Wo" (The US Base Problem Is a Problem for All of Japan: Going Beyond Sympathy and Criticism). *Journalism* (Asahi Shimbun) 304 (September 2015).

———. "Chiiki to Anzen Hoshō: Okinawa no Kichi Mondai wo Jirei to Shite" (Regions and Security: Okinawa's Base Problems). *Multidisciplinary Research for Regions Bulletin of the Institute of Regional Research* (Institute of Regional Research, Dokkyo University) vol. 8 (March 2015).

———. *Sengo Okinawa to Beigun Kichi: Juyō to Kyozetsu no Hazama de 1945–1972* (Postwar Okinawa and US Military Bases: Between Acceptance and Rejection, 1945–1972). Tokyo: Hōsei University Press, 2012.

Takahashi Hiroshi. *Ningen Shōwa Tennō* (Emperor Shōwa: Human Being). Tokyo: Kōdansha, 2011.

Tanaka Akihiko. *Nicchū Kankei 1945–1990* (Sino-Japanese Relations 1945–1990). Tokyo: University of Tokyo Press, 1991.

Tanino Sakutarō. *Ajia Gaikō: Kaiko to Kōsatsu* (Asian Diplomacy: Recollections and Thoughts). Tokyo: Iwanami Shoten, 2015.

Tōgō Kazuhiko and Hatano Sumio, eds. *Rekishi Mondai Handobukku* (Historical Memory Problems Handbook). Tokyo: Iwanami Shoten, 2015.

University of Tokyo Institute for Advanced Studies on Asia (Tanaka Akihiko's office and Matsuda Yasuhiro's office) and University of Tokyo Graduate School Interfaculty Initiative in Information Studies (Harada Shiro's office). Database: Sekai to Nihon (The World and Japan). http://www.ioc.u-tokyo.ac.jp/~worldjpn.

Vogel, Ezra. *Deng Xiaoping and the Transformation of China*. Cambridge: Belknap of Harvard University Press, 2011. Japanese edition translated by Masuo Chisako and Sugimoto Takashi (Tokyo: Nikkei, 2013).

Wakamiya Yoshibumi. *Sengo 70nen Hoshu no Ajiakan* (The Conservative View of Asia 70 Years After the War). Tokyo: Asahi Shimbun, 2014.

Yoshida Shien. *Chiisana Tatakai no Hibi: Okinawa Fukki no Urabanashi* (Small Battles Daily: The Inside Story on Okinawa's Reversion). Tokyo: Bunkyō Shōji, 1976.

Yoshida Yutaka. *Nihonjin no Sensōkan: Sengo-shi no naka no Henyō* (The Japanese View of War: Changes over the Course of Postwar History). Tokyo: Iwanami Shoten, 2005.

Yoshino Sakuzō Kōgiroku Kenkyūkai, ed. (Iokibe Kaoru, Sakuuchi Yūko, and Fushimi Taketo, primary eds.). *Yoshino Sakuzō Seiji-shi Kōgi: Yanaihara Tadao, Akamatsu Katsumaro, Oka Yoshitake Nōto* (Yoshino

Sakuzō Seiji-shi Kōgi [Yoshino Sakuzō Political History Lectures]: Akamatsu Katsumaro, Oka Yoshitake, and Yanaihara Tadao's Notes). Tokyo: Iwanami Shoten, 2016. Particularly Iokibe Kaoru's "Yoshino Sakuzō Seiji-shi no Shatei" (The Range of Yoshino Sakuzō's Political History).

Yoshitsugu Kōsuke. *Ikeda Seikenki no Nihon Gaikō to Reisen: Sengo Nihon Gaikō no Zahyōjiku 1960–64* (Japanese Foreign Policy Under Prime Minister Ikeda and the Cold War: The Parameters of Postwar Diplomacy, 1960–64). Tokyo: Iwanami Shoten, 2009.

Zhao Ziyang. *Zhao Ziyang Gokuhi Kaisō Roku* (Zhao Ziyang's Top Secret Memoirs). Tokyo: Kōbunsha, 2010.

About the Authors

Hosoya Yūichi is professor in Keio University's Faculty of Law. He is author of *Meisō suru Igirisu* (Brexit and the Crisis of Europe), *Anpo Ronsō* (available as *Security Politics in Japan,* JPIC Japan Library), and *Rekishi Ninshiki towa Nanika* (Historical Awareness from the Russo-Japanese War to the Pacific War).

Iokibe Kaoru is professor in the Faculty of Law at the University of Tokyo Graduate Schools for Law and Politics. He is author of *Jōyaku Kaisei-shi* (Renegotiating Japan's Unequal Treaties) and coauthor and coeditor of *Yoshino Sakuzō Seiji-shi Kōgi* (Yoshino Sakuzō Political History Lecture Notes) and *Jiyū-shugi no Seijika to Seiji Shisō* (Liberalist Politicians and Political Thought).

Kawashima Shin is professor in the Graduate School of Arts and Sciences at the University of Tokyo. He is author of *Chūgoku Kindai Gaikō no Keisei* (The Making of Modern Chinese Foreign Policy), *21 seiki no Chūka: Xi Jinping Chūkoku to Higashi Ajia* (The Sinic World in the Twenty-First Century: Xi Jinping's China and East Asia), and *Chūgoku no Furontea* (Chinese Frontiers).

Komiya Kazuo is a part-time lecturer at Aoyama Gakuin University, Komazawa University, and Senshu University. He is author of *Jōyaku Kaisei to Kokunai Seiji* (The Domestic Politics of Treaty Revision), coauthor and coeditor of *Jinbutsu de Yomu Kindai Nihon Gaikō-shi* (Major Figures in Modern Japanese History), and coauthor of *Jiyū-shugi no Seijika to Seiji Shisō* (Liberalist Politicians and Political Thought).

Miyagi Taizō is professor in the Faculty of Global Studies at Sophia University. He is author of *Sengo Ajia chitsujo no Mosaku to Nihon* (Japan and the Search for a Postwar Asian Order), *Kaiyō Kokka Nihon no Sengoshi* (available as *Japan's Quest for Stability in Southeast Asia,* Routledge), and *Gendai Nihon Gaikō-shi* (Modern Japanese Foreign Policy).

Murai Ryōta is professor in the Faculty of Law, Political Science Department, Komazawa University. He is author of *Seitō Naikakusei no Tenkai to Hōkai* (The Development and Collapse of Party Government) and coauthor of *Kokkyō wo Koeru Rekishi Ninshiki* (Historical Awareness Without Borders) and *Daini no Sengo no Keisei Katei* (Japan's Second Postwar Restart).

Nishino Jun'ya is professor in the Faculty of Law at Keio University. He is author of *Chōsen Hantō to Higashi Ajia* (The Korean Peninsula in East Asia), contributing author of *Chōsen Hantō no Chitsujo Saihen* (The New Order on the Korean Peninsula), and coauthor and coeditor of *Tenkanki no Higashi Ajia to Kita-Chōsen Mondai* (North Korea in a Changing East Asia).

Satō Susumu is professor in the Faculty of International Politics and Economics at Nishogakusha University. He is author of *Sengo Nihon to Ajia* (Postwar Japan in Asia), and coauthor of *Reisen Henyō-ki no Nihon Gaikō* (Japanese Foreign Policy at the End of the Cold War) and *Dai-Nippon Teikoku no Hōkai* (The Japanese Empire's Collapse).

Taira Yoshitoshi is research associate at the Dokkyo University Institute of Regional Research and part-time lecturer at Hōsei University. He is author of *Sengo Okinawa to Beigun Kichi* (Postwar Okinawa and the US Bases), contributing author of *Anzen Hoshō Seisaku to Sengo Nihon* (National Security Policy in Postwar Japan), and coeditor of *Taiwa: Okinawa no Sengo* (Conversation About Postwar Okinawa).

Takeda Tomoki is professor in the Faculty of Law, Political Science Department, at Daito Bunka University. He is author of *Shigemitsu Mamoru to Sengo Seiji* (Shigemitsu Mamoru in Postwar Politics), coauthor and coeditor of *Nihon Seitō-shi* (History of Japanese Political Parties), and coauthor of *Shōwa-shi Kōgi* (Shōwa History Lectures, vols. 1–2).

Watanabe Tsuneo is senior fellow at the Tokyo Foundation and senior research fellow at the Sasakawa Peace Foundation. He is author of *2025nen Beichū Gyakuten* (When China Overtakes America in 2025) and *Ima no Amerika ga Wakaru Hon Saishiban* (Understanding America, updated), and contributing author of *Reisengo no NATO* (NATO After the Cold War).

NB: Author information is as of the date of writing the Japanese original.

Index

shaping the current global order, 143–144; shifting foreign policy following, 183. *See also* Soviet-Japanese relations
collapsed empire, 48
colonialism: elements of the Abe Statement, 121–122; European remorse and reconciliation, 134–137; Japanese reconciliation, 48; Korean perspective on reconciliation, 97–98; Korea's demand for reparation, 71; as obstacle to Korean-Japanese reconciliation, 103; postwar historical research on reparations, 174–175; shared interests in Korean-Japanese relations, 140–141; writings on historical memory, 153–154
comfort women, 97, 117, 121, 126–127, 136, 140–141, 147, 156, 166
Communist Party's Okinawa Prefectural Committee, 82
compensation, 50, 61(n9), 100. *See also* reparations
constitutional issues, 60; Article 9, 15, 92; drafting and promulgation, 169; impact on postwar policy, 18, 30, 35, 52, 55; Meiji Constitution, 3–4
constitutional separation of state and faith. *See* Yasukuni Shrine
Council on the Investigation of the Greater East Asia War, 31. *See also* Investigation Council for the War
coups and coup attempts, 6–7
Crimea (Ukraine), 112
crimes against peace, 16

Dai-Nihon Genron Hōkokukai (Greater Japan Patriotic Press Association), 21
daimyo, 2
Damousi, Joy, 151
demobilization and repatriation research, 167–168
democracy, 6, 179; China and Taiwan's postwar governments, 107–108; constitutional debate, 3–4; Korean-Japanese relations, 110–111, 112–113
Democratic Party of Japan (DPJ), 86, 87

Democratic People's Republic of Korea (DPRK). *See* North Korea
Deng Xiaoping, 59, 69–71, 74, 108
Depression (1929), impact of, 25, 189
detainee repatriation, 167–168
Diet, building, 52
diplomacy: conflicting perception of historical events, 181–183; postwar historical research, 162, 170–178. *See also* San Francisco Peace Treaty; *specific countries*
diplomatic history, 21–23
Dower, John W., 169
Duan Qirui, 5

economic conditions: Okinawans' demands for US military reduction, 84–85; postwar historical research, 164
economic cooperation, 71–72, 74, 178–179
economic growth and development: China's perception of Japanese aggression, 102; Japan's development assistance to China, 108; Japan's winner status accounting for, 11; Korean-Japanese relations, 103, 109–110; Okinawa's development independent of US presence, 86–87; postwar reconstruction of political and economic ties, 49–50; research on Japan's postwar trajectory, 169–170
education: China's anti-Japanese programs, 107; historical narrative curricula, 8–9; postwar reconciliation initiatives, 115; textbook controversies, 48, 67–76, 89–90
Ekstein, Modris, 152
emperor: radio broadcast, 165; responsibility for war, 35; system, 2–3, 5, 14, 52; visit to China (1992), 67, 77
Endō Ken, 152
ethical remorse, 30–31
European Union (EU), 136

fascism: historical view, 39; Konoe administration, 46(n60)

Hosoya Chihiro, 161, 171, 175
Hosoya Yūichi, 95–96, 97, 98, 100,
105, 109, 111, 113, 118, 119–120,
128–129, 131, 134–138, 143–144,
148
House of Councilors: Committee on
Foreign Affairs, 61(n9); Committee
on Social and Labor Affairs,
63(n19); election, 57, 142
House of Representatives, 33, 40,
45(n44, 45), 55, 84, 126; Committee
on Social and Labor Affairs,
63(n19); Legislation Bureau, 57
Hozumi Shigetō, 21
Hu Yaobang, 73, 74, 75–76
Huanggutun incident (1928), 16
Hughes, Charles Evans, 23
human rights issues, 124, 194; comfort
women, 126; European remorse and
reconciliation, 134–135, 137;
shared interests in Korean-Japanese
relations, 140–141

Ienaga Saburō, 51
Iida Seizō, 23
Iimura Jō, 33
Ikeda Hayato, 49–50
Ikeda Shintarō, 163
Imperial Household Agency, 59, 72
Imperial Japanese Army's Asia policy,
162
Imperialism, 38, 124
Inamine Keiichi, 85
Inayama Yoshihiro, 59
independence movement, Okinawa's,
88–89
individual responsibility issue, 34–
35
Indonesia, coup, 53
Inoki Takenori, 163
Inoue Masaya, 176
internal understanding of history, 48
International Conference on Military
Trials (London, 1945), 16
International Military Tribunal for the
Far East. *See* Tokyo Trials
international relations: Abe Statement
addressing Japan's stance on the
international order, 130, 132; Abe
Statement on regional balance and
regional order, 133–134; China's
values politics, 138–140; European

view of Japanese and Asian
historical narratives, 134–138; Five-
Power Treaty, 5–6; historical
memory issue as foreign policy,
41(n2); Japan's postwar foreign
policy path, 157–158; the postwar
global order, 143–148; postwar
historical research on reparations,
174–175; reflections on the causes
of the war, 37–38; Tokyo Trials,
17–20
International Relations Research
Society. *See* Kokusai Kankei
Kenkyūkai
Inukai Tsuyoshi, assassination (1932),
6
Investigation Council for the War
(initially the Council on the
Investigation of the Greater East
Asia War), 14, 31–38, 39
Iokibe Makoto, 162, 168, 170–171
Ishibashi Tanzan, 22
Ishida Ken, 170
Ishihara Shintarō, 66
Ishii Itarō, 29
Itabashi Takumi, 170
Italy, 27, 36, 170
Itō Junji, 152
Itō Masanori, 22
Itō Takashi, 168–169
Itochu Corporation, 71
Iwate Yasukuni suit, 55
Iwo Jima, 76

Jager, Sheila Miyoshi, 153
Japan: as peace-loving nation, 15, 18,
53–54, 149–150, 179, 188, 191; as
victim, 1, 8, 57; Basic Act on
Education, 89
Japan Association of International
Relations, 51
Japan Center for Asian Historical
Records, 115
Japan-China: Joint Communiqué
(1972), 56, 101, 122, 144; Joint
Declaration on Building Partnership
(1998), 101, 144; Joint History
Research Committee, 96, 109; Joint
Statement on Mutually Beneficial
Relations Based on Common
Strategic Interests (2008), 101;
Peace, Friendship, and Exchange

About the Book

Memories can be shared—or contested. Japan and Korea, just one case in point, share centuries of intertwined history, the nature of which continues to be disputed, particularly with regard to World War II.

The authors of *History, Memory, and Politics in Postwar Japan* explore Japan's historical narratives, and their impact on both domestic politics and diplomatic relations, as they have evolved from 1946 to the present. Presenting the results of more than a decade of collaborative research, their book is a rich contribution to our understanding not only of Japanese politics, but also of how the historical narratives that we embrace have far-reaching consequences.

Iokibe Kaoru is professor in the Faculty of Law at the University of Tokyo Graduate Schools for Law and Politics. **Komiya Kazuo** is lecturer at Aoyama Gakuin, Komazawa, and Senshu universities. **Hosoya Yūichi** is professor in Keio University's Faculty of Law. **Miyagi Taizō** is professor in Sophia University's Faculty of Global Studies.

Heterick Memorial Library
Ohio Northern University

DUE	RETURNED	DUE	RETURNED
1.		13.	
2.		14.	
3.		15.	
4.		16.	
5.		17.	
6.		18.	
7.		19.	
8.		20.	
9.		21.	
10.		22.	
11.		23.	
12.		24.